STUDENT'S BOOK
with Workbook Digital Pack

5

CEFR C1



# TH!NK

SECOND EDITION

Herbert Puchta,
Jeff Stranks &
Peter Lewis-Jones

CAMBRIDGE
UNIVERSITY PRESS

# CONTENTS

**C** Cheering someone up and sympathising about past situations; Life's ups and downs; A helping hand; Adjectives to describe uncomfortable feelings; Talking about past ability
**D** Introducing news; Ways of speaking; News mad?; Verb + noun collations with *make, take, play, do, give*; Cause and effect linkers; Sharing news

| PRONUNCIATION | THINK! | SKILLS |
|---|---|---|
| Intonation: showing emotions | **Train to THINK:** Questioning widely accepted theories<br>**Values:** Relationships | **Reading** Article: The power of siblings  Website page: Siblings: what's the big deal?<br>**Writing** An email  **Listening** Soap opera: *People next door* |
| Different ways of pronouncing *c* and *g* | **Train to THINK:** The rule of threes | **Reading** Article: Time for a change?  Article: The power of dreaming<br>**Writing** A proposal  **Listening** Radio programme about staying awake |
| C1 Advanced practice | | |
| Unstressed words in connected speech | **Train to THINK:** Behaviour based on myths rather than facts<br>**Values:** How do we feel about luck? | **Reading** Article: Blessings in disguise  Article: Blog: Serendipity<br>**Writing** A story  **Listening** Radio show about luck and lucky charms |
| Telling jokes: pacing, pausing and punchlines | **Train to THINK:** Divergent thinking | **Reading** Article: You have to laugh, don't you?<br>Article: The world of comedy: Trevor Noah<br>**Writing** A review  **Listening** Jokes |
| C1 Advanced practice | | |
| Connected speech feature: elision | **Train to THINK:** Red herrings | **Reading** Article: Man on a wire  Article: Wim Hof: The iceman<br>**Writing** A newspaper article  **Listening** Extreme sports |
| Modal stress and meaning | **Train to THINK:** Making logical conclusions (syllogisms)<br>**Values:** Teamwork | **Reading** Article: To tweet or not to tweet?<br>Article: Fame – a blessing or a curse?<br>**Writing** An essay  **Listening** Radio programme about Liverpool F.C. |
| C1 Advanced practice | | |
| Connected speech feature: assimilation | **Train to THINK:** Understanding irony<br>**Values:** Valuing the beauty around us | **Reading** Article about beauty  Blog: What's beautiful for you?<br>**Writing** A formal letter  **Listening** Podcast about beauty regimes |
| Stress in multi-syllable words | **Train to THINK:** Making logical deductions about unknown words<br>**Values:** Learning another language | **Reading** Article: The Rosetta Stone  Article: Multilinguals have multiple personalities<br>**Writing** A report from a graph  **Listening** The Somerton Man |
| C1 Advanced practice | | |
| Unstressed syllables and words: the /I/ phoneme | **Train to THINK:** The *ad hominem* fallacy | **Reading** Article: Miscarriages of justice<br>Book review: *The Spirit Level* by Richard Wilkinson and Kate Pickett<br>**Writing** An essay  **Listening** Radio programme about disciplining teenagers |
| Lexical and non-lexical fillers | **Train to THINK:** Doing something for the 'right' reasons | **Reading** Meeting summary: what to drop?  Article: Pick up your guitar and (learn to) play<br>**Writing** An essay  **Listening** Life after school |
| C1 Advanced practice | | |
| Intonation: mean what you say | **Train to THINK:** Do as I say, not as I do<br>**Values:** Modern life | **Reading** Article: Internet rage  Article: Explaining the modern world: veganism<br>**Writing** A blog post  **Listening** Radio phone-in about the stresses of modern life |
| Shifting word stress | **Train to THINK:** Appropriate sampling | **Reading** Article: Wanted: real-life heroes  Article: I just wrote to say … Thank you!<br>**Writing** An article  **Listening** Presentation about an inspirational man |
| C1 Advanced practice | | |

# WELCOME

## A LESSONS IN LIFE

### Saying *yes* and adding conditions

**1** W.01 **Read the dialogue and complete each space with one word. Listen and check.**

**Andy** This is hopeless. I give [1]________________ .

**Meg** What's the problem?

**Andy** This new phone I bought. I just can't [2]________________ used to it.

**Meg** Why not?

**Andy** It's so different from my old one. Nothing's where it was before.

**Meg** Well, it's a different manufacturer, for one thing. But it can't be that different.

**Andy** Well, I promise you it is. And I haven't got time to be re-learning everything.

**Meg** Well, you'll never know how to use it [3]________________ you keep trying to work it out.

**Andy** Yes I know! But it's frustrating! These things are [4]________________ to be easy to understand, aren't they?

**Meg** Didn't the assistant at the shop give you any help?

**Andy** Yeah, she ran [5]________________ a few things with me and pointed out the most important features, but …

**Meg** But what?

**Andy** I didn't really pay a lot of attention. I thought it'd be easy!

**Meg** You never learn, do you?

**Andy** Can you [6]________________ a look at it? Help me find my way around it? You're good at things like this.

**Meg** OK, I'll help you, [7]________________ you promise me one thing.

**Andy** What's that?

**Meg** I'll get it to work for you as [8]________________ as you …

**2** **Complete Meg's last line. Compare with the rest of the class.**

**3** SPEAKING **Work in pairs and discuss.**

1. When was the last time you had a problem with technology? What happened? Did you manage to solve it?
2. How often do people ask you to help them with technology problems?
3. How easy do you find it to explain such things to other people?

**4** **Complete the sentences with your own ideas and then compare with a partner.**

1. I'll help you with your homework provided …
2. You can borrow my laptop as long as …
3. I'll tell Mum what you did unless …
4. Help me clear up this mess. Otherwise …

### *get used to*

**5** **Complete with the missing verbs then add some ideas of your own.**

*What people said about the first mobile phones:*

People will never get used to

0 __*texting*__ rather than speaking to others.

1 __________ videos on such a small screen.

2 __________ photos on a phone.

3 __________ to music through headphones.

4 __________ such a small keyboard.

5 ________________________

6 ________________________

7 ________________________

**6** SPEAKING **Work in pairs. Discuss the latest item of technology that you have. Talk about features:**

you've already got used to.
you're not used to yet.
you think you'll never get used to.

## Secrets of love

**7** **Read the essay quickly. What are the writer's grandmother's secrets to a successful marriage?**

**8** **Read the essay again and answer the questions.**

1 What did other people think about how quickly the writer's grandparents got married?
2 Why does the writer's grandmother say respect is important?
3 Why does she say patience is important?
4 What does she say about having children?

**9** SPEAKING **Work in pairs and decide what you think the secrets of a good friendship are.**

**My grandparents have been together for 50 years. It's amazing, isn't it? My granddad and grandma met when he was 19 and she was 18. He asked her to marry him two weeks later, she said 'yes' and they got engaged. They were married six months after that, although everyone else thought they were mad. Her parents warned her that it wouldn't last and predicted that they'd split up before they turned 20. Well, they didn't. They proved everyone wrong and half a century on they're more in love than ever.**

I'm thinking of getting married before too long, so I asked my grandma what the secret to a long and happy marriage is and if she had any advice. She had loads. One of the most important things, she said, was respect. Without respect, there's no chance of a relationship surviving. You both have to be able to accept the other person for who they are and give them room to do the things they need to do. She also highly recommended patience. She said that it was impossible to live with someone day in, day out for 50 years without falling out occasionally. But, with patience, she said that she and my grandfather have always been able to work things out. She said that having children had been a really important part of their marriage. However, she said she believed it was something that shouldn't be rushed into. They'd waited five years before starting a family. She felt it had given them plenty of time to really get to know each other. She also said that she knew many happy couples who hadn't had children.

But the most important secret of all, she said, was something she couldn't really put into words. It was the feeling she had when she first saw my granddad. She said that from that moment on she knew they'd be together forever. And she wasn't wrong.

## Friendship idioms

**10** **Put the words in order to make friendship idioms.**

1 cry / shoulder / to / a / on / have/ to
2 hip / the / joined / at / be / to
3 air / to / clear / the
4 on / a / get / fire / like / house / to / on
5 out / fall to
6 someone / out / to / inside / know
7 in / look / pod / two / to / peas / a / like
8 the / bury / hatchet / to

**11** **Complete the mini-dialogues with friendship idioms from Exercise 10.**

1 A 'I was so upset last week when my dog was knocked over by that car.'
B 'You should have called me. You know you always have my ______________________.'

2 A 'I really hate it when we ______________________.'
B 'Well, let's stop arguing and be friends again.'

3 A 'Anna and Lily seem to be getting on much better these days.'
B 'Yes, it's a relief that they have finally decided to ______________________ and cooperate at work.'

4 A 'There will be lots of useful presentations to go to at this conference.'
B 'Yes, but we shouldn't feel we have to be ______________________ while we're there. We can meet up afterwards to discuss them.'

**12** SPEAKING **Work in pairs. Think of someone you know well.**

Talk to your partner about the person using as many idioms as you can from Exercise 10.

# B CHALLENGES

## The bucket list

**1** W.02 **Listen to the dialogue and answer the questions.**

1 What is a bucket list?
2 Which of the things in the photos has Angus already put on his bucket list?

**2** W.02 **Read the dialogue and complete it with the words in the list. There are two extra words. Then listen and check.**

bet | chance | coming | having | it online
manage | problem | reckon | right | to come

**Joanna** What are you writing, Angus?
**Angus** Actually, I'm compiling a bucket list.
**Joanna** A bucket list? Seriously?
**Angus** Yeah. A list of things you should do before you reach a certain age. I'll be 20 in a few years' time so I thought I'd try [1] ____________ up with 20 things to do before I'm 20.
**Joanna** But bucket lists are things people make up when they think they're getting really old.
**Angus** Maybe, but I don't want to get to 20 and regret not [2] ____________ made the most of my teenage years.
**Joanna** So what's on it?
**Angus** So far, not a lot. Let's see. Get a photograph published in a national newspaper or magazine. Do you [3] ____________ I could do that?
**Joanna** No [4] ____________ . Your photos are brilliant.
**Angus** Thanks, Joanna. Then, I've got to do a solo wild-water canoe trip.
**Joanna** Cool. You could wear a helmet camera, record it all and then post [5] ____________ . If you survive, that is!
**Angus** Ha, ha! That's not a bad idea. I'll add it to my list.
**Joanna** So what else have you got on your list?
**Angus** The only other thing is ... just a moment. Ah yes. I want to visit every country in Europe before I'm 20.
**Joanna** Really? Do you know how many countries there are in Europe?
**Angus** Er, no, not really. I mean, no I don't. But there can't be that many.
**Joanna** Sorry Angus, you've got no [6] ____________ at all. You'll never [7] ____________ that. You haven't got the time, or the money frankly.
**Angus** Yeah, I think you're probably [8] ____________ . But I need something on my list. I'm running out of ideas. Maybe you could help.

**3** **Work in pairs. Help Angus with his list. Think of five more things he could put on it.**

## Verbs with *-ing* or infinitive

**4** **Here are some of the things that Angus' canoe instructor said to him. Complete them with the correct form of the verb in brackets.**

1 Don't forget ____________ (hold) on to the paddle all the time
2 This is something you'll remember ____________ (do) for the rest of your life.
3 Stop ____________ (worry). It's perfectly safe.
4 Try ____________ (take) a deep breath and see if that helps calm you down.
5 I've decided ____________ (cancel) today's canoeing because of the weather.

## Issuing and accepting a challenge

**5** **Match the sentences 1–4 with possible replies a–f. There may be more than one possibility.**

1 I challenge you to sing a song in another language.
2 Do you reckon you could spend a day without using your phone?
3 I bet you can't think of four countries that begin with 'E'.
4 I bet I can stay awake for more than 24 hours.

a I think you're (probably) right.
b That's too easy.
c I bet I can.
d You'll never manage to do it.
e Of course I can.
f I'm sure I could.

**6** **Write down five challenges that your partner could do in class.**

**7** **Work in pairs and challenge each other.**

## Our greatest challenge

**8** **Read the blog quickly. What does the writer believe is our greatest challenge?**

*MY* **BLOG** ABOUT NEW POSTS SUBSCRIBE

I'm only 20 years old and I've got a really bad feeling about the future of our world. I know that sounds very dramatic, but sometimes I just can't see that there's really that much to look forward to. The way things are going, it's very likely there'll be nothing left of the natural world for our grandchildren to enjoy. I keep hoping that we'll finally come to our senses and start fiercely protecting all that we have left, but every time I see the news, there are even more stories about the destruction of our planet. It's got to the point now where I dread opening the newspaper. The latest story that got me worked up was about a golf course that they're about to start building up the coast from where I live. They've been trying to get permission for years, but it had always been denied on the grounds that the area they want to develop is a protected breeding site for thousands of seabirds. I always imagined that 'protected' meant the land could never be touched. Apparently, it doesn't. The developers must have found the right amount of money needed to get that so-called protection lifted.

I believe that more than ever our greatest challenge is to defend the natural world from man's greed. This world doesn't just belong to a powerful few. It isn't theirs to exploit. This world belongs to all of us – every man, woman and child; every animal, bird and insect. This is a challenge that we must meet now if there's any hope for the future of our world.

**9** **Read the blog again and answer the questions.**

1 What story did the writer read about recently that has got her so concerned about the world?
2 Why is she so upset about it?
3 Who does she believe the world belongs to?
4 Which of the things she says do you agree with? Which do you disagree with? Why?

**10** **Complete the sentences so that they're true for you.**

What's wrong in the world

1 I'm feeling quite apprehensive about ...
2 I'm also a bit unsure about ...
3 I'm really worried about ...

The hope I have for the world

4 I've got a really good feeling about ...
5 I feel quite positive about ...
6 I believe our greatest challenge is ...

**11** SPEAKING **Work in pairs. Compare your ideas.**

## Phrases for talking about the future

**12** SPEAKING **Work in pairs. Read these imaginary news headlines and discuss them. Do they refer to good or bad news? Why? Can you agree on a ranking of the stories from 1 to 5 (1 = the worst news; 5 = the best news)?**

1 Real Madrid *are about to* spend money on a big-name player.
2 The President *is off to* Turkey for trade talks.
3 The ice caps *are on the point of* disappearing forever.
4 University fees *are likely to* increase by 25 percent next year.
5 This summer *is certain to* be the hottest ever recorded.

**13** **Match the words in italics in Exercise 12 with their meaning.**

will definitely ☐
will happen very soon ☐
will probably ☐
is starting a journey/trip ☐

**14** **Think of three current news stories about the near future and complete the sentences.**

1 ______________ about to ______________
2 ______________ off to ______________
3 ______________ on the point of ______________
4 ______________ likely to ______________
5 ______________ certain to ______________

**15** SPEAKING **Work in pairs. Compare your sentences and decide who has the best news story and who has the worst.**

# C EMPATHISING

## Cheering someone up and sympathising about past situations

**1** W.03 **Listen to the dialogue and answer the questions.**

1 Why is Tom miserable?
2 What does Abi promise him for the next time?

**2** W.03 **Read the dialogue and complete it. Listen again and check.**

**Abi** [1] ____________________ , Tom. You look miserable.
**Tom** I am miserable.
**Abi** Poor you. What's up?
**Tom** My job interview.
**Abi** Oh [2] ____________________ . So it didn't go well, then?
**Tom** Well, I thought I did fine, but it [3] ____________________ they need someone fluent in French and that my French isn't good enough.
**Abi** What a shame. I'm so sorry, Tom. I know how much you wanted that job.
**Tom** And now I've got to [4] ____________________ the whole process again. Look for jobs online, write a letter of application, go to the interview. Just the thought of it [5] ____________________ me ____________________ .
**Abi** I know, but try not to let it [6] ____________________ you ____________________ .
**Tom** I just feel like I've [7] ____________________ my parents.
**Abi** Why?
**Tom** Well, I think they're really ready for me to move out and if I'd got the job, I would have been able to afford to rent a place of my own.
**Abi** Look, don't [8] ____________________ yourself. You did your best and that's all you can do. Sometimes things just don't [9] ____________________ the way we hope.
**Tom** I know. You're right. I just wish I'd taken some extra French lessons for the last month.
**Abi** Don't [10] ____________________ on it. What's done is done. You're going to get a job soon, I promise.
**Tom** Thanks, Abi. You're a really good friend. I hope you know that.

**3** SPEAKING **Work in pairs. What would you say to Tom to cheer him up?**

**4** **Match 1–8 with a–h to form expressions for cheering someone up or expressing sympathy.**

| | |
|---|---|
| 1 Oh | a you |
| 2 What a | b terrible |
| 3 Poor | c get you down |
| 4 How | d there |
| 5 Cheer | e the bright side |
| 6 Hang in | f dear |
| 7 Don't let it | g up |
| 8 Look on | h shame |

**5** WRITING **Work in pairs. Choose one of the situations below and write a dialogue of 8–10 lines between the person who's upset and the person who's trying to make them feel better.**

1 You really thought you had a chance of getting into the school tennis team, but the coach didn't seem to agree and you haven't been picked.
2 You were off on holiday, but on the way to the airport your train broke down and you missed your flight. You've had to return home as there isn't another flight for a month.
3 You bought a skateboard, but the first time you went on it, you fell off, broke your arm and completely ruined the skateboard.

## Life's ups and downs

**6** **Complete the questions with the words in the list. There are two extra words.**

blamed | expectations | get | hardest | let | taken | wants | way

1 When was the last time you felt nothing was going your ____________________ ?
2 Have you ever ____________________ someone for something and then found out that they didn't do it? What was it? Did you apologise?
3 Can you think of a time when you ____________________ someone down?
4 Have you ever tried your ____________________ to do something and still not succeeded? What was it? Did you give up or keep on trying?
5 Can you think of something that didn't live up to your ____________________ ? What was it?
6 What things tend to ____________________ in your way when you're trying to study?

**7** SPEAKING **Work in pairs and discuss the questions. Give details.**

## A helping hand

**8** **Read the article quickly and put the suggested titles in order from most to least suitable for you.**

The kindness of strangers ☐
A nightmare journey ☐
Life with an autistic child ☐

Life with my autistic six-year-old son is a constant adventure. There are times when it's more fun than you can possibly imagine and then there are times when you get desperate, knowing there's very little you can do to bring him out of one of his frequent tantrums. You can't help feeling a little guilty when other parents look at you as if to suggest you should be doing more to make your child behave better.

So it was with a certain amount of trepidation that I boarded a coach with him for the first time recently, knowing that there would be someone who knew nothing about our daily challenges sitting beside us for the next eleven hours. Sure enough, our problems started before the coach had even left, as I tried to fasten my son's seat belt and he started crying really loudly. But far from feeling awkward, the young woman sitting on the other side leant over with a smile and helped me with the task. The effect on my son was nothing short of a miracle. He stopped crying immediately. He'd made a new best friend. I never got to know this woman's name or anything about her, but for the duration of the journey her charm worked wonders. Every time my son threatened to kick off, the woman was able to calm him down before things got too out of hand. She even succeeded in getting my son to eat a sandwich.

Thanks to the compassion, patience and understanding of a woman I'd never met before, we managed to get through the journey without major incident and, for once, I didn't feel like a complete failure as a mum.

**9** **Read the article again and answer the questions.**

1 How does the writer describe life with an autistic child?
2 How was she feeling about the journey and why?
3 How did the stranger help her child?
4 How do you think you'd have reacted if you'd been sitting next to the child? How would you have felt?

## Adjectives to describe uncomfortable feelings

**10** **Complete the sentences with the words in the list.**

ashamed | awkward | desperate
guilty | puzzled | stuck

1 It was quite an embarrassing situation and I felt a bit ______________ .
2 Even though it wasn't my fault, I still felt ______________ for some reason.
3 We were in danger. I had absolutely no idea what to do. I was ______________ and started to panic.
4 It was a really strange situation. How could it have happened? I was ______________ .
5 I had no idea how to even start doing my maths homework. I was ______________ .
6 Why did I say such a mean thing? I'd never said anything like that before and I felt ______________ of myself.

**11** SPEAKING **Work in pairs. Think of specific situations (real or imaginary) for each of the adjectives in Exercise 10.**

*I once went to school with two different shoes on. I felt quite embarrassed.*

## Talking about past ability

**12** **Which of these things might the stranger have said to her husband when she got home after the journey? Tick all that apply. Then compare with a partner.**

1 I managed to watch two films on my tablet.
2 I got a good night's sleep.
3 Between us, we were able to get his seat belt on.
4 I succeeded in finishing my book.
5 I managed to keep the little boy happy.
6 I succeeded in finding those chocolates you like from that little shop in the city centre.

**13** SPEAKING **Work in pairs. Imagine you've just been on a terrible flight. Agree together on all of the things that went wrong. Complete the sentences.**

1 I only managed …
2 I didn't succeed …
3 I wasn't able …
4 I was able …
5 I didn't manage …

# D BUT IS IT NEWS?

## Introducing news

**1** **Does your school have a school newspaper? If so, what kind of stories does it feature? Do you read it?**

**2** **Read the dialogue and complete it with the words in the list. There are four extra words.**

about | certainly | done | exactly | keep
made | make | out | run | time | told | up

**Jim** Have you heard [1] ______________ Mr Wilson?

**Sam** No, what's he done?

**Jim** He's finally announced that he's retiring because he wants to become a politician.

**Sam** So the school's deepest secret is finally [2] ______________ .

**Jim** I guess it is.

**Sam** Well, I suppose it's [3] ______________ we put him in the school paper.

**Jim** What?

**Sam** I think we should [4] ______________ a story on him in this month's edition.

**Jim** It's hardly news, is it?

**Sam** Well, he is a teacher here. I think we could do a really funny piece on him about how he's tried to [5] ______________ his politics out of his teaching when we all knew how strongly he felt about it. He might be Prime Minister one day.

**Jim** There's no way that's a news story.

**Sam** It is. This is [6] ______________ the kind of news story we want. Do you know how many complaints were [7] ______________ about last month's edition? Students don't want to read advice on how to revise or a report on the latest school trip to some theatre somewhere. They want a bit of gossip about their teachers.

**Jim** Well, I'd just like to say that I'm really against running this story.

**Sam** Well, I'm not and as editor of the magazine, I get the final say. This story is going in. My mind's made [8] ______________ .

**3** **Who do you agree with most, Jim or Sam? Why?**

**4** **Match the sentence halves.**

1 Have you
2 Have you heard about
3 Did you
4 Guess
5 You'll never believe

a Mr Dawes?
b what?
c what I heard.
d heard?
e know … ?

**5** **Put the lines in order to make the dialogue.**

A Absolutely. Let's send some chocolates too.
A Have you heard about Mr Dawes?
A Yes, it was. He's in hospital.
A He's broken his arm and two of his ribs.
A Apparently, he's fallen off his bike.

B That's awful. How is he?
B No, what happened?
B No way! Was it serious?
B Good idea.
B We have to send him some flowers.

**6** **Work in pairs. Choose one of the expressions from Exercise 4 and use it to start a short dialogue (8–10 lines).**

## Ways of speaking

**7** SPEAKING **Complete the school news story headlines with the missing verbs in the correct form. There are three extra words.**

announce | apologise | complain | confess
introduce | recommend | regret | warn

1 Local residents ______________ about students dropping litter in the street
2 Miss Wales ______________ four books that all Year 10 students should read over the holidays
3 Headteacher ______________ new French teacher
4 Mr Owen ______________ plans for the new school play
5 Student ______________ to breaking classroom window

**8** SPEAKING **Work in pairs. Decide which of the stories in Exercise 7 you'd put in the school newspaper. Give your reasons.**

## News mad?

**9** **Read the blog entry quickly. What does the writer suggest C means?**

**EMMA'S BLOG** LATEST POSTS

**Is it just me or has the world gone news mad? It's so easy to get word out these days that every time you turn on a screen there's news waiting to be read or heard. There's no escaping it. Just turn on the TV. There are so many 24-hour news channels all competing with each other to see who can get to a story first. I could swear sometimes they break the news before it's even happened. And when there's no breaking news I find myself panicking. What's happened? Is the world still out there?**

In fact, I'm beginning to fear that I may have become addicted to news. I spend far too much time checking every news feed that appears on my internet browser when I should be working, and as a result I find myself working way past midnight in order to meet my deadlines. And then, of course, it's a new day with new news to catch up on.

But it's not just world news which invades our every waking moment; people's personal news is equally omnipresent. With social media it's so easy to keep in touch with every friend you've ever made in your life. Just post what you've been up to on your wall and with one click of a button, everyone who knows you, knows what you've been up to, whether or not they even really care. And it's just as easy for them to comment immediately on your news – anything from a simple C (which means they can't really be bothered) to a 140-character summary of what they really think. Be careful, though; say something stupid and before you know it, it's been retweeted halfway around the world. Consequently, you've become news, and not in a good way.

**10** **Read the blog again and answer the questions.**

1 How does the writer feel when there's no breaking news?
2 How is her addiction to news affecting her working life?
3 What warning does the writer give about tweeting?
4 Which, if any, of the writer's opinions do you agree with? Explain your reasons.

## Verb + noun collocations with *make, take, play, do, give*

**11** **Complete the news headlines with the present simple form of *make, take, play, do,* or *give*.**

1 The headteacher ______ a speech to the whole school
2 Many people go to Portugal in the winter ______ advantage of the good weather
3 The Olympic Committee ______ a decision on next Olympics
4 Canada ______ a deal with Britain over trade
5 FIFA ______ advice from leading activist on racism
6 Bono ______ a part in peace talks
7 Hundreds of people ______ complaints to the police about the party

**12** SPEAKING **Work in pairs. Make news headlines using these four verb / noun pairs.**

do research | give money
make progress | take revenge

## Cause and effect linkers

**13** **Rewrite the sentences using the words in brackets.**

1 The weather was so hot that thousands took to the beach. (due to)
2 There will be another match as the first one ended in a draw. (consequently)
3 The president is taking a break as she has just had a baby. (because)
4 So many people protested that the FIFA have reversed their decision. (as a result of)

## Sharing news

**14** **Complete the sentences with the words in the list. There are three extra words.**

break | find | get | give
keep | let | pass | show

1 You're going to be late home. How do you ______ your parents know?
2 How do you ______ in touch with old friends?
3 Your mum asks you to ______ on a message to your sister. How do you do it?
4 You need to ______ in touch with your best friend immediately. How do you do it?
5 You've done really badly in your school tests. How do you ______ the news to your parents?

**15** SPEAKING **Work in pairs and discuss the questions.**

# 1 FAMILY MATTERS

**OBJECTIVES**

**FUNCTIONS:** using emotive language

**GRAMMAR:** talking about habits; adverbs to express attitude

**VOCABULARY:** personality (1); personal conflict

**Get THINKING**

Watch the video and think: is having a sibling a good thing?

A

C

B

D

## READING

1 **Look at the photos. Who might say each of these things?**

1 I love having so many brothers and sisters.
2 The kids all play together so well, and they help each other, too!
3 We tend to argue a lot, but that isn't such a bad thing.
4 It's cool to be an only child.
5 My sister's always teasing me – I'd like a brother as well!
6 Maybe she needs a brother or sister.

2 SPEAKING **Work in pairs or small groups. Discuss your answers in Exercise 1.**

3 **How might having or not having siblings affect our life and personality, do you think? Read the article on page 13 quickly and check your ideas. Discuss in pairs.**

4 1.01 **Read the article again. Where do these sentences come from? Match with A–F in the article. There are two sentences you won't use. Then listen and check.**

1 Having siblings can help you become more skilled socially.
2 No doubt, future research will provide some explanation for this question.
3 This is not to say that an only child will necessarily be unhealthy.
4 In this sense, they have a role model who is more or less their own age, rather than an adult one.
5 After all, people are complex and see themselves in that way.
6 It's one area where arguably the only child has an advantage over people who have siblings.
7 But that's only part of the story.
8 Their findings do not provide us with a very clear-cut answer.

5 SPEAKING **Work in pairs. Discuss the following questions.**

1 Do you have siblings? If not, who in your family does (e.g. your mother, your father)? Do any of the research findings seem correct about you/them?
2 How important do you think it is whether you're an only child or have siblings? Give reasons.

# THE POWER OF SIBLINGS

Many people dislike any suggestion that human beings can be easily categorised. **[A]** But whether we like it or not, we all fall into one of these two categories: either we are an only child or we have siblings (brothers and sisters). But does it really matter which of these categories each of us is in, and if it does matter, how much and in what way? Many researchers in human psychology have attempted to answer these questions. **[B]** But, overall, the consensus seems to be that it's better to have siblings. Here we take a look at a few advantages. See if you agree!

## Siblings can make you smarter

A 2007 study conducted in Norway found that older siblings tend to have a higher IQ than younger ones. This might be due to the fact that first-born children have all their parents' attention, whereas later siblings clearly have that attention divided. **[C]** Interestingly, it also discovered that the higher the test scores of the eldest sibling, the better the scores of the younger brothers and sisters, too. This could be a result of genetics, or because smart older siblings encourage the younger ones to be and act smart, too.

## Younger siblings teach the older ones empathy

We used to think that it was younger siblings who learn from the older ones and don't give much back in return. But there's evidence to suggest that younger siblings help their older brother or sister develop empathy and not be as self-centred as an only child. These traits, of course, carry over into adulthood, and it's known that empathy is a determining factor in adult happiness.

## Having siblings helps you learn how to manage relationships

**[D]** Here, it's a case of the more siblings, the better. More brothers and sisters means more time spent in negotiating relationships, arguments, competition, conflict resolution, etc., which leads to learning how to accept the people around you and perhaps be less demanding. A study by The Ohio State University suggests that for each sibling you have, your chance of getting divorced as an adult will fall by as much as two percent.

## A good sibling relationship brings mental health benefits

A Harvard University study followed around 300 men and discovered that having a close relationship with a brother or sister when they were young resulted in 93 percent of them feeling positive when they were older. However, the reverse is also true: poor sibling relationships in childhood and adolescence seem to produce adults who are insecure and, in some cases, depressed.

## Your siblings can make you physically healthier, too

There's evidence that kids watch their brothers and sisters eating and copy how they eat, more so than they copy their parents. **[E]** Children with siblings also run around a lot, playing games and so on. So general health and weight management in particular can be helped by having siblings.

So, if you believe the scientific research out there, it could seem that if you're an only child, you're in danger of missing out! That said, we have to remember that it isn't easy to make definite claims in an area as complex as this. Studies have to be carried out over many years, and there are always many personal, family and cultural aspects that have an effect on whether or not siblings are a good thing. **[F]**

## Train to TH!NK

### Questioning widely accepted theories

*Although we often draw conclusions based on what we've read, heard or observed, it does not mean these conclusions are always 100 percent correct. The article talks about possible advantages/disadvantages of having siblings or not. There will always be plenty of exceptions.*

6 **Which of these examples contradict claims made in the article?**

1 My youngest child Tom is way smarter than his older brother Andy, and he always helps him with homework and things.

2 We've got four children, and Mary, the eldest, is the one who has the fewest friends.

3 Steve didn't have a close relationship with his brothers when he was younger, but he's a great friend to me. He's always upbeat and positive.

7 SPEAKING **Work in pairs. Think of people you know who contradict the claims made in the article.**

8 SPEAKING **Work in pairs. What other theories about families have you heard or read about? Can you think of people you know who contradict these theories?**

## GRAMMAR
### Talking about habits

Grammar video ▶ 02

**1 Match the example sentences with the descriptions. Then complete the rule.**

1 For each sibling you have, your chance of getting divorced as an adult will fall by as much as two percent.
2 My brother's always teasing me.
3 We used to think that it was younger siblings who learn from the older ones.
4 Older siblings tend to have a higher IQ than younger ones.

a ☐ Talks about a habit in the past.
b ☐ Expresses irritation about the habit of another person.
c ☐ Uses a future construction to talk about what we might expect from someone's behaviour.
d ☐ Talks about something that is often (but not always) true.

**RULE:** There are a number of ways we can talk about habits:

- *used* + [1]______________ or *would* + infinitive to talk about habits in the past.
- *always* + [2]______________ tense to refer to behaviour which irritates us.
- [3]______________ + infinitive to refer to habits in general (not the future).
- [4]______________ *(not) to* + infinitive to refer to the way a person is likely to behave.

**2 Complete each space in the text with one word.**

My little brother really used [1]______________ annoy me – and I mean *really annoy* me! Every little thing he did, every little noise he made with his mouth and every little thing he said [2]______________ drive me crazy. We [3]______________ to fight all the time and get in big trouble with our parents. It always ended up with both of us being grounded. It was terrible. These days things have improved and we tend [4]______________ get on a lot better. I'm not sure what changed, but I probably worked out that life would be a lot less stressful if I could try to find him less irritating. It isn't always easy. I mean, he still [5]______________ to say silly stuff and I find myself getting annoyed, but I [6]______________ just get up and walk away now. There is one thing that does get me really angry, though: he's [7]______________ walking into my bedroom without knocking, despite the big 'Keep Out' sign on the door. When he does that, I tell him to 'get lost'. He knows I mean it and tends [8]______________ to hang about. It's important to make sure that he still knows who's boss!

**3** WRITING **Look at the cartoon. What are the dog and the cat thinking? Write three sentences for each. Use the structures for talking about habits from Exercise 1.**

→ workbook page 10

## VOCABULARY
### Personality (1)

**4 Find the parts in the article on page 13 where these things are said. What word in the article is used instead of the underlined phrase in each sentence?**

1 People who didn't have good sibling relationships when they're younger often feel <u>unsure of themselves</u>.
2 Having siblings means time spent arguing and resolving problems, so you become less <u>likely to put yourself first.</u>
3 The first-born can become not as <u>concerned only with themselves</u> because they've got siblings.

**5 Match the adjectives and the definitions.**

demanding | insecure | outgoing
rebellious | respectful | self-centred
traditional | unconventional

1 show admiration and consideration for someone
2 not do things in the usual or expected way
3 only think about oneself
4 like to cause trouble by not doing as you're told
5 not like change very much
6 be very sociable
7 expect a lot of time and attention from others
8 often feel very unsure of oneself

**6** WRITING **Write five sentences about the habits of people you know. Use personality adjectives.**

*My sister is really outgoing. She loves talking to people and she knows everyone at school.*

**7** SPEAKING **Read your sentences to your partner but don't say the personality adjective! Can your partner guess the adjective?**

→ workbook page 12

## LISTENING

### What's on

7.00 – 7.30 pm **People Next Door**

Things have not been easy between Emma and Jack recently, especially since the accident. Jack's hoping that an evening out with friends will lighten things up. But will it? The country's favourite soap opera moves on.

**8** SPEAKING **Look at the photo and read the TV listing. In pairs, discuss the questions and make notes.**

1 How do you think the people in the photo are related?
2 What do you think they're talking about?
3 How are they feeling? Why?

**9** 1.02 **Listen to a scene from *People Next Door*. Check your predictions from Exercise 8.**

**10** 1.02 **Listen again and mark the statements T (true) or F (false).**

1 Emma is talking to her mum on the phone. ☐
2 Jack and Emma are fifteen minutes late. ☐
3 Emma's brother is younger than she is. ☐
4 Jack is an only child. ☐
5 Emma phones her sister every day. ☐
6 Jack feels that Emma's family phone her too often. ☐

**11** SPEAKING **In pairs, discuss what you think about Jack's attitude and about Emma's attitude in this scene.**

## FUNCTIONS

### Using emotive language

**12** **Look at the sentences from the listening. Who says each one, Emma or Jack?**

a I'm tired of this family. I'm tired of always waiting while you talk to your sister.
b Why do you have to talk to each other all the time?
c I don't understand. I'm sorry we're going to be late but …
d I don't want to go anymore. I really don't.
e Tell me it isn't someone in your family!
f That can wait, can't it?

**13** **Match each of the sentences with the emotive technique it uses.**

1 ☐ question tags
2 ☐ repetition of a word (or phrase)
3 ☐ rhetorical questions (questions for which you don't expect an answer)
4 ☐ emphatic use of the auxiliary verb in statements
5 ☐ phrases such as *tell me, I don't understand, you can't be serious* or *you must be joking*

**14** WRITING **Work in pairs. Remind yourselves how the scene ended and then write the next eight lines of dialogue. Use emotive language.**

**PRONUNCIATION**
Intonation: showing emotions Go to page 120.

## THINK values

### Relationships

**15** WRITING **Think about your family and your friends. Giving examples to support your choices, write about someone who:**

1 you can tell anything to.
2 you find it difficult to talk to.
3 is really fun to be with.
4 is quite boring to be with.
5 you have the most in common with.
6 you have the least in common with.
7 knows you the best.
8 doesn't know you at all.

**16** SPEAKING **Work in pairs. What could you do to improve your relationship with one of the people you wrote about in questions 2, 4, 6 or 8? Take turns to suggest some ideas to your partner. Would you be interested in trying any of these ideas? Why/Why not?**

# SIBLINGS:
## WHAT'S THE BIG DEAL?

Chatting with my friend Jen the other day, I got quite a surprise – in fact, what she said was really eye-opening for me. She was talking about how her older sister sometimes gets on her nerves and she's always getting into fights with her brothers, but then suddenly she said that even so, she felt sorry for me because I'm an only child. Now I've heard this stuff before, and it always annoys me. I honestly don't understand why people think this way – that somehow not having brothers or sisters is some kind of disadvantage. I've always found it to be quite the opposite! Anyway, I just smiled at Jen and kept quiet. I didn't want to say something I might regret later. But I'm really interested to hear your views about this. Hopefully, I'll hear from some of you who are 'onlies' and also from some who have siblings. **Greg**

Hi, Greg. First of all, we have to acknowledge that all of us can only ever experience either being an only child or having siblings – and since we can't experience both, it's obviously very hard to compare them. Like you, I'm an 'only' and I know lots of other onlies, too. So, I know exactly where you're coming from. I'm really OK with not having brothers or sisters. Lots of people think onlies are spoiled or lonely, but I don't think that's true about me. For sure, some onlies are spoiled, but I'd guess there are people with siblings who are, too. **Robyn**

I've got a sibling and frankly I wish I didn't! A younger brother who makes my life miserable most of the time. He's undoubtedly my parents' favourite, and when I ask them to have a word with him, ask him to behave more considerately, they just tell me to let him be. If I try to talk to him, explain how annoying he can be, it only makes things worse. Still, only a couple of years and I'll be off to university and a long way away, and I won't have to put up with him anymore. **Cathy**

Wow, Cathy. Understandably, you're upset and that's a shame. But I think your post helps us to see that it isn't just a question of whether or not you've got siblings. Let's face it, there are nice siblings and some not-so-nice ones. Some onlies might be lonely not because there aren't any siblings around, but because they aren't much good at making friends. Admittedly, some are spoiled, but there are plenty who aren't – that depends totally on the parents, in my opinion, not on how many kids there are in the family. **Matt**

Spot on, Matt. Not so long ago, I read that some psychologist back in the 19th century (!!) created the idea of the 'only-child syndrome' – that an only child is spoiled, lonely, selfish and what-have-you. But he was looking at kids living on farms, with no other kids around them. That isn't really how things are now, and since these days more and more people are having just one child, inevitably we're going to see more and more onlies – it won't be a bad thing for anyone. **Greg**

## READING

**1** SPEAKING **Work in pairs. How is life different for someone who is an only child and for someone who has siblings?**

**2** **Read the web page quickly. Does the article mostly discuss being an only child or having siblings?**

**3** 1.04 **Read the web page again and listen. Mark the statements T (true) or F (false).**

1 Greg thinks being an only child is a disadvantage. ☐
2 Robyn is an only child. ☐
3 Robyn believes it's possible for people with siblings to be spoiled. ☐
4 Cathy's parents are not sympathetic to her problem with her brother. ☐
5 Cathy thinks she'll never get away from her brother. ☐
6 Matt thinks the attitude of parents is more important than whether or not you're an only child. ☐
7 Greg thinks the 19th century research is no longer relevant. ☐
8 Greg thinks that the increase in the number of onlies could become a problem. ☐

**4** 1.04 **Read and listen again. Underline any statements that you strongly agree or disagree with. Compare with a partner.**

## SPEAKING

**5** **Work in groups of four. Take turns to talk about a problem you have with a brother or sister. This can be real or imaginary. Give each other advice on how to deal with the problem.**

Think about:

- what exactly it is they do.
- how to describe their behaviour.
- how this makes you feel.
- what you've done to try and improve the situation.
- how they've reacted to this.
- what tactics you might try in the future.

# GRAMMAR
## Adverbs to express attitude

**6 Complete the sentences with the words in the list. Check your answers in the web page.**

admittedly | hopefully
obviously | undoubtedly

1 ______________ , I'll hear from some of you who are 'onlies'.
2 It's ______________ very hard to compare them.
3 He's ______________ my parents' favourite.
4 ______________ , some are spoiled, but there are plenty who aren't.

**7 Find four more examples of adverbs to express attitude in the web page and use them to complete the rule.**

**RULE:**
Words like *undoubtedly, hopefully, admittedly, obviously,* [1]______________ , [2]______________ , [3]______________ and [4]______________ are used to express how we feel about what we're saying.
We usually put them at the start of the clause or immediately after the initial verb.

**8 Change the underlined word into an adverb and use it to make one sentence.**

1 Your new haircut looks terrible. I'm being frank about this.
2 My brother might lend me his jacket. I live in hope.
3 I will not pass the test because I didn't study enough. This is inevitable.
4 I'm good at languages, but my sister is better than me at Maths. This is something I have to admit.
5 You're angry with me for being mean to my sister. I understand that.
6 I would never hurt my sister. I'm being honest about this.
7 My brother is jealous of me. It's obvious.
8 We'll be tired when we arrive. There's no doubt about this.

→ workbook page 11

# VOCABULARY
## Personal conflict

**9 Match the sentence halves. Use the web page to help you.**

1 My little sister really *gets on* ☐
2 Dad said he wants to *have a* ☐
3 Please don't say anything. You'll only *make* ☐
4 I'm really angry, but I don't want to *say something* ☐
5 I really can't *put up* ☐
6 My elder sister *made* ☐
7 Why don't you just *let* ☐
8 He's always *getting into* ☐

a *word* with me. What could it be?!
b *I might regret.*
c *my life miserable* when we were younger.
d *him be* and get on with your own life?
e *fights* with the other kids.
f *with* all that noise anymore!
g *my nerves* when she keeps taking my things.
h *things worse* for me.

**10 Choose the correct words to complete the expressions.**

1 Mrs Gibson is making my *time / life / days* miserable. She's always picking on me.
2 The teacher had a word *on / to / with* Angela about her attendance and punctuality.
3 Never reply to an angry email immediately in case you *say / reply / tell* something you might regret.
4 I hate the way he drums his fingers on the table. It really *goes / gets / puts* on my nerves.
5 That's the fourth time you've come in without knocking. I won't put *with / up with / up on* it anymore!
6 I was only trying to help, but judging by her reaction, I think I've just *done / made / caused* things worse.
7 If Jason wants to spend all day watching TV, just let him *alone / be / do*. It's his life, not yours.
8 He and his sister are always getting *into / in / with* fights with each other about who sits where at the table.

**11 SPEAKING Complete the questions with the missing words and then discuss them with a partner.**

1 What sort of things really get on your ______________ ?
2 Have you ever said anything you later ______________ ? What was it and what was the consequence?
3 Have you ever had to have a ______________ with someone? Why? What happened next?
4 Can you think of a time when you tried to help someone but only made things ______________ ? What happened?
5 What kind of behaviour do you find difficult to put ______________ with?

→ workbook page 12

# Literature

1 **What do you think might be the pleasures and the difficulties of being part of a family with either five sisters or five brothers?**

2 1.05 **Read and listen to the extract. What do you learn about the relationship between Jane and Elizabeth, and about their individual characters?**

# Pride and Prejudice

*by Jane Austen*

**Mr and Mrs Bennet, who live in Longbourn, are not very rich. They have five daughters – Jane, Elizabeth, Mary, Lydia and Kitty – and hope to see them all married. Lydia has run away with a soldier but then married him. Elizabeth has a love-hate relationship with the rich and (in her opinion) arrogant Mr Darcy. Mr Darcy's wealthy friend, Mr Bingley, loves Jane but Mr Bingley's sisters do not like her very much. Darcy has just helped Bingley to propose to Jane and she has happily accepted him.**

Bingley, from this time, was of course a daily visitor at Longbourn, coming frequently before breakfast, and always remaining till after supper […].

Elizabeth had now but little time for conversation with her sister; for while he was present, Jane had no attention to bestow on anyone else; but she found herself considerably useful to both of them in those hours of separation that must sometimes occur.

In the absence of Jane, he always attached himself to Elizabeth, for the pleasure of talking of her; and when Bingley was gone, Jane constantly sought the same means of relief.

'He has made me so happy,' said she, one evening, 'by telling me that he was totally ignorant of my being in London last spring! I had not believed it possible.'

'I suspected as much,' replied Elizabeth. 'But how did he account for it?'

'It must have been his sister's doing. They were certainly not very pleased about his acquaintance with me, which I cannot wonder at, since he might have chosen so much more advantageously in many respects. But when they see, as I trust they will, that their brother is happy with me, they will learn to be contented, and we shall be on good terms again; though we can never be what we once were to each other.'

'That is the most unforgiving speech,' said Elizabeth, 'that I ever heard you speak. Good girl! It would upset me, indeed, to see you again being misled by Miss Bingley's pretended good opinion.'

'Would you believe it, Lizzy, that when he went to town last November, he really loved me, and nothing but a persuasion of my being indifferent would have prevented his coming down again!'

'He made a little mistake to be sure; but it is to the credit of his modesty.' […]

Elizabeth was pleased to find that Bingley had not said anything about the interference of Mr Darcy; for, though Jane had the most generous and forgiving heart in the world, she knew it was a circumstance which would make her think badly of him.

'I am certainly the most fortunate creature that ever existed!' cried Jane. 'Oh! Lizzy, why am I singled out like this from my family, and blessed above them all! If I could only see you as happy! If there were only such another man for you!'

'If you were to give me forty such men, I never could be so happy as you. Till I have your disposition, your goodness, I never can have your happiness. No, no, let me look after myself; and, perhaps, if I have very good luck, I may meet with another Mr Collins in time.'

The situation of affairs in the Longbourn family could not be long a secret. Mrs Bennet was privileged to whisper it to Mrs Phillips, and she took the opportunity, without any permission, to do the same to all her neighbours in Meryton. The Bennets were speedily pronounced to be the luckiest family in the world, though only a few weeks before, when Lydia had first run away, they had been generally believed to be marked out for misfortune.

3 **Read the extract again. Complete the sentences with your own ideas.**

1 Elizabeth was useful to both her sister and to Mr Bingley by …
2 Bingley's sister … his relationship with Jane.
3 Jane hopes that in the future, she and Bingley's sister will …
4 Elizabeth thinks that Jane's attitude towards Miss Bingley …
5 Jane really wants Elizabeth to …
6 Other people start to see the Bennet family as …

4 SPEAKING **Compare your ideas in Exercise 3 with a partner.**

5 VOCABULARY Match the highlighted words or phrases in the extract with the definitions.

1 explain
2 chose someone (or something) for special attention or privilege
3 bad luck
4 getting information that makes you believe something that's untrue
5 happen
6 say something very quietly to another person
7 get on well; have a good relationship
8 knew absolutely nothing

6 SPEAKING Work in pairs. Discuss the questions.

1 Which of the two – Jane or Elizabeth – do you think is older? Why?
2 Imagine you are Elizabeth and someone asks you about Jane's personality. How would you describe her?
3 Now imagine you're Jane. What would you say about Elizabeth?
4 What evidence is there in the extract that Jane and Elizabeth have a very close relationship?

## WRITING
### An email

7 INPUT Read the email and answer the questions.

1 How is the writer related to Sam?
2 How was Sam's relationship with his siblings when he was young? What reason is given for this?
3 How did Sam fall out of favour with his family?
4 What things happened in Sam's life that his parents never knew about?
5 What is the writer now determined to do?

8 ANALYSE Read the email again. In what order is the following information mentioned?

- [ ] what she plans to do with this information
- [ ] what the scandal was
- [ ] how she made the discovery about her great-uncle
- [ ] the consequence of the scandal
- [ ] the little she already knew about her great-uncle
- [ ] the evidence she found about his life

9 Complete with the missing words. Then check in the email. What effect do the missing words and expressions have on the sentences?

1 She was very old – over a hundred, __________ __________.
2 Anyway, __________ __________ __________ __________ that he'd done something terrible.
3 My mother had __________ __________ known what it was __________ __________.
4 It turns out that, __________, he was a conscientious objector.
5 Sadly, __________ __________ he never made up with his parents.

10 Use the words and expressions from Exercise 9 to make these sentences less certain.

1 He wasn't very well liked by other members of the family.
2 He was a hero in the First World War.
3 He'd spent some years in prison.
4 I never found out if it was true.

Diana
Diana@thinkmail.com

Hi Diana,

I think I told you my great-aunt May died recently. She was very old – over a hundred, I believe. I was helping my mother clear out some of her things when we came across some really interesting papers all about her brother Sam, my great-uncle. I'd heard a few things about him from my grandmother over the years, but on the whole he wasn't talked about much in the family. He was the youngest of five children and generally considered to be the favourite of my great-grandparents. I think the others felt he was quite spoiled.

Anyway, there was a rumour that he'd done something terrible and that's why his name was never mentioned. But my mother had never really known what it was for sure. Well, guess what – we found out everything in a small leather briefcase in my great-aunt's attic. May was the only family member that he'd kept in touch with and he'd written her dozens of letters over the years.

It turns out that, apparently, he was a conscientious objector in World War II and had refused to fight. He was 18 when the war broke out and his parents obviously felt that he'd brought great shame on the family. They sent him away to live with a distant relative in the Scottish Highlands. He eventually became a policeman and made quite a name for himself. In the briefcase, there were loads of newspaper cuttings about things he'd done and even a medal he'd won for bravery.

Sadly, it seems he never made up with his parents and they never got to meet any of the five children he went on to have. I've now made it my mission to try and find some of my missing Scottish relatives.

I'll keep you posted on what I find out! Have you ever made any interesting discoveries about people in your family?

Must run but looking forward to hearing from you soon!

Lots of love, Helen

11 PRODUCE Write an email.

You have recently found out about an interesting relative of yours. Write an email to a friend (220–260 words) about the relative. Write about:

- how the person is related to you.
- how they got on with other members of the family.
- what they did that was interesting.

# 2 SWEET DREAMS

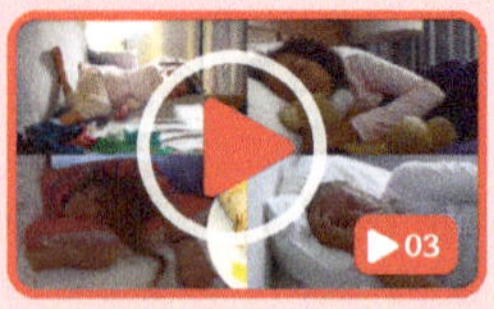


**Get THINKING**

**Watch the video and think: do you get enough sleep?**

**OBJECTIVES**

**FUNCTIONS:**
giving advice

**GRAMMAR:**
past tense with hypothetical meaning; adverbs for modifying comparatives

**VOCABULARY:**
sleep; idioms with *sleep* and *dream*

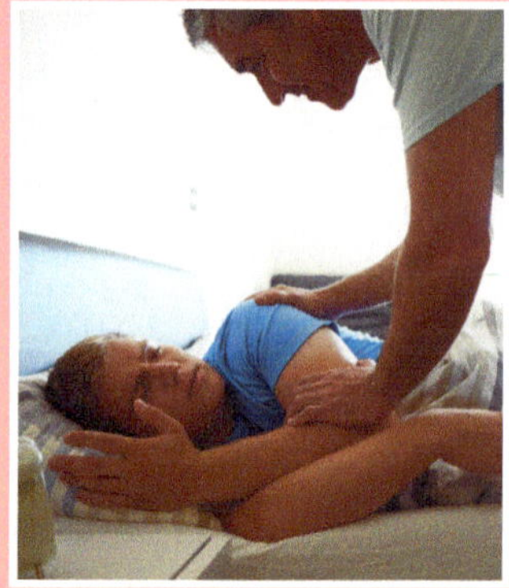

## READING

1 **Look at the photos. Can you relate to any of these situations? Read the quiz below and choose your answers.**

2 SPEAKING **Work in pairs. Compare your answers and decide who's the best sleeper.**

3 2.01 **Read and listen to the article on page 21 and mark these sentences T (true), F (false) or DS (doesn't say).**

1 Hannah Kidner would like to see schools starting later. ☐
2 She believes that a lack of sleep is responsible for students not doing as well. ☐
3 Hannah has the support of several of her teachers. ☐
4 Teenagers have different sleep rhythms to those of adults. ☐
5 The school in the study used to start at 8 am. ☐
6 Some people feel teenagers are responsible for their own lack of sleep. ☐
7 Headmasters can choose when their schools start and finish. ☐
8 Hannah has been successful with her petition. ☐

4 SPEAKING **Work in pairs and discuss the following questions.**

1 How many hours' sleep do you usually get? Do you feel it's too little, too much or just right?
2 How regular are your sleep patterns?
3 What time does your school day start? Would you be in favour of a later/earlier starting time? Why/Why not?

## ARE YOU A HEALTHY SLEEPER?

**1 You wake up half an hour late for school. You think …**
a) I should go to bed earlier.
b) It's time I bought a new alarm clock.
c) That's unusual. I don't usually oversleep.

**2 It's 7 am and your dad is yelling at you to get out of bed. You think …**
a) I wish I could have another hour in bed.
b) OK, OK! I'm getting up.
c) Why's he shouting? I'm already up.

**3 You turned off your light half an hour ago. You think …**
a) If only my mind wasn't on that computer game. I want to go to sleep.
b) I'd prefer it if you didn't ask me silly quiz questions. I'm quite a light sleeper and I'm about to fall asleep.
c) Nothing. You're fast asleep and snoring loudly.

**4 It's 11 pm and your mum suggests it's time you went to bed. You think …**
a) No way. I'm snapchatting Rachel.
b) OK, I'll read for half an hour before I turn my light off.
c) I'm on my way right now.

# TIME FOR A CHANGE?

**In February 2019, the UK government debated a motion calling for the starting time of secondary schools in the UK to be moved back to 10 am. The debate was a direct result of an online petition with nearly 188,000 signatures set up by teenager Hannah Kidner.**

Hannah believes that teenagers are getting too tired as a result of having to wake up for school starts as early as 8.30 am. She also claims that if schools were to allow teenagers a later starting time, they would see greater productivity among the pupils and ultimately better exam results. But it isn't just about improving academic performance; many are worried that a lack of sleep is also causing a growing number of health problems in young people, especially when it comes to mental health issues such as exhaustion and depression.

But a later school starting time isn't just the wish of a teen who would like to lie in under the covers for longer every morning. The arguments behind the motion are backed up by extensive scientific research.

It has long been recognised that teenager sleep patterns are different to those of adults and younger children. There is a proven biological reason behind the stereotypical image of the teenager who goes to bed late and doesn't want to wake in the morning, and it's all down to a hormone called melatonin. The release of melatonin is the body's way of letting us know we are falling asleep and should be taking ourselves to bed.

In teenagers, the release of melatonin happens, on average, two hours after it does in an adult, meaning that teens feel tired later than adults do. Since teenagers need between eight and ten hours of sleep per night, the knock-on effect is that they won't want to rise so early the following morning; however, because of early school starts, they need to. The result is a generation of over-tired school children nodding off and taking naps in classrooms all over the country.

A long-term study at a British state school found that by allowing students to start school an hour and a half later at 10 am, there was more than a 50 percent reduction in the number of students who were getting ill. Not only did the later starting time produce healthier pupils, but it also led to better academic results, too.

While the call for the government to recommend an earlier start time in schools was welcomed by many – school children and scientists included – there were those who believed there are plenty of other reasons to explain a generation of over-tired teens. Many took to Twitter to join in the debate, claiming reasons such as soft-parenting and a late-night addiction to gaming as the real causes for teenage tiredness.

The final outcome of the parliamentary debate, however, was somewhat of a disappointment for Hannah, as politicians could see no real reason to officially change the school starting time. They voted to stick with the current policy, which allows all schools to decide when they open and close. This means that Hannah still has the option to try to convince the headteacher of her school to set a 10 am start, but without any official political instruction to back her up, it would seem unlikely that a change will be made.

## Train to TH!NK

### The rule of threes

*The rule of threes states that ideas should be considered from three different perspectives.*

*The more perspectives you can view a problem from, the better your overall understanding. For example, imagine an aeroplane is flying through heavy turbulence.*

- *An experienced pilot would see it as a normal occurrence and put on the seatbelt sign.*
- *A nervous flyer might convince themselves the plane is about to crash.*
- *A fan of rollercoasters might enjoy the thrill of it.*

**5 A teenager is still asleep at 11 am on a Saturday. Who might have the following opinions of the situation?**

1 What's the problem? I'm tired.
2 We need to understand that teenage sleep patterns are different to those of adults.
3 He's so lazy these days.

**6 SPEAKING Make notes on how each of the following people might respond to the statement 'Schools should start at 10 am'. Then compare with a partner.**

a teenager a parent a teacher an economist a doctor

**PRONUNCIATION**

Different ways of pronouncing *c* and *g*

Go to page 120.

## GRAMMAR

### Past tenses with hypothetical meaning

1 **Complete the sentences from the quiz on page 20 with the verbs in brackets. Then complete the rule with *past* and *present*.**

1 It's time I ______________ a new alarm clock. (buy)
2 I wish I ______________ have another hour in bed. (can)
3 If only my mind ______________ on that computer game. I want to go to sleep. (not be)
4 I'd prefer it if you ______________ me silly quiz questions. (not ask)

> **RULE:** With certain expressions, like *It's time, I'd prefer it if, I wish* and *If only*, we use the [1] ______________ simple tense to talk about how we would like [2] ______________ situations to be different.
> With *I'd rather* and *I'd prefer*, we use the infinitive when the subject of the second verb is the same as the subject of *I'd rather* and *I'd prefer*. Also, with *I'd rather, I'd prefer* and *It's time*, we use the infinitive when there is no second subject.
> *It's time to go.* *I'd prefer to eat now.*
> *It's time we left.* *I'd prefer it if we ate now.*

2 **Complete the dialogue with the correct forms of the verbs in the list.**

be | get up | go on | not have | not talk | respect | show

**Dad** Come on, Ella. It's time you [1] ______________ .
**Ella** ZzzzzzzzZzzzzzzz.
**Dad** Did you hear me, Ella? You've got fifteen minutes until the school bus arrives.
**Ella** What?! No! If only it [2] ______________ the weekend. If only I [3] ______________ school today. If only …
**Dad** Ella!
**Ella** Dad, I'd prefer it if you [4] ______________ my melatonin levels.
**Dad** And I'd prefer it if you [5] ______________ such nonsense.
**Ella** It isn't nonsense. It's science. Melatonin. It's why I need so much sleep.
**Dad** I've never heard of it.
**Ella** Then maybe it's time you [6] ______________ the internet and read about it.
**Dad** And maybe it's time you [7] ______________ your dad a bit of respect. Now get out of bed!

3 SPEAKING **Think about your own sleeping habits and complete the sentences so that they are true for you. Compare with a partner.**

1 I wish I could …
2 If only school …
3 I'd rather … today.
4 I wish the teachers …

→ workbook page 18

## VOCABULARY

### Sleep

4 **Match the words on the left with those on the right to make sleep-related collocations and phrasal verbs. Then check in the quiz and article on pages 20 and 21.**

1 nod — a the covers
2 fall — b loudly
3 lie — c off
4 a light — d asleep
5 fast — e a nap
6 snore — f asleep
7 under — g sleeper
8 take — h in

5 SPEAKING **Work in pairs and discuss the meaning of each of the collocations and phrasal verbs in Exercise 4, using the context provided by the quiz and article to help you.**

6 **Which noun collocates with all of these: *a lack of, over, skip, get enough, get seven hours*?**

7 SPEAKING **Complete the questions with collocations and phrasal verbs from Exercises 4 and 6, in the correct form. Then ask and answer in pairs.**

1 Do you ever ______________ in the afternoon or do you prefer to just sleep at night?
2 Have you ever ______________ during a lesson at school? Did anyone notice? What happened? How did you feel?
3 Do you like to ______________ at the weekend? Or do you get up early? What does it take to get you out from ______________ ?
4 Do you know anyone who ______________ when they sleep? What's the best way to prevent this?
5 Are you a ______________ or is it difficult for you to wake up when you're ______________ ? Is noise or light more likely to wake you up?
6 Have you ever ______________ and been late for something really important? What happened?

→ workbook page 20

## LISTENING

**8** SPEAKING **Work in pairs and discuss.**

1 What's the longest you've ever gone without sleep?
2 Which of these problems do you think people experience when they don't get enough sleep over an extended period of time?

- [ ] hallucinations
- [ ] headaches
- [ ] a decrease in physical abilities
- [ ] problems sleeping
- [ ] memory loss
- [ ] slow reactions
- [ ] impatience

**9** 2.03 **Listen to a radio programme about a teenager called Randy Gardner who set a world record for staying awake. Which of the problems in the list above did he experience? Did he have any other problems?**

**10** 2.03 **Listen again and choose the correct answers.**

1 Why is it not a good idea to try to beat Randy's record?
 a It's much too dangerous.
 b Scientists have said it would be impossible to beat.
 c The Guinness World Records won't accept it.
2 How many people would you need to set a new world record for the biggest sleepover?
 a 2,003
 b 2,004
 c 2,005
3 How many of Randy's friends took part in the experiment?
 a 2
 b 3
 c 4
4 How did Dr Dement find out about the experiment?
 a The story was on the national news.
 b He lived locally.
 c Randy wrote to him to ask for his help.
5 How long was it before Randy started having problems with his speech?
 a after one day
 b after two days
 c after three days
6 What happened to Randy after five days?
 a He had trouble with his short-term memory.
 b His basketball skills got worse.
 c He didn't want to eat.
7 How long did Randy sleep for at the end of the experiment?
 a 11 hours
 b 14 hours
 c 25 hours
8 What effect did the experiment have on Randy?
 a He had strange dreams for many years after.
 b He found it difficult to stay awake.
 c He suffered from insomnia.

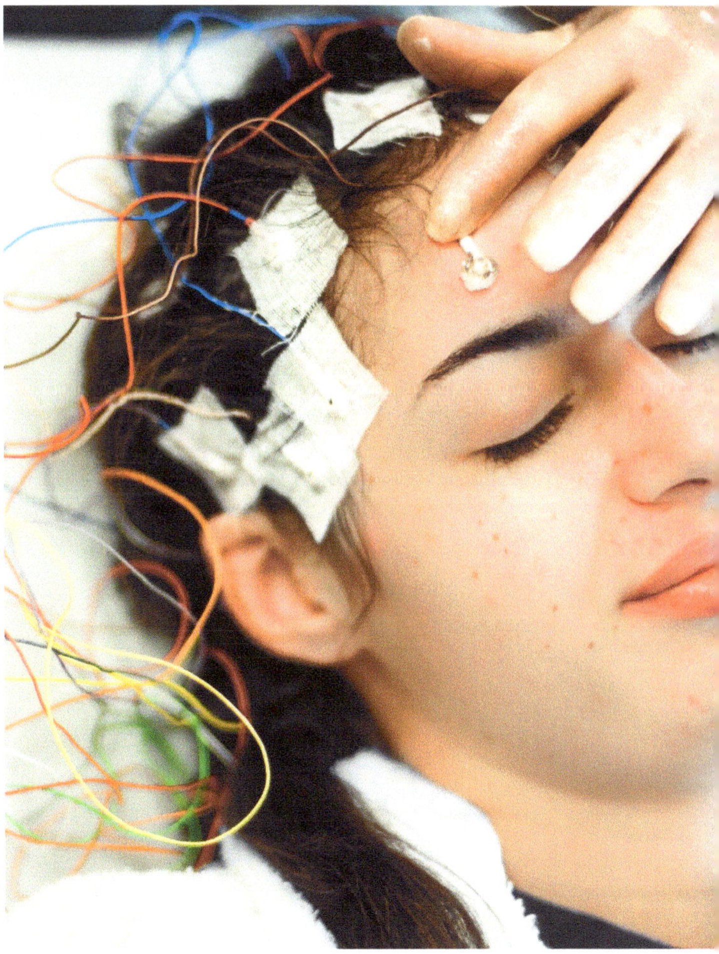

## FUNCTIONS
### Giving advice

**11** 2.03 **Listen to the radio programme again. What does the presenter do when he can't get to sleep?**

**12** 2.03 **Complete the advice with the missing words. Then listen again and check.**

1 I find that b__________ a c__________ seems to work.
2 I wouldn't recommend t__________ to b__________ that particular record.
3 You might want to consider d__________ something e__________ .
4 Try not to g__________ l__________ in it!

**13** SPEAKING **Work in pairs. Think of two pieces of advice for each of these people.**

1 Dan finds it hard to get to sleep at night.
2 Anna keeps falling asleep in lessons
3 Ben's dad snores so loudly Ben can hear him in his bedroom.

*I find that ...*
*I'd recommend/I wouldn't recommend ...*
*You might want to consider ...*
*Try not to ...*

# READING

1 SPEAKING Work in pairs. Answer the questions in the quiz.

## HOW MUCH DO YOU KNOW ABOUT … DREAMS?

**1 What percentage of people remember their dreams when they wake up?**
a) 40%
b) 50%
c) 60%

**2 How long does the average person spend dreaming every night?**
a) less than one hour
b) between one and two hours
c) more than two hours

**3 How much time does the average person spend dreaming in their lifetime?**
a) one year
b) three years
c) six years

**4 How many dreams does the average person have a night?**
a) fewer than four
b) between four and seven
c) more than seven

**5 What percentage of dreams are negative?**
a) 25%
b) 50%
c) 75%

**6 What percentage of people dream in colour?**
a) 88%
b) 94%
c) 99%

2 2.04 Read and listen to the article to check your answers.

## THE POWER OF DREAMING

**Everyone dreams – that's a fact! So don't believe those people who say they don't. They are probably among the 60% who forget their dreams as soon as they wake up. Are you one of these people? Do you remember your dreams?**

Most sleep specialists agree that dreaming is essential. Research shows that dreaming is a way of allowing our brains to process memories and organise all of the information we pick up around us in our everyday life and discard anything that is irrelevant. It is also widely believed that dreams allow us to deal with emotions and work out problems that might seem to be far more difficult to solve when we are awake. In other words, dreams offer a sort of subconscious nightly therapy session. Most of us will spend an average of about an hour and a half dreaming every night. Over a lifetime, that works out at around six full years of just dreaming! Imagine that! Each night we will have between four and seven different dreams, although it is unusual we will remember more than the last one when we wake up.

Dreams have always been a source of fascination. Most people say they like dreaming and we often awake feeling good about where we've been and what we've seen. More often than not, we will want to share our dreams with family or friends, only to see the dreams frustratingly disintegrate from our memories as we try to recall them. Dreams can also be a source of inspiration, and many artists and poets have woken up with a vision for their new work in their head. Interestingly, several inventions are said to have also been the result of a dream; Larry Page says his idea for Google came in a dream. Likewise, Dmitri Mendeleyev thought up the periodic table while taking a nap.

But some dreams are not nearly as helpful as others. In fact, it's been estimated that about half of our dreams are not very pleasant at all and we will often find ourselves in awkward or compromising situations in them. Often the levels of frustration are increased when we try to change the course of a dream but find we have little power to do anything. Sleep paralysis is a particularly nasty phenomenon that affects some people. It's a condition in which you feel 100% awake but are absolutely unable to move your body. Although the paralysis may only last seconds, it gives the sensation of lasting for a lot longer. Those who experience it say sleep paralysis is considerably more frightening than the worst nightmare. And then there are those dreams that seem to predict the future and leave us feeling uneasy about the day to come. There are several famous examples of people who really did dream about what was going to happen. For example, Abraham Lincoln foresaw his own assassination and several people reported having dreams that predicted the tragedies of the sinking of the *Titanic* and the 9/11 attacks.

There are many odd and fascinating facts about dreams that scientists are still investigating. Why is it, for example, that 12% of people say they only dream in black and white? And what is it that makes some people act out their dreams by sleepwalking? One thing is for sure: for as much we understand dreams, there is still a whole lot more to be discovered. So, dream on!

# SPEAKING

3 Which information in the article do you find most interesting and/or surprising? Why?

4 Do you believe our dreams are trying to tell us something? Give examples to support your opinion.

# GRAMMAR

Grammar video ▶ 04

## Adverbs for modifying comparatives

**5 Put the words in brackets back into the example sentences. Then read and complete the rule.**

1 Sleep paralysis is more frightening than the worst nightmare. (considerably)
2 Dreams allow us to deal with emotions and work out problems that seem to be more difficult to solve when we are awake. (far)
3 But some dreams are not as helpful as others. (nearly)

**RULE:** As well as using *a lot* and *much* to emphasise a comparison, we can use other adverbs, such as *considerably, far, significantly, extensively, notably, way* and *drastically*. By using these words, we achieve a greater level of variety in our speaking and writing.

- *Notably* and *Significantly* are used in more [1]*formal / informal* spoken contexts and in writing.
- *Way* is used in more [2]*formal / informal* spoken contexts.
- To emphasise a(n) *(not) as … as* construction, we can use *not nearly, nothing like* and *nowhere near*.

**6 Complete with the missing words.**

Why are other people's dreams not [1]n_____________ as interesting as mine? My dreams are [2]c_____________ more exciting than most other people's, but no one seems interested in hearing about them. It's strange. Anyway, the other day I had a really weird dream. It was [3]w_____________ more weird than my usual dreams. I was on a bus to school. It wasn't my normal bus though. In fact, it was nothing [4]l_____________ my normal bus at all. It was [5]n_____________ slower for a start and it was [6]s_____________ older, too, but it was definitely the school bus and all my friends were on it. Suddenly, I heard a really horrible noise. It was like a bee buzzing, only it was [7]f_____________ louder. It was really creepy, but it was [8]n_____________ near as scary as what happened next. What did happen next? I can't remember. It was frightening though. It really was.

**7 Complete the second sentence so that it has a similar meaning to the first. You must use between three and six words including the word given.**

1 I feel a lot less tired than I did five minutes ago. **NOWHERE**
I feel _____________________ now as I did five minutes ago.
2 My bed is nothing like as comfortable as yours. **WAY**
Your bed _____________________ mine.
3 My dreams were far more exciting when I was a child. **NEARLY**
My dreams these days are _____________________ when I was a child.
4 I hope tonight is much less warm than last night. **NOTHING**
I hope tonight _____________________ as it was last night.

**8 WRITING Write a short text about a dream you can remember (or make one up). Include modifying comparatives.**

**9 SPEAKING Tell your dream to a partner. Whose dream was the strangest?**

→ workbook page 19

# VOCABULARY

## Idioms with *sleep* and *dream*

**10 Complete the sentences with either *sleep* or *dream(s)*.**

1 It's a difficult decision. *Let me* _____________ *on it* and I'll let you know tomorrow.
2 It isn't such a big problem – certainly nothing to *lose* _____________ *over*.
3 I can't believe I'm getting the chance to study in Italy! That's *beyond my wildest* _____________.
4 You really think I'd do that?! *I'd never* _____________ *of doing* something so mean. He's my brother.
5 I'd love to be a teacher. It's my _____________ *job*.
6 I can't believe I've been signed by Liverpool. *It's a* _____________ *come true*.
7 We've got an early start in the morning and you need to *get your beauty* _____________.
8 Do you imagine I'd buy you a sports car? *In your* _____________!

**11 Which expressions in italics in Exercise 10 could be replaced with these words?**

1 more or better than I could ever hope for
2 no way
3 the realisation of my ultimate ambition
4 give me some time to think about it
5 sleep well so that you're fresh and at your best the next day
6 worry too much about
7 It's just not in my character to do
8 perfect profession

**12 SPEAKING Work in pairs and discuss the questions.**

1 What's your dream job?
2 What would be a dream come true for you?
3 What would you never dream of doing?
4 Which of the idioms in Exercise 10 can you translate directly into your language? How would you translate the other ones?

→ workbook page 20

**TH!NK**

**Different ways of sleeping**

# Culture

**1 Scan the article for the answers to the following questions.**

1 What caused a change in sleeping patterns across a number of countries?
2 How long, on average, do people sleep for?

## Sleep in different cultures

It is quite apparent that there are significant differences in sleep patterns in different parts of the world, and that sleep patterns have also changed over time. Traditions, cultural values and local conditions and environments all have a bearing on sleep practices and attitudes.

One major source of these differences is the widespread availability of artificial light, which, since its introduction in the mid-nineteenth century, has led to dramatic changes in sleep patterns in the industrialised world. It is thought that today we sleep at least an hour less each night than was the custom just a century ago, and probably several hours less than before industrialisation and electricity. According to some studies, artificial lighting has encouraged people to go to bed later and to sleep in a single concentrated burst throughout the night (monophasic sleep), rather than the more segmented and broken-up sleep patterns (polyphasic or biphasic sleep) that were previously the norm.

During the long nights of the winter months, our prehistoric ancestors – and, according to some researchers, more recent ancestors up until about two hundred years ago – may have broken sleep up into two or more chunks, separated by an hour or two of quiet restfulness. In nomadic societies, even today, it is more common for people to have this kind of biphasic sleep, or sometimes even more flexible and fragmented polyphasic sleep periods, sleeping on and off throughout the day or night, depending on what is happening.

Even within the developed world, there are significant differences in sleep patterns. A study carried out in ten countries in 2005 revealed some of these regional variations. For instance, while the average time the study participants slept was about 7.5 hours a night, the results from individual countries varied from 6 hours 53 minutes in Japan to 8 hours 24 minutes in Portugal. Over 42% of Brazilians took regular afternoon naps, compared to only 12% of Japanese people. Over 32% of Belgians complained of insomnia and other sleep problems, while only 10% of Austrians claimed not to sleep well.

In the past, particularly in many Mediterranean countries, people used to take frequent naps during the day, or 'siestas', although, in the hustle and bustle of the modern world, it is less ubiquitous than it once was. Naps are also common in parts of Africa and China.

The experience of Japan is a clear example of the way a change in culture can affect sleep patterns. In the post-war years, Japan was keen to rebuild and reassert itself and, as one expression of patriotism, Japanese workers were encouraged to start work early (and often finish late as well). The *inemuri* (a nap taken at work in order to increase productivity) was encouraged as a way for an employee to demonstrate their commitment, even though it probably degraded the quality of night-time sleep even more. Today, sleep is perhaps more undervalued in Japan than anywhere else, and sleep deprivation is endemic.

It is clear, then, that there are cultural and historical differences in the amount of sleep we get and the way we get it. Yet one thing is for sure: the need for sufficient sleep, however we may define this, is universal and unchanging.

**2** 2.05 **Read and listen to the article again. Then answer the questions.**

1 How has the number of hours we sleep changed over the centuries?
2 What's the difference between monophasic and polyphasic sleep?
3 Which country was found to sleep the least?
4 In which countries is it usual to have a short sleep in the afternoon?
5 Why are naps becoming less common?
6 Why was the *inemuri* introduced in Japan?
7 What effect did it have?

3 SPEAKING **Work in pairs and discuss the questions.**

1 What sleeping habits are typical in your country?
2 Which of the habits mentioned in the article would be unusual in your culture?
3 In what way do you think sleeping habits have changed over the last few decades?

4 VOCABULARY **Match the highlighted words or phrases in the article to the definitions.**

1 ordinary, everyday
2 not given enough importance
3 in one time rather than separated out into several short chunks
4 consisting of several separate parts
5 difficulty sleeping
6 to have an influence or effect on
7 loyalty
8 found everywhere

## WRITING
### A proposal

5 INPUT **Read the proposal and answer the questions.**

1 What problem is the proposal trying to tackle?
2 What recommendation does it make?

6 ANALYSE **Read again and answer the questions.**

1 How well does the proposal answer the question?
2 How varied is the language?
3 How well organised is it?

7 PLAN **When writing a proposal, the key things to mention are:**

- a specific problem
- a summary of the problem and the proposed solution to it
- an idea for a solution
- justification of why it's a good solution

**Match each of these areas to the paragraphs A–D in the proposal.**

8 PRODUCE **Write a proposal supporting the idea that the school day should start two hours later. Use the stages outlined in Exercise 7 to help you organise your ideas.**

Write a proposal supporting the idea that your place of work should introduce a nap room for employees.

**A** A recent study has shown that less than half of all Americans are getting enough sleep each night and that an overtired workforce is costing the economy millions of dollars in lost productivity each year. Clearly, anything that is losing big business so much money warrants investigation.

**B** Among several ideas that have been put forward, one of the most popular has been the introduction of nap rooms in many businesses across the US. As the name suggests, a nap room is a place where employees can have a short rest during the working day in order to recharge their batteries. A nap room can be anything from a designated dark room with several beds to specially designed sleep pods.

**C** The idea is that rather than falling asleep at their desk, tired workers can take time out in the nap room if they need to do so. Those companies that have installed one are already reporting rises in the effectiveness of their workforce.

**D** Lack of sleep is clearly a widespread problem among the population and the introduction of a nap room in our offices would greatly benefit the well-being of the staff. If we could be offered a quiet room where we could catch up on sleep during breaks, we would see an overall improvement in our performance and efficiency, which in turn would increase the company's productivity.

# C1 Advanced

## READING AND USE OF ENGLISH

### Part 1: Multiple-choice cloze

→ workbook page 25

1 **For questions 1–8, read the text below and decide which answer (A, B, C or D) best fits each gap. There is an example at the beginning (0).**

0 A over B in C (across) D into

Anyone who googles the word 'dreams' will come [0] ___C___ thousands of sites that offer to interpret your dreams. However, there is no system of dream interpretation that is [1]_____ up by scientific research. Consequently, many of these sites offer nothing more than guesswork, and, indeed, the interpretations do not [2]_____ much from those that were around thousands of years ago. So, for example, if you dream that you are being chased, you are supposedly fleeing from uncomfortable [3]_____ . Many people dream that an authority [4]_____ asks them for personal identification but they are unable to [5]_____ it – this, it is suggested, indicates that you are struggling to [6]_____ a feeling of social inadequacy. There is as yet no scientific data to [7]_____ these ideas. However, some scientists are gathering reports from dreamers that, in the future, will [8]_____ a correlation to be made between dreams and actual waking experiences.

| | A | B | C | D |
|---|---|---|---|---|
| 1 | held | pushed | backed | grown |
| 2 | differ | change | resemble | offer |
| 3 | remembrances | remembers | memories | recalls |
| 4 | individual | character | officer | figure |
| 5 | manufacture | discover | search | produce |
| 6 | overdo | overcome | overreact | oversee |
| 7 | suppose | discover | support | report |
| 8 | allow | make | research | provide |

## READING AND USE OF ENGLISH

### Part 4: Key word transformation

→ workbook page 71

2 **Complete the second sentence so that it has a similar meaning to the first sentence, using the word given. Do not change the word given. You must use between two and five words, including the word given. Here is an example (0).**

0 Thieves broke into our school last night.
**BROKEN**
Our school ___was broken into by___ thieves last night.

1 I really think my mother should buy a new car.
**TIME**
It's ______________________ a new car.

2 My sister sings very well and could become a star.
**SUCH**
My sister is ______________________ she could become a star.

3 'Have you taken your medicine?' my mother asked me.
**IF**
My mother asked me ______________________ my medicine.

4 Before, I wanted to go to the museum, but now I don't want to go anymore.
**MIND**
I have ______________________ going to the museum.

5 Everyone knows that she is considering an attempt at the world record.
**KNOWN**
She ______________________ considering an attempt at the world record.

6 Please do not stop the work you are doing.
**CARRY**
Please ______________________ work.

# TEST YOURSELF UNITS 1 & 2

## VOCABULARY

**1 Complete the sentences with the words/phrases in the list. There are four extra words/phrases.**

asleep | dream | insecure | lie-in | miserable | nerves | nod off | oversleep
rebellious | sad | sleep | take a nap | traditional | unconventional

1 My aunt's very ______________ . She got married in a bright red dress and with dyed silver hair.
2 I'd love to be someone who designs beds. It would be my ______________ job.
3 I've got nothing to do tomorrow morning, so I'm going to have a ______________ .
4 Don't worry about it. It's nothing to lose ______________ over.
5 He might seem very confident, but underneath he's quite ______________ and worries a lot.
6 My younger sister is quite ______________ and doesn't like being told what to do.
7 I often ______________ when I'm watching TV. It's so annoying as I miss the end of the programme.
8 I wish he'd stop asking so many annoying questions. He's really getting on my ______________ .
9 I'm going to set my alarm for 7 am because I don't want to ______________ .
10 My older brother was really mean when we were younger and he made my life ______________ .

/10

## GRAMMAR

**2 Complete the sentences with the words/phrases in the list. There are two extra words/phrases.**

considerably | get rid of | got rid of | hopefully | nowhere near | regrettably | to have | understandably

1 It's time we ______________ this old TV.
2 Boys tend ______________ more friends than girls when they're younger.
3 ______________ , we had to come home three days early from our holiday.
4 It's ______________ as hot as it was yesterday.
5 ______________ , no one is very happy about the fare increase on the buses.
6 It's ______________ hotter today than it was yesterday.

**3 Find and correct the mistake in each sentence.**

1 Manchester United are nowhere nearly as good as Barcelona.
2 My younger brother always is taking my things without asking.
3 I'd prefer it if we leave half an hour earlier.
4 Not many of the birds sadly were able to survive.
5 I wish I don't have so much homework.
6 Being the oldest in the family, my brother will be the most traditional.

/12

## FUNCTIONAL LANGUAGE

**4 Choose the correct options.**

1 A I *find / discover* that adding eggs helps make a lighter cake.
B *Inform / Tell* me you haven't done that! I'm allergic to eggs.
2 A Try not *worrying / to worry* too much. It's only a bike.
B But *what / how* about work tomorrow morning? How am I going to get there?
3 A You might want to *think / consider* inviting Dan to your party.
B I plan to invite him. I really *do / plan*. I just haven't seen him in a while.
4 A I'd recommend *to put / putting* your books away. Why don't you watch a bit of TV instead?
B I don't *get / understand*. Are you telling me not to study?

/8

**MY SCORE** /30

22–30 | 10–21 | 0–9

# 3 LUCKY FOR SOME?

**Get THINKING**

Watch the video and think: how lucky are you?

**OBJECTIVES**

**FUNCTIONS:** giving encouragement to someone who's feeling nervous

**GRAMMAR:** mixed conditionals (review); alternatives to *if*

**VOCABULARY:** phrasal verbs; expressions with *luck*

## READING

1 SPEAKING **Look at the photos. For each one:**

1 describe what you think is happening/has happened.
2 say what might happen next.
3 say how each person could possibly be unlucky.
4 say how each person could possibly be lucky.

2 **Read the magazine article quickly.**

1 Match the stories (1–3) to the photos.
2 How does each person think they were lucky?

3 3.01 **Read again and listen. Mark the statements T (true) or F (false).**

1 The large school was Molly's first choice. ☐
2 Molly's interview at the large school was unsuccessful. ☐
3 Molly was not very good at the interview as she was too nervous. ☐
4 It was dark, and Suzanne fell over and hurt her ankle. ☐
5 Suzanne would not have met her husband if she had not broken her ankle. ☐
6 Edwin had lost his sight in a bad accident a few years earlier. ☐
7 Edwin went to stand under the tree to avoid being hit by lightning. ☐
8 After Edwin had had a rest in bed, he could see again. ☐

4 SPEAKING **Work in pairs and discuss the questions.**

1 In your opinion, who was the luckiest person: Molly, Suzanne or Edwin? Who was the least lucky?
2 Which story do you like the most/least? Why? Compare with a partner.
3 Can you think of any other blessings in disguise that you or people you know have experienced?
4 One of these stories is a true story. Which one do think it is?

# Blessings in disguise

### 1 Just a phone call away

During my last year at college, just over two years ago, I started to apply for teaching jobs. Two schools in my home town offered me an interview. The first was a large school with 1,200 pupils and the second was a smaller one with 500 pupils. I really wanted to work at the large school because I thought it was a better place overall. The interview there went well and the next day they phoned to offer me a job. Of course, I accepted their job offer immediately. I quickly phoned the other school to turn down the interview but no one answered the phone. The next morning, I got a phone call from the headteacher of the large school. She said that there was no longer a vacancy there as the teacher had decided to stay on and didn't want to leave after all. I went to the job interview at the small school and I got the job. I still work there and I love it, so it all worked out in the end. If somebody had picked up the phone that afternoon, I would not have this wonderful job. ***Molly***

### 2 Every cloud has a silver lining

It was my 21st birthday. I wanted to do something different – something that I would remember for the rest of my life, so I arranged to go rock climbing with some friends. We went to Malham Cove in the Yorkshire Dales. The sun was shining and it was a beautiful day. When we set off, we were all laughing and chatting. Then suddenly, I fell over. I landed badly on my ankle and I couldn't walk. I needed to go to hospital, but my friends and I didn't have a car. Another climber at the cove, James, had a car. 'I'll give you a lift to the hospital,' he said, and so my friends helped me to the car and we set off for the hospital. This was not how I wanted to spend my birthday! At the hospital, we learned that my ankle was broken. That evening, we had my birthday party as planned and James stayed for that, too. In the end it was a very special day because it was the day that James and I met. A year later we got married. If I had not fallen, I would not be married to James. ***Suzanne***

### 3 Miracles do happen

I read an amazing story about an elderly man who was blind and deaf. His name was Edwin Robinson, and he had lost his sight in a very serious accident. Then, one fateful night, nine years after his accident, there was a terrible thunderstorm. He was wandering around outside in the field near his house looking for his hen, and swinging his white metal stick as he walked along. When it began to rain heavily, he sheltered under a tree. Seconds later, he was struck by lightning and fell to the ground. For twenty minutes, he lay there unconscious. When he came to, he stumbled back to the house. Understandably, he felt very tired, so he went to bed for a nap. When he woke up that evening, he discovered that he could see and hear again. It was unbelievable! When his wife came into the room, he said, 'I can see you! I can see the house. I can read. If the hen didn't run away all the time, I wouldn't have been out in that storm!' It was incredible. ***Scott***

## Train to TH!NK

### Behaviour based on myths rather than facts

*Sometimes we change our behaviour or make a decision because of a myth or false belief. These myths can range from culturally shared false beliefs, such as 'breaking a mirror means bad luck' to more personal ones, such as 'I wear my lucky T-shirt to every football match that my team plays in'.*

*Most of us are aware that such behaviour has no actual influence on the outcome of an event, but despite this, we still act as if the false belief we have is fact.*

**5** SPEAKING **Work in pairs. Read this dictionary definition of a myth and answer the questions.**

> **myth** *noun* (FALSE IDEA)
> **a commonly believed but false idea:**
> *Statistics disprove the myth that women are worse drivers than men.*

1 According to the dictionary entry, who are worse at driving: women or men?
2 If someone believes women are worse drivers than men, how might this affect their behaviour?

**6** **Which of these myths do you feel are personal beliefs and which are widely held ones?**

1 I always put my left leg into the bath first.
2 If I spill salt accidentally, I throw it over my shoulder and make a wish.
3 I never walk under a ladder. It brings bad luck.
4 I never travel on Friday 13th. It's an unlucky day.
5 I tap my phone three times before I turn it on.
6 I always use the same pen to do my exams.

**7** SPEAKING **Discuss in pairs. Which myths do you or people you know have? How do these myths affect your/their behaviour?**

## GRAMMAR
### Mixed conditionals (review)

1 **Match the beginnings and endings of these sentences from the article. Then complete the rule with *present* and *past*.**

1 If somebody had picked up the phone that afternoon, ☐
2 If I had not fallen over, ☐
3 If the hen didn't run away all the time, ☐

a I would not be married to James.
b I would not have this wonderful job.
c I wouldn't have been out in that storm.

**RULE:**
Mixed conditionals are used:
- to connect an imaginary past (*had* + past participle) with a [1]_____________ result (*would* + infinitive) as in sentences 1 and 2.
- to connect a hypothetical present (past simple) with a [2]_____________ result (*would have* + past participle) as in sentence 3.

**PRONUNCIATION**
Unstressed words in connected speech
Go to page 120.

2 **Choose the correct options.**

1 My cousin lived in Chicago for five years as a child. If she *didn't live / hadn't lived* there, she *wouldn't speak / wouldn't have spoken* English as well as she does.
2 Yo-Yo Ma plays the cello exceptionally well. He *wouldn't be / wouldn't have been* as famous as he is if he *didn't learn / hadn't learned* from such a young age.
3 I don't feel very well. If I *hadn't eaten / didn't eat* two bars of chocolate, *I'd be / I'd have been* OK now.
4 I'm never on time. If I *wasn't always / hadn't always been* late, I *wouldn't get / wouldn't have got* in trouble with the teacher yesterday.
5 She was really rude to me. We *would still be / would still have been* friends now if she *didn't say / hadn't said* those things.
6 I'm not very good at football. If I *was / had been* a better player, I'm sure I *would have been chosen / would be chosen* for the school team last week!

3 **Rewrite the sentences using a mixed conditional structure.**

0 I'm tired today because I didn't sleep well last night.
*If I'd slept well last night, I wouldn't be tired today.*
1 I know how to play the game. My friend explained it to me yesterday.
2 I haven't got any money. I didn't buy a present for my mum.
3 My sister had an accident. She's in hospital.
4 He's a very talented tennis player. He won four tournaments last year.
5 I missed the train. I'm not in Manchester yet.

4 WRITING **Write two mixed conditional sentences about yourself or someone you know.**

1 If _____________________, I wouldn't be here now.
2 _____________________ if I'd had a bit more luck.

→ workbook page 28

## VOCABULARY
### Phrasal verbs

5 **Replace the words in bold with phrasal verbs from the list in the correct form.**

come to | fall over | pick up
run away | set off | stay on
turn back | turn down | work out

1 Everything **went well** in the end and I was happy.
2 I couldn't go on. It was too cold and dark so I **went back home**.
3 The dog **escaped** and I found him two days later.
4 I **continued** at university for another year.
5 I fainted, and when I **became conscious again**, the horse had gone.
6 I didn't want the job so I **didn't accept** their offer.
7 I **slipped** and broke my arm.
8 We **left** at six o'clock in the morning. It was still dark.
9 If only she had **answered** the phone this morning, we wouldn't have missed each other.

6 SPEAKING **Work in pairs and answer the questions.**

1 Have you ever set off for a trip and forgotten something?
2 Have you ever fallen over and broken an arm or a leg? How did it happen?
3 Have you ever turned down an invitation to a party and regretted it later? What happened?

7 WRITING **Use phrasal verbs from Exercise 5 to write two more questions for your partner.**

8 SPEAKING **Work in pairs. Ask and answer your questions.**

→ workbook page 30

# LISTENING

A

D

B

E

C

F

**9** **Can you name the people in the photos above? What's the connection between the famous people and the objects?**

**10** 3.03 **Listen and check your ideas from Exercise 9.**

**11** 3.03 **Listen again to Holly, Nick and Antony and answer the questions.**

1 Who carried a compass with him everywhere?
2 Who likes to use a winning ball?
3 Whose plane crash resulted in him finding a new career?

**12** 3.03 **Listen again. Complete each sentence with between one and three words.**

1 When Charles Dickens travelled anywhere, he took a ______________ with him.
2 Charles Dickens always ______________ facing north.
3 Roald Dahl was a ______________ when his plane crashed.
4 The famous writer C.S. Forester published Roald Dahl's story ______________.
5 If Richard Gasquet wins a point, he wants to use ______________ again.

# VOCABULARY

## Expressions with *luck*

**13** SPEAKING **Read the sentences. What do the underlined phrases mean? Discuss in pairs.**

1 A Your pen must have broken. You've got ink all over your shirt.
B Oh no! I've got an interview this afternoon! It's just my luck.
2 He always wears those shoes when he plays. He thinks they bring him luck.
3 A Does the number 21 bus stop here?
B Yes – and you're in luck. Look, there's one coming now.
4 A I missed the last train by 15 seconds!
B Oh, bad luck. What did you do – walk home?
5 A I failed my driving test.
B Oh, sorry to hear that. Better luck next time.
6 A Did you get wet on your walk?
B No! As luck would have it, we got home just before the rain started.
7 A It was my first ever go at one of those competitions, and I won!
B Huh! Beginner's luck.
8 A Dad's agreed to drive me to football practice. I think I'll ask him if he can pick me up, too. I don't feel like walking home.
B That might be pushing your luck. He'll be watching TV later.

→ workbook page 30

# SPEAKING

**14** **Work in pairs and answer the questions.**

1 Have you ever had bad luck that turned into good luck? When/How?
2 Do you or does anyone you know have any things that they do to bring them good luck?
3 Give an example of a time when you've pushed your luck.

# TH!NK *values*

## How do we feel about luck?

**15** **Make notes on how you'd feel in each of these situations.**

1 You know someone who, in the past, said things about you that you didn't like. You hear that they had some bad luck – they slipped and broke their right arm just before an important exam.
2 You hear that someone you like very much has just won a competition and the prize is a week's holiday in a wonderful place.
3 You take a multiple-choice test. You don't know many of the answers at all but you guess them. You discover that you got a score of 17 out of 20.

**16** SPEAKING **Work in pairs. Compare your answers to Exercise 15 and then discuss these questions.**

1 What would be the best response to each situation?
2 Is this a true reflection of how you really feel?
3 What, if anything, would be an inappropriate response?

## READING

1 **Look at the title of the blog. Have you ever seen this word before? What do you think it means?**

2 **Read the blog quickly to check your ideas from Exercise 1.**

3 3.04 **Read and listen to the blog again and answer the questions.**

1 What was the wildlife photographer hoping to do?
2 What was lucky about the photo he took?
3 How do translators feel about the word 'serendipity'?
4 What example is mentioned of serendipity in science?
5 What example is given of serendipity in history?
6 What example of serendipity does the writer give from her own experience?

4 **Are these things examples of serendipity or not? Why/Why not? Put a tick (✓) or a cross (✗) in the box. Then compare with a partner.**

1 ☐ You've lost a ring at home. You look everywhere for it. Then a family member comes in and says: 'Look! I found your ring in the car.'
2 ☐ A footballer tries to kick the ball to score a goal. He kicks it very badly, but accidentally passes it to another player in his team, who scores.
3 ☐ You're looking for a book in your room. You look on a shelf and see a DVD that you thought you'd lost.

5 SPEAKING **Work in pairs. Discuss your answers to the questions.**

1 How would you translate the word 'serendipity' into your language?
2 Do you know of any examples of serendipity from a film/book/TV show?
3 Have you experienced serendipity in your own life (or has someone you know)?

# Janet's 'odd word' blog.

**This week: 'serendipity'.**

## Serendipity

A wildlife photographer was waiting, hoping to get a shot of a relatively rare bird, a particular kind of heron. He'd waited several frustrating hours with no luck at all. He needed a photo soon, otherwise it would be too dark and he would have to come back the next day and start all over again. Suddenly, to his delight, a heron settled on a branch right in front of him. He raised his camera, focused in and took the shot just before the heron flew away. Feeling particularly pleased with himself, the photographer looked at the image. To his astonishment, he saw that behind the heron, his photograph had also captured a very, very rare woodpecker flying past. He hadn't seen it, but without even trying, he'd photographed an even rarer bird than the one he was aiming for.

This is an example of serendipity – a word which, according to some translators, is among the ten most difficult English words to define and translate. It means something like 'the fact of finding interesting or valuable things by chance'. The key thing is that if you come across something fortuitous by chance, it's serendipity, provided that you weren't consciously trying to find that thing at the time.

Cases of serendipity can be found in numerous fields, such as science. Back in the 1800s, a man called Horace Wells was at a demonstration of laughing gas (ether and nitrous oxide). After being given the gas, the patient started laughing, as expected. But then he suddenly fell over and cut his leg rather badly. To everyone's surprise, the man reported that he couldn't feel any pain. Wells hadn't been looking for it, but he'd made a medical discovery – certain gases reduce and can even almost eradicate pain. Had Wells not been there that night, anaesthesia might have taken longer to be discovered.

History offers further examples. In 1856, 18-year-old William Perkin wanted to make a drug form of quinine to cure malaria. Instead, he discovered the colour purple. He failed to make quinine and instead got a thick brown liquid in the bottom of the beaker. However, when he washed the beaker with alcohol, the brown liquid turned into a beautiful bright purple. William forgot about malaria and made a lot of money from his new purple dye instead. He was looking for one thing and found another.

Most of us can probably think of at least one example of serendipity in our own lives. A friend of mine was trying to come up with an idea for an online article but got completely stuck. Frustrated, she decided to go out to a local café. She sat there and as she was sipping her coffee, she heard two people talking behind her. A man was telling a story that sounded so unbelievable that she knew it had to be true. She asked the people if she could interview them for the article – unless she got their permission, she wouldn't be able to use their story. They agreed and her article turned out to be one of the top trending articles of the week.

## GRAMMAR
### Alternatives to *if*

Grammar video ▶07

**6 Complete the sentences from the blog on page 34 by writing one word in each space.**

1 He needed a photo soon, ______________ it would be too dark.

2 If you come across something fortuitous by chance, it's serendipity, ______________ that you weren't consciously trying to find that thing at the time.

3 ______________ she got their permission, she wouldn't be able to use their story.

**7 Read these sentences. Underline the word(s) that could be replaced with *if*. Then complete the rule with *unless, otherwise, as long as* and *suppose*.**

1 You can borrow it as long as you're careful with it.

2 Suppose you were on holiday – what would you be doing now?

3 Imagine you could live anywhere in the world – where would you live?

**RULE:** There are many alternatives to *if*, including *provided that, as long as, unless, otherwise, suppose* and *imagine*.

- We use *provided that* and [1]______________ in the same way as *if*, but they make the main clause even more dependent on the condition.
- The word [2]______________ is used after an order or suggestion to indicate what the result will be if the order or suggestion isn't followed.
- When we use the word [3]______________ instead of *if*, it gives the verb that follows a negative meaning.
- *Imagine* and [4]______________ are often followed by a second or third conditional clause.

**8 Choose the correct options.**

1 Everything will be fine *as long as / suppose / unless* you're very careful.

2 *Imagine / Provided that / Unless* you could meet someone famous – who would you choose?

3 We'll arrive before eleven o'clock *provided that / unless / otherwise* the traffic is bad.

4 Go to bed early, *unless / as long as / otherwise* you'll be tired tomorrow.

**9 Rewrite the sentences using the word in brackets.**

1 I always enjoy eating out in restaurants if the food's good. (as long as).

2 I never work at the weekend if I don't have to. (unless)

3 Everyone deserves some good luck. If not, it isn't fair. (otherwise)

4 I don't mind working hard if I get good exam results. (provided that)

→ workbook page 29

## WordWise
### Expressions with *over*

**10 Complete these sentences from the unit with words and phrases from the list.**

all over | all over again
fell over | just over | overall

1 But then he suddenly ______________ and cut his leg rather badly.

2 ______________ two years ago, I started to apply for teaching jobs.

3 Your pen must have broken. You've got ink ______________ your shirt.

4 I really wanted to work at the large school because I thought it was a better place ______________ .

5 He would have to come back the next day and start ______________ .

**11 Choose the correct options.**

1 It rained a bit, but we had a good weekend *overall / all over.*

2 We weren't listening, so the teacher had to tell us *overall / all over again.*

3 It was really windy last night and a lot of trees *all over / fell over.*

4 It took us *just over / all over* five hours to drive home.

5 Look at this mess! There are books and clothes *all over / just over* the floor.

→ workbook page 30

## WRITING
### A story

**12 PLAN You are going to write a story. It must begin or end with this sentence:**

*It was the luckiest day of my life.*

1 Decide whether to base this on a true story or an invented one. Make sure there's luck involved.

2 Think about and make notes on the following:

- the background (where you were, what was happening, etc). Use narrative tenses.
- how the event proved to be lucky and changed things in your life. Try to use conditionals and some of the 'luck' vocabulary in the unit.

**13 PRODUCE Write your story (250–300 words).**

# DEVELOPING SPEAKING

**1** 3.05 **Look at the photos. What do you think the girl and the man are doing? What do you know about the shamrock? Read, listen and check your ideas.**

**Jo:** Dad, what am I going to do? I've got my driving test on Saturday and I'm still making mistakes. I so want to get my licence and I'm going to fail, I know I am!

**Dad:** Calm down, Jo! I'm sure you'll be fine. After all, everyone makes mistakes now and again.

**Jo:** But Dad, I can't afford to fail. If I go off to university without a driving licence, then I won't have as much freedom as I hoped!

**Dad:** Oh, we'll sort something out. And like I said, you'll be fine … assuming the examiner isn't concentrating at the time.

**Jo:** What?

**Dad:** I'm joking, Jo. Try not to worry so much! You can pass even if you make a mistake.

**Jo:** Oh? So how do you know that?

**Dad:** Experience. When I did my test, I did 35 miles an hour in a 30-mile-an-hour zone for about two minutes. Luckily, the examiner didn't notice! I think it was my lucky shamrock that did it.

**Jo:** Your lucky shamrock? I didn't know you had something like that, Dad.

**Dad:** Well, kind of, you know. You can take it on Saturday. If you want to borrow it, that is.

**Jo:** I don't think a lucky charm is going to make a difference. Either I drive well enough to pass or I don't.

**Dad:** But Jo, what have you got to lose? I think having the shamrock will help you keep calm. It certainly won't do you any harm.

**Jo:** Maybe you're right. OK, I'll take it along. Now, can we do another ten minutes' practice, please?

**2** 3.05 **Read and listen to the dialogue again and answer the questions.**

1 When is Jo's test and why is it important for her?
2 What mistake did her father make in his test?
3 Why does Jo agree to take the charm with her?

## Phrases for fluency

**3 Find these expressions in the dialogue. Who says them? How do you say them in your language?**

1 After all
2 now and again
3 we'll sort something out
4 assuming …
5 …, that is
6 What have you got to lose?

**4 Use the expressions in Exercise 3 to complete the dialogues.**

1 A Do you go there very often?
B No, only ______________ .

2 A You should ask Sarah to go to the cinema with you. ______________ ?
B Well, nothing I guess, ______________ I ask her and she says yes!

3 A Your Spanish is amazing!
B Not really. ______________ , my mum is from Peru.

4 A You've invited 50 people to the party? We can't provide food for 50 people!
B Oh, don't worry – ______________ !

5 A Do you want to watch that film on TV?
B Yes – if it's OK with you, ______________ .

## FUNCTIONS

### Giving encouragement to someone who's feeling nervous

**5 Complete what Jo's father says when Jo tells him she thinks she'll fail her test.**

Dad: '______________ , Jo! I'm sure you'll ______________ .'

**6 Which of these expressions could also be used to give someone encouragement when they're feeling nervous?**

- You've got this!
- What a nightmare!
- Take a deep breath.
- I've got my fingers crossed for you.

**7** ROLE PLAY **Work in pairs.**
**Student A: Tell student B something that you feel nervous about.**
**Student B: Give encouragement to student A using and expanding on the expressions in Exercises 5 and 6.**
**Then switch roles. Who did the best job of encouraging their partner?**

Possible topics:

- you're about to sing in front of the whole school
- you're about to take a university entrance exam
- you're about to play in a crucial football or basketball match.

# LIFE COMPETENCIES

**We all worry sometimes. We worry about what's happening now, or what might happen in the future, or even about things we've done in the past. But it's important not to let worry dominate our lives.**

1 ▶ 08 Watch the vlog. What is Annie's biggest worry?

2 ▶ 08 Watch the vlog again. Make notes about what Annie says under the headings.

My worries
Clothes –
Social media –
The future –

3 SPEAKING Work in pairs. What advice would you give Annie?

## TIPS ON NOT WORRYING TOO MUCH

- If you are worried about something, share it as soon as possible with someone you trust – a problem shared is a problem halved.
- Live as much as you can in the present – the past is over and the future will take care of itself.
- Do regular exercise. It's been shown that the more you exercise, the less you tend to worry or lose sleep.

4 SPEAKING Read the blog post. Work in pairs or small groups. Discuss which of the quotes in the blog you think:

- is most useful.
- is least useful.
- is the funniest.
- is the best.

## Me and my world

5 Make a list of five things you tend to worry about. Rank them in order of how important you think they are (1=least important; 5=most important).

6 SPEAKING Compare your list with a partner. How could you reduce the amount of time you spend worrying?

## Don't worry, be happy

**Are you a worrier? I am and have been for most of my life, though as I've got older, I've managed to cut down the amount of time I spend worrying about 'what might happen' or 'what someone might think', and so on.**

One of the things that's helped me is reading the thoughts of wiser people – here is a small selection of some of my favourite quotes about 'worry'.

A There have been hundreds of terrible events in my life, and most of them never actually happened. *Mark Twain*

B If you ask what is the single most important key to longevity, I would have to say it is avoiding worry, stress and tension. And if you didn't ask me, I'd still have to say it. *George Burns*

C If you want to test your memory, try to recall what you were worrying about one year ago today. *Joseph Cossman*

D Worry never robs tomorrow of its sorrow, it only saps today of its joy. *Leo Buscaglia*

E Worry often gives a small thing a big shadow. *Swedish proverb*

F That the birds of worry and care fly over your head, this you cannot change; but you can prevent them from building nests in your hair. *Chinese proverb*

G If there is no solution to the problem, then don't waste time worrying about it. If there is a solution to the problem, then don't waste time worrying about it. *The Dalai Lama*

H Worry has never done anyone any good, and it is very much worse than mere dissipation of psychic energy, for it substantially curtails the joy and fullness of life. *Meher Baba*

# 4 HAVING A LAUGH

**OBJECTIVES**

**FUNCTIONS:**
responding to jokes

**GRAMMAR:**
emphatic structures; boosting

**VOCABULARY:**
laughter; idioms with *laugh* and *joke*

**Get THINKING**

**Watch the video and think: what sorts of things make you laugh?**

## READING

1 SPEAKING **Rank these situations from most (1) to least (6) enjoyable for you. Compare your ideas with a partner.**

- ☐ your best friend telling a funny story at break time in school
- ☐ your little brother or sister getting scared by a fake spider
- ☐ your dad telling you the same joke for the tenth time
- ☐ watching your favourite comedy series
- ☐ being asked to tell a joke to a crowd of people
- ☐ standing with a group of friends who are all laughing at a joke that you don't get

2 SPEAKING **Work in pairs. Look at the photos on this page. Why do you think the people are laughing in each one?**

3 4.01 **Read and listen to the article on page 39. Number the situations in the photos in the order that they are referred to in the article.**

4 **Read the article again. In which paragraph (A–E) are the following points made? Some paragraphs include more than one point.**

1. We have a strong tendency to laugh together with other people. ☐
2. Laughing can be a way of reducing physical pain. ☐
3. Artificial laughter can be as useful as real laughter. ☐
4. Laughter brings benefits in several different areas of our lives. ☐
5. A marriage can benefit from laughter. ☐
6. Laughter is known to have positive effects on our future health. ☐
7. Laughter can help to reduce our stress levels. ☐
8. Laughing about anything at all is good for us. ☐

5 SPEAKING **Work in pairs and discuss the following questions.**

1. How many times do you think you laugh in a day?
2. What are the things that most often make you laugh?
3. Which of the three benefits mentioned in the article can you relate to? Give examples.
4. Can you think of a time when you found yourself laughing at something that wasn't really funny?

# You have to laugh, don't you?

**A Imagine there was a medicine that improved your physical and mental health at the same time; that had no negative side effects; that was easy to use; that helped you get on better with people; and, best of all, that was totally free. Great, right? Well, there is such a medicine, and it's available to all of us, all of the time – it's called laughter. There's evidence, both scientific and experiential, that laughter is a determining factor in our physical, mental and social wellbeing.**

## Good for your body

**B** Whether you just [1]*get the giggles* or you [2]*burst out laughing* when you [3]*find something funny*, laughter does several beneficial things to your body. Firstly, it releases endorphins – chemicals which make us feel good and which can also act as painkillers. Secondly, laughing increases blood flow and relaxes our heart muscles – things that together can help reduce the risk of a heart attack. Thirdly, it relieves physical stress – a person's muscles can be more relaxed for as long as 45 minutes after a good laugh. As if all this wasn't enough, laughing burns calories, too – not many, it's true, but hey, every little helps to keep you slimmer and fitter!

## Good for your mind

**C** Having a good [4]*sense of humour* helps to maintain a positive state of mind, too. When you [5]*get a joke* (it doesn't have to be [6]*hilarious*, just [7]*amusing* or [8]*witty* is good enough) and it makes you laugh or simply smile, you relax a bit. And it's relaxation that helps us deal with difficult emotions like sadness, anxiety or anger. Of course, it doesn't have to be a joke – it can be an amusing comment, a cat video on YouTube, or some slapstick comedy on stage or TV. It doesn't matter – anything that makes you laugh will do. What laughter does is allow us to get a better perspective on our problems, and then we can deal with them better. It's no surprise that many people find that 'laughter therapy' helps with their problems.

## Good for your relationships

**D** You must have watched comedy programmes with a pre-recorded, fake laughter track. Some people find it very annoying, so why do the programme producers add this artificial laughter? Because they know that laughter is contagious – if you hear someone laughing, you're probably going to laugh along. The truth is, laughter does bring people together. A lot of this doesn't come from comedy programmes or jokes, but just from being with people you like and sharing humorous times. And there's evidence that our closest relationships – with parents, siblings and partners – are improved with shared laughter. As the old saying goes: 'The couple that laughs together, stays together.'

## It doesn't even need to be real

**E** Have you ever been in a group of people where someone tells a joke, they get to the [9]*punchline* and everyone laughs, but you don't get it? You'll probably laugh anyway – and that laughter, even if it's fake, will still have a positive effect on you. The endorphins will kick in, your blood flow will increase, any stress that you're feeling will diminish a bit, and the people you're with (and you too) will feel more connected. So, all you have to do is laugh! Find things to laugh about, be with the people who make you laugh, and laugh for no reason at all as often as you can. Laughter definitely is one of the best medicines.

## Train to TH!NK

### Divergent thinking

*Sometimes, we laugh about something because of incongruity: our brains are hard-wired to follow a logical progression of thought, and if something challenges this order, the effect can often lead to some very creative ideas. This is sometimes referred to as divergent thinking, and the effect can be humorous.*

6 **Look at the question and the three answers.**

What can you do with a one pound coin?

a buy a bottle of water with it
b use it to make a decision (heads or tails)
c put it under the leg of a wobbly chair

1 Which is the most obvious?
2 Which is the funniest?
3 Which is the most creative?

7 SPEAKING **Work in pairs and discuss. How many ideas can you come up with for each one?**

1 What can you do with a pair of ripped jeans?
2 What's your excuse for not handing in your homework?
3 What things can money not buy?

# GRAMMAR
Grammar video ▶10

## Emphatic structures

1 **Complete the sentences from the article on page 39 with the missing words. Then complete the rule with *it's*, *what* and *all*.**

1 ______________ laughter does ______________ allow us to get a better perspective on our problems.
2 And ______________ 's relaxation ______________ helps us deal with difficult emotions.
3 So, ______________ you have to do ______________ laugh!

**RULE:** To make our language more emphatic we can use cleft sentences:
Cleft sentences with [1]______________ shift the focus of attention to the end of the sentence.
Cleft sentences with [2]______________ shift the focus of the attention to the beginning of the sentence.
Cleft sentences with [3]______________ have the meaning of *the only thing*.

**Look**
Another way we can add emphasis is by adding *do* or *does* to a positive statement, for example *Laughter **does** bring people together.*

2 **Rewrite the sentences using the words in brackets.**

1 Adults forget how it feels to be a child. (What …)
2 I don't like the way he always interrupts me when I'm telling a joke . (It's … that …)
3 I only watch comedy shows on TV. (All …)
4 You have to remember that many people don't find those kinds of jokes very funny. (What …)
5 Dad, he's laughing at you, not your joke. (It's … that …)
6 You only need to say sorry and she'll forgive you. (All …)

3 SPEAKING **Complete the sentences so that they are true for you. Then discuss with a partner.**

1 What really makes me laugh …
2 It's … that makes me cross.
3 All I want for my birthday this year …
4 It's … that causes most of the problems in the world.

→ workbook page 36

# VOCABULARY

## Laughter

4 **Look back at the words and phrases in italics in the article on page 39 and write the correct number (1–9) next to the definition.**

a to suddenly laugh very hard ☐
b very, very funny ☐
c funny, in a way to make you smile ☐
d understand [a joke] ☐
e to see the funny side of something ☐
f the last line of a joke ☐
g the ability to see the funny side of things ☐
h funny in a clever way ☐
i start to laugh again and again, in a quiet but uncontrolled way ☐

5 **Complete each space with one word, using your answers to Exercise 4 to help you.**

My dad is terrible at telling jokes. His jokes are never very funny; at best, they're just [1]______________ . The problem is no one ever really [2]______________ his jokes. The fact that he often forgets the [3]______________ clearly doesn't help. When he gets to the end of the joke, he [4]______________ laughing because he thinks his jokes are always completely [5]______________ . Of course, we all start getting the [6]______________ , which makes him think that we [7]______________ his joke funny. He doesn't realise it's him we're laughing at, not his joke. Luckily, our very clever mum is usually around to say something [8]______________ – unfortunately, Dad doesn't always understand!

6 **Answer the questions. Make notes.**

1 What sort of things give you the giggles? What do you do to try to stop them?
2 What kind of jokes do you find funny?
3 Which things do you think we shouldn't laugh at?
4 Do you prefer to tell jokes or to hear them?
5 What do you do if you don't get a joke that someone tells you?

7 SPEAKING **Compare your answers with other students. Can you find anyone who shares your sense of humour?**

→ workbook page 38

# SPEAKING

8 **Think about funny things that happened this week. Make notes on:**

1 two things you did that made other people smile.
2 two funny things that you shared or saw online.
3 two things that made you smile.
4 two things that you found hilarious.

9 SPEAKING **Work in pairs and compare your answers. Who has the funniest anecdote?**

## LISTENING

10 4.02 **Listen to three jokes and match each one with a picture. There is one extra picture.**

A ☐

B ☐

C ☐

D ☐

11 4.02 **Listen again and make notes on the following for each joke.**

1 Who are the main characters?
2 What happens?
3 What's the punchline?
4 Why is it funny?

12 4.02 **Listen again and rate each of the jokes from 5 (hilarious) to 0 (I didn't get it).**

Joke 1 ☐ Joke 2 ☐ Joke 3 ☐

13 SPEAKING **Work in groups of three. Choose one of the jokes and tell it to the others.**

## FUNCTIONS

### Responding to jokes

14 4.03 **Read and listen to four jokes. What do the people think of them? Choose 😊 or 😔 or 🤨.**

1
*Why is 6 afraid of 7?*
*Because 7 8 9.*

2
*What do you call a deer with no eye?*
*No idea.*

3
*I phoned the local hospital. I said, 'Is that the local hospital?' The woman said, 'Well, it depends where you're phoning from.'*

4
*Knock, knock!*
*Who's there?*
*Tank.*
*Tank who?*
*You're welcome.*

15 4.03 **Complete the phrases in order to make the responses. Listen again and check.**

1 That's a g________ o________ .
2 Ha ha. V________ f________ .
3 I m________ r________ that one.
4 I d________ g________ it.

16 SPEAKING **Work in pairs. Discuss these questions. Think about the jokes you heard in Exercises 10 and 14.**

1 Which of the jokes, if any, did you find funny? Did you dislike any of them? Why?
2 Some people have said that the joke about the elderly couple could be considered to be in bad taste. What do you think?
3 Which of these jokes work in your language?
4 Are there any jokes that you know that wouldn't work in English?

17 SPEAKING **Work in pairs. Think of a joke and practise telling it in English.**

18 SPEAKING **Tell your joke to another pair. Respond appropriately to each other's jokes. Whose joke was the funniest?**

**PRONUNCIATION**
Telling jokes: pacing, pausing and punchlines
Go to page 120.

## READING

1 SPEAKING **Work in pairs. Ask and answer the questions.**

1 Which comedy shows do you enjoy watching? Why?
2 Who are the most famous comedians in your country? Are there many international comedians?
3 Are there daily comedy shows in your country? How popular are they?

2 **Read the article quickly and answer the questions.**

1 In what ways is Trevor Noah unusual?
2 Apart from hosting a comedy show, what other things has he done?
3 What examples are given of how he's been successful?

3 4.05 **Read the article again and listen. Answer the questions.**

1 Who were Trevor Noah's parents?
2 Why did his parents keep their relationship secret?
3 Why does he speak so many languages?
4 What was his book *Born a Crime* about?
5 Why did he first go on stage as a stand-up comedian?
6 How did he start to learn how to be a talk-show host?
7 What happened when he took over *The Daily Show*?

## SPEAKING

4 **Work in pairs. Make a list of the three most popular comedians from your country. What makes them so entertaining?**

5 **Work in groups. Agree together on the best comedian from your country.**

# THE WORLD OF COMEDY: TREVOR NOAH

**Since 2015, Trevor Noah has been hosting *The Daily Show*, a well-known comedy programme on US TV. He took over from the very successful Jon Stewart, and since then, the show has definitely gone from strength to strength. So who is Trevor Noah?**

Trevor Noah is South African. He was born in Soweto, a township near Johannesburg, in 1984. He's the son of a black Xhosa woman and a white Swiss man. In South Africa in those days, under apartheid, relationships between people of different skin colours was banned, and his parents had to keep their relationship secret. This fact of his birth certainly accounts for many things about him: for example, the fact that he speaks several languages, including English, Zulu, Xhosa, Sotho, Tsonga, Tswana, Afrikaans and Swiss German; the fact that when he started as a comedian, a lot of his comedy referred to the racial situation in his home country; and his international outlook (he says of himself: 'I've always wanted to be a comedian in the world. I don't want to be labelled a South African comedian.').

In 2016, he published a highly successful book entitled *Born a Crime: Stories from a South African Childhood*, and it became an immediate bestseller in New York and beyond, containing stories of his early life in South Africa as the apartheid regime came to an end and the new freedoms that followed; stories like eating caterpillars at a time when his family was extremely poor, or being thrown out of a car driven by gangsters.

In his late teens, Noah appeared in a South African soap opera, and later, when his friends dared him to, he went on stage as a stand-up comedian for the first time. This led to numerous appearances on all kinds of TV shows in South Africa – for example, he took part in a reality dancing show in 2008 – and his career began to take off. In 2010, he was offered the opportunity to run his own talk show, *Tonight with Trevor Noah*, which gave him the chance to acquire the skills of being a talk-show host.

Noah's reputation grew and soon he attracted the attention of people outside his native country. In 2012, he appeared on a famous US show, *The Tonight Show With Jay Leno* – the first African comedian to do so. The following year he got his own TV show in the US, and then, crucially, in 2014 he was invited to appear on Comedy Central's *The Daily Show* with Stewart.

Then, in 2015, Noah took over after Stewart's retirement. Although viewing figures dropped a little at first (not surprising, given how popular Stewart had been), the show still had an excellent audience and Noah was offered a five-year renewal in 2017. His story is unquestionably one of success and recognition (in 2018, he was listed in *Time* magazine's 100 most influential people). Who knows where he will go next.

## GRAMMAR
### Boosting

**6 Rewrite the sentences from the article to include the word in brackets. Then complete the rule with *before*, *after* and *between*.**

1 The show has gone from strength to strength. (definitely)
2 This fact of his birth accounts for many things about him. (certainly)
3 Then, in 2014 he was invited to appear on Comedy Central's *The Daily Show*. (crucially)
4 His story is one of success and recognition. (unquestionably)

**RULE:** When we want to make a statement stronger, we can use an adverb such as *unquestionably, definitely, crucially* or *certainly*.
These adverbs come:
[1] ______________ the verb *to be*
[2] ______________ other verbs
[3] ______________ auxiliary and main verbs
Other common adverbs include *undoubtedly, undeniably, clearly, absolutely, utterly, entirely, essentially, exactly, literally* and *totally*.

**7 Put the words in order to make sentences.**

My favourite comedian is Amy Schumer.
1 the / undeniably / she / world / of / funniest / is / actors / one / the / in / .
2 is / film / undoubtedly / best / *I Feel Pretty* / her / .
3 I've / is / seen / funniest / it / literally / the / film / ever / .
4 playing / she / ordinary people / loves / clearly / .
5 convincing / her / was / *Thank You for Your Service* / performance / in / utterly / .
6 day / an / win / she / definitely / one / Oscar / will / .

**8 WRITING Write four sentences about a comedian or actor that you really like, using adverbs to make your statements stronger. Keep their name a secret! Read your sentences to your partner. Can he/she guess who you're describing?**

→ workbook page 37

## VOCABULARY
### Idioms with *laugh* and *joke*

**9 Match the sentence halves.**

1 The team really are *a laughing* ☐
2 Your exam result *is no* ☐
3 I love this programme. I *laugh my* ☐
4 When we saw we were wearing the same dress, we *burst out* ☐
5 It was very funny to hide my shoes, but *joking* ☐
6 He might think it's funny now, but he'll be *laughing* ☐
7 I can't believe United paid £30 million for him. *It's a* ☐
8 They call you a nerd because you study hard, but you'll *have* ☐

a *laughing*. What else could we do? It was too late for either of us to change.
b *on the other side of his face* when his parents read his school report.
c *joke*. He's rubbish – not even remotely worth that amount.
d *head off* every time I watch it.
e *the last laugh* when you get into the best university in the country and they all fail their exams.
f *aside*, I need to leave. Where are they?
g *stock*. They haven't won a game for more than a year.
h *laughing matter*. 30 percent is just not good enough.

**10 Complete with the missing words from the idioms in Exercise 9.**

1 Have you heard Sarah's new joke? I laughed my ______________ when she told me.
2 I got a one percent pay rise. One percent! It's a ______________ !
3 I know you think I've got no talent for acting, but I'll ______________ the ______________ when I'm rich and famous.
4 You can't wear that Wonderwoman costume to the end-of-year ball. You'll be the ______________ of the party.
5 Yes, I know it's funny to laugh at me in a suit, but ______________ , do you think it's appropriate for a job interview?
6 You'll be laughing on the ______________ of your ______________ when I'm your boss one day.
7 These new tax rules are no ______________ . Many families will find themselves a lot poorer.
8 When she slipped on the banana skin, I ______________ laughing. I couldn't help myself.

**11 WRITING Write a reply to each of the sentences. Use one of the idioms in each one.**

1 He thinks it's funny to drive his Porsche around town at 100 km per hour.
2 Did you think the film was funny?
3 Nigel's parents aren't going to be happy when they see what he's done to their car. I can't believe he isn't more worried. He still seems to think it's funny.

→ workbook page 38

# Literature

1 How good do you think three middle-aged English men (in the 19th century) might be at cooking? How often do you imagine they cook for themselves? Under what circumstances might you expect them to cook?

2 4.06 Read and listen to the extract and make a list of the things they put into the Irish stew.

## Three Men in a Boat

### (to say nothing of the dog)

*by Jerome K. Jerome*

**In this famous, late-nineteenth century novel, a man called J and his two friends Harris and George decide to take a holiday to improve their health. They travel along the River Thames in a small boat (and they take their dog, Montmorency, with them). They are not very good sailors, or cooks, and the novel tells of their many odd adventures.**

It was still early when we got settled, and George said that, as we had plenty of time, it would be a splendid opportunity to try a good, slap-up supper. He said he would show us what could be done up the river in the way of cooking, and suggested that, with the vegetables and the remains of the cold beef and general odds and ends, we should make an Irish stew.

It seemed a fascinating idea. George gathered wood and made a fire, and Harris and I started to peel the potatoes. I should never have thought that peeling potatoes was such an undertaking. The job turned out to be the biggest thing of its kind that I had ever been in. We began cheerfully, […], but our light-heartedness was gone by the time the first potato was finished. The more we peeled, the more peel there seemed to be left on; by the time we had got all the peel off and all the eyes out, there was no potato left – at least, none worth speaking of. George came and had a look at it – it was about the size of a peanut.

He said:

'Oh, that won't do! You're wasting them. You must scrape them.'

So we scraped them, and that was harder work than peeling. […] We worked steadily for twenty-five minutes, and did four potatoes. […] I never saw such a thing as potato-scraping for making a fellow in a mess. It seemed difficult to believe that the potato-scrapings in which Harris and I stood, half smothered, could have come off four potatoes. […]

George said it was absurd to have only four potatoes in an Irish stew, so we washed half-a-dozen or so more, and put them in without peeling. We also put in a cabbage and a few peas. George stirred it all up, and then he said that there seemed to be a lot of room to spare, so we looked through both the baskets, and picked out all the odds and ends and the remnants, and added them to the stew. […] Then George found half a tin of salmon, and he emptied that into the pot.

He said that was the advantage of Irish stew: you got rid of such a lot of things. I fished out a couple of eggs that had got cracked, and put those in. […]

I forget the other ingredients, but I know nothing was wasted; and I remember that, towards the end, Montmorency, who had evinced great interest in the proceedings throughout, strolled away with an earnest and thoughtful air, reappearing, a few minutes afterwards, with a dead water rat in his mouth, which he evidently wished to present as his contribution to the dinner; […].

We had a discussion as to whether the rat should go in or not. Harris said that he thought it would be all right, mixed up with the other things, and that every little helped; but George stood up for precedent. He said he had never heard of water rats in Irish stew, and he would rather be on the safe side, and not try experiments.

3 Read the extract again. Mark the statements T (true), F (false) or DS (doesn't say).

1 George said they should make Irish stew using just some beef and vegetables. ☐
2 After the men peeled the potatoes, they were very small. ☐
3 Scraping the potatoes was the most difficult work they'd ever done. ☐
4 George wanted to look for other things to put in the stew because he thought it was too small. ☐
5 Montmorency killed a rat. ☐
6 The men didn't put the rat in the stew because there was no room for it. ☐

4 VOCABULARY Match the highlighted words or phrases in the extract with the definitions.

1 left over; more of something than you need or want
2 to take off a layer of something by rubbing with a hard or sharp object
3 remove the skin (of a vegetable or fruit)
4 not take any risks
5 in a smooth and regular way, without hurrying
6 various small things of different kinds
7 everything, no matter how small, was useful
8 got something out (usually with fingers)

5 SPEAKING Work in pairs. Discuss the questions.

1 Do you think the men enjoyed their meal when they finally ate supper? Why/Why not?
2 What was the worst meal you have ever eaten or cooked? Why was it so bad? Tell your partner about it.

## WRITING
### A review

6 INPUT Read the review and tick (✓) the adjectives that the reviewer would agree describe the book.

- [ ] entertaining
- [ ] boring
- [ ] old-fashioned
- [ ] hilarious
- [ ] depressing
- [ ] exciting

7 ANALYSE Read the review again and underline:

- two examples of cleft sentences.
- four examples of boosting adverbs.

8 Rewrite these sentences from the review using a cleft sentence to add emphasis.

1 The three of them decide that they are over-worked and in need of a holiday.
*What the three of them decide ...*
2 You get the strangest looks when you suddenly burst out laughing.
*It's when you ...*
3 Some of my friends [...] said it was too old-fashioned and that the plot moved far too slowly.
*What some of my friends said was ...*

**Note:** It's good to use boosting and cleft sentences in your review to give it more impact. But be careful not to use too many. This could result in your writing sounding artificial.

9 PLAN Match each paragraph with its function. Then match the functions with advice for writing a review.

- [ ] a description of what the writer likes/doesn't like
- [ ] a brief synopsis of the story
- [ ] a recommendation

1 Don't give too much away.
2 Say who it might appeal to.
3 Don't forget to give reasons for your opinions.

[A] Jerome K. Jerome is sitting in the living room of his house, describing an ever-growing list of illnesses from which he fears he is suffering to his sympathetic friends Harris and George. The three of them decide that they are over-worked and in need of a holiday. After deciding that a vacation in the countryside would be too dull and a voyage at sea too dangerous, they decide that a boating trip up the River Thames from London to Oxford would be perfect. So the next Saturday, accompanied by Jerome's dog Montmorency, they set off for a fortnight of amusing storytelling and mild misadventure, all set in the background of the idyllic English countryside.

[B] Originally published in 1889, *Three Men in a Boat* was recently voted number 33 on the *Guardian*'s list of the 100 greatest novels of all time and there's one simple reason for this: it's utterly brilliant. What I like most about it is the perfect mixture of travel guide, which is what it was originally intended to be, and comedy – two of my favourite genres. The book is laugh-out-loud funny, which can be quite embarrassing if you're reading it on a crowded underground train on your way to college! You get the strangest looks when you suddenly burst out laughing.

[C] Clearly, though, it isn't for everyone. Some of my friends didn't find it so humorous and said it was too old-fashioned and that the plot moved far too slowly. But it's exactly this lazy boat ride of a journey that makes it so good. If you're looking for a highly enjoyable cruise into the eccentricities of the English, with a cast of undeniably colourful characters, then this might just be the book for you.

10 PRODUCE Write a review of a book or film (220–260 words).

- Give a short summary.
- Say how you feel about it.
- Say whether you'd recommend it and, if so, to whom.

## LISTENING

### Part 3: Multiple choice

→ workbook page 43

1 4.07 **You will hear part of a podcast interview in which the actor Daniela Merchant is talking about a book she's read that discusses the role of luck in people's lives. For questions 1–6, choose the answer (A, B, C or D) which fits best according to what you hear.**

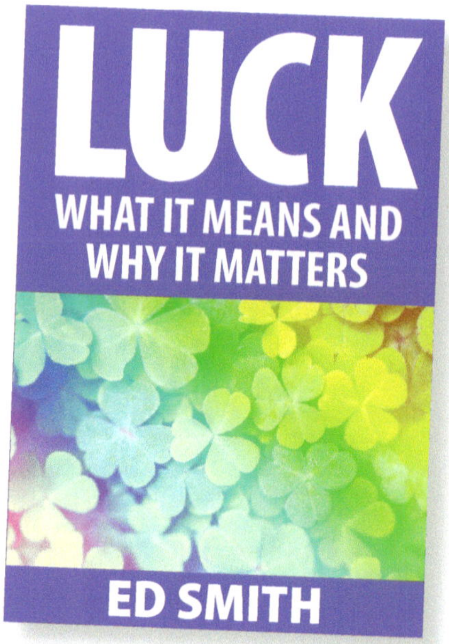


1 Daniela's main criticism of the beginning of the book she's read is that the writer
A tries to blame other people's actions for his own misfortunes.
B fails to explain the exact circumstances behind an incident.
C seems unable to come to terms with a past disappointment.
D assumes that the reader is familiar with his previous books.

2 In terms of the difference between luck and fate, Daniela feels that the book
A could make it clearer what the two terms mean.
B should have considered a wider range of situations.
C makes an interesting point about people's attitudes.
D relies too heavily on the writer's personal experiences.

3 Daniela agrees with the interviewer's point that
A natural ability is still regarded as necessary for success.
B it's becoming more acceptable to make mistakes these days.
C most people think success or failure is largely a matter of chance.
D society is becoming less tolerant of those who use bad luck as an excuse.

4 Daniela explains that the second half of the book highlights
A how family values can inform our decisions.
B how some factors of our birth influence our lives.
C how each generation tends to view things differently.
D how inherited features are more important than upbringing.

5 Daniela believes that her acting career has been successful because
A she adopted an exceptional actor as her role model.
B she did her training at a particularly prestigious college.
C she was able to appreciate and learn from the work of others.
D she benefited from an unplanned change in her training course.

6 Daniela's overall assessment of the book she's read is that
A it's more likely to appeal to a younger readership.
B some parts of it are more clearly written than others.
C it's entertaining, but shouldn't be taken too seriously.
D the writer argues too strongly for the main idea behind it

## WRITING

### Part 2: A proposal

2 **Write an answer to the following task.**

A local school has a piece of land that it wants to build on. In preparation for a meeting to discuss the plans for the project, the school has asked students to write a proposal. In your proposal, explain what type of building you think it should be and why, how to make sure all students in the school benefit from it, and suggest ways in which the building could be used by the local community outside school hours.

**Write your proposal (220–260 words).**

# TEST YOURSELF UNITS 3 & 4

## VOCABULARY

**1 Complete the sentences with the words in the list. There are four extra words.**

away | beginner's | giggles | in | matter | off | on | over | punchline | stock | through | to | trick | turn

1 You need to go to the supermarket? Well, you're ______________________ luck. I'm just about to drive to town.
2 I loved that film. It was so funny that I laughed my head ______________________ .
3 Don't wear that shirt. You'll be the laughing ______________________ of the party.
4 He wanted to offer me the job, but I decided to _______________ it down.
5 I can't believe I won. I've never played cards before. It must be ______________________ luck.
6 Oh no! Where's my bag? That boy has run _______________ with it.
7 When the patient came _______________ , the nurse asked him if he could remember his name.
8 I'm terrible at telling jokes. I always forget the ______________________ .
9 You've broken the window. I don't think this is a laughing ______________________ .
10 I always get the ______________________ when Mr Harrison tells me off. I just can't help laughing.

/10

## GRAMMAR

**2 Complete the sentences with the words/phrases in the list. There are two extra words/phrases.**

all | could speak | didn't speak | don't speak | hadn't spoken | it | speak | what

1 Unless you _______________ to the headmaster first, you won't be able to use the hall for the party.
2 _______________ was Dave who suggested the idea.
3 If I _______________ Spanish fluently, they wouldn't have offered me the job. I can't wait to start!
4 _______________ annoyed me most was the wait.
5 Imagine you _______________ another language, which language would you choose?
6 If you _______________ to her so rudely yesterday, you might still be friends.

**3 Find and correct the mistake in each sentence.**

1 I'll do certainly all I can to help you.
2 Unless we don't leave now, we'll miss the train.
3 If I hadn't eaten so much, I wouldn't have felt so ill now.
4 It was the journey what was most fun.
5 He's made clearly a lot of enemies.
6 Provided that you could go anywhere in the world, where would you go?

/12

## FUNCTIONAL LANGUAGE

**4 Choose the correct options.**

1 That's a great joke. I must *learn / remember* that one. Thanks.
2 Ha, ha! That's a *fun / good* one.
3 Thanks for explaining the joke. I just didn't *catch / get* it at first.
4 Ha ha – very *funny / hysterical*.
5 A I can't believe I didn't win the poetry competition.
B *Never / Don't* mind. You can always try again.
6 A Can you believe we lost the match in the last minute?
B That really is *bad / worse* luck.
7 He'd never played football before and scored three goals. Talk about *starter's / beginner's* luck.
8 I've missed the bus by a minute. *Only / Just* my luck!

/8

**MY SCORE** /30

22–30 | 10–21 | 0–9

# 5 WHAT A THRILL!

**OBJECTIVES**

**FUNCTIONS:** giving and reacting to an opinion

**GRAMMAR:** participle clauses; verbs of perception with infinitive or gerund

**VOCABULARY:** thrill seeking; idioms with *hot* and *cold*

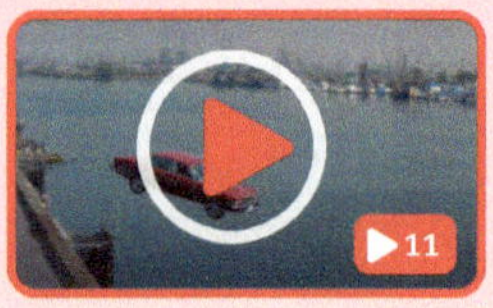


**Get THINKING**

**Watch the video and think: which stunts do you enjoy watching?**

## READING

1 **Look at the photos. Tick (✓) the adjectives and phrases that you'd use to describe these activities.**

| | | | |
|---|---|---|---|
| challenging | ☐ | rewarding | ☐ |
| dangerous | ☐ | boring | ☐ |
| terrifying | ☐ | awesome | ☐ |
| exciting | ☐ | unsafe | ☐ |
| not for me | ☐ | awe-inspiring | ☐ |

2 SPEAKING **Work in pairs. Think of three reasons why people might want to do these activities and three reasons why they might not.**

3 **Compare your ideas with others in the class.**

4 **Read the article quickly. How does Philippe Petit describe himself?**

5 🔊 5.01 **Read the article again and listen. Put these events in the order that they happened.**

☐ Petit takes his high-wire act to Australia.
☐ Petit's mental state is assessed.
☐ Petit learns his skill from Rudy Omankowsky Jr.
☐ Petit lies down on the wire.
☐ Petit is arrested.
1 Petit practises his skill at his parents' home.
☐ Petit starts his walk between the Twin Towers.
☐ Petit walks across the towers of the Notre-Dame cathedral.
☐ Petit and his team fly over the Twin Towers in a helicopter.
☐ The team fire an arrow between the Twin Towers.

6 SPEAKING **Work in pairs and discuss the questions.**

1 Would you like to do something like this? Why/Why not?
2 On the day Petit walked between the Twin Towers, how do you think he felt
   a as he stepped onto the wire?
   b half way into his walk?
   c at the end of his walk?
3 Make a list of three other high-wire walks Petit could do. How exciting, dangerous, challenging and terrifying would they be? Rank them from 1 (least) to 5 (most) for each adjective in turn.

**PRONUNCIATION**

Connected speech feature: elision Go to page 120.

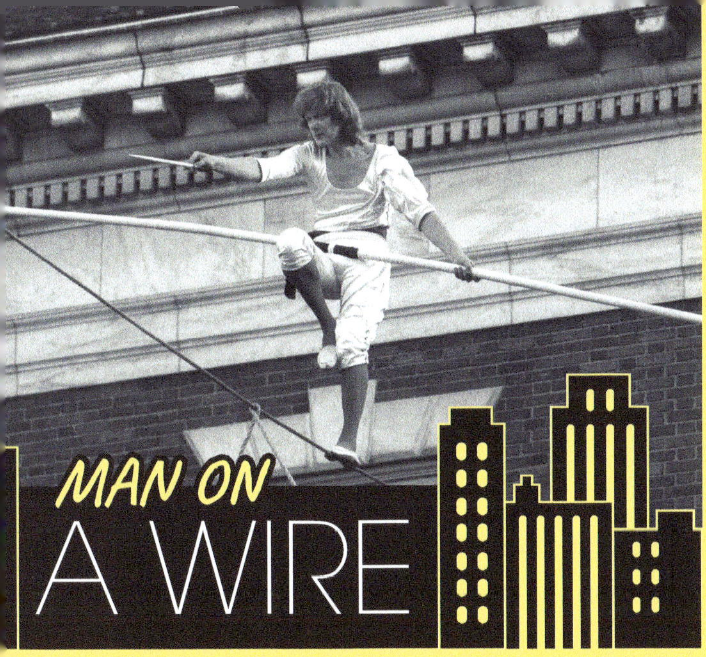

# MAN ON A WIRE

**In the early morning rush hour on 7th August 1974, commuters in New York City stopped their mad dash to work to look up in the sky. Way up above them there seemed to be someone walking between the recently constructed Twin Towers of the World Trade Center. As the crowds grew larger, the person stopped walking and lay down as if he were floating in thin air.**

Four hundred metres above, French-born Philippe Petit looked down on the people below. They were his audience and looked like ants to him. Petit had started his stunt at 7 am, when he first walked out onto the thin wire that passed between the towers. For the next three quarters of an hour, he entertained the New Yorkers below him by walking between the towers, often stopping to sit or lie down on the wire. Eventually, having made eight crossings, Petit took a bow and walked back inside. Arriving safely back on solid ground, Petit handed himself over to the police who were waiting for him.

Since the authorities thought anyone attempting such a death-defying feat must be crazy, he was first taken to a mental-health hospital to determine whether or not he was mad. When they decided he wasn't, he was charged with public disorder offences, but all charges were dropped soon after and Petit was a free man, able to enjoy all the publicity and fame that his tight-rope walk had earned him.

Petit's audacious act had been many months in the planning. With a small group of friends, he had made many plans, assessing and minimising the risks of the challenge he had set himself, including hiring a helicopter, from which they took photos of the towers from above. When he was completely sure that everything was in place, Petit and his team set about preparing for the main event. One member of his team had an office inside one of the towers and the night before, he was able to sneak the team and their heavy equipment up to the top floors of the tower, which were still under construction. Knowing they had a lot to do, the team worked quickly throughout the night. First, they shot an arrow (to which a line was attached) across to a contact on the roof of the other tower. Then, they used this line to pull across a heavy wire. Finally, this wire was secured tightly between the two towers. Petit was ready to step out and introduce himself to the world. Had they not prepared so diligently, the walk might well have ended in disaster.

But the walk between the Twin Towers was not the Frenchman's first daredevil act. Petit had always been a risk-taker, ever since he had first tied a rope between two trees in his parents' garden and practised walking between them. As a young man living in Paris, he met a Czech tight-rope walker called Rudy Omankowsky Jr., who showed him how to prepare ropes for large-scale walks. His first big appearance came in June 1971 when he walked between the two towers at the front of the Notre-Dame cathedral in Paris. Two years later, he was in Sydney to walk along the pylons of the famous harbour bridge. Like the Twin Towers, neither of these walks had permission from the authorities, but Petit has always refused to accept that he is just a stuntman willing to take risks to make himself famous – he insists that he is a performing artist.

## Train to THINK

### Red herrings

*A red herring is often introduced to deliberately cause a distraction from the main issue by appearing to have some actual importance when, in fact, it has none. By thinking critically, we can train ourselves to identify red herrings quickly and not be misled by them. This ultimately places us in a better position to make decisions based only on the facts that are truly important to the issue.*

7 **Read the text in the box and answer the question. Which sentence does not show how Petit has inspired modern daredevils?**

A He has shown that with good preparation, anything is possible.
B He has also had two films made about him.
C He showed how doing such stunts would not get you into trouble with the law.

8 WRITING **Work in pairs. Write a multiple-choice question for the article. Include a red herring.**

9 SPEAKING **Work with another pair. Identify each other's red herring.**

Philippe Petit is an inspiration to many of today's daredevils. His careful planning showed how it was possible to achieve the most audacious of stunts without putting any other person's life in danger. He has also been the subject of at least two films. His exploits have often caused the authorities many headaches. Although, in theory, such actions might be illegal, it would make the authorities very unpopular if they charged these daredevils with a crime.

## GRAMMAR
### Participle clauses

Grammar video ▶12

**1 Look at the sentences from the article. What meanings do the participle clauses (in bold) express? Decide if they mean *at the same time* (a), *after* (b), *because* (c) or *if* (d). Then complete the rule with *reasons, time, the same, results, conditions, present* and *past.***

- ☐ **Having made** eight crossings, Petit took a bow and walked back inside.
- ☐ **Had they not prepared** so diligently, the walk might well have ended in disaster.
- ☐ **Arriving** safely back on solid ground, Petit handed himself over to the police.
- ☐ **Knowing** they had a lot to do, the team worked quickly throughout the night.

**RULE:** We form participle clauses with the present or past participle.

Participle clauses are used to:

- talk about [1]__________ relationships (things happening at the same time, or one after the other).
  *He was looking down at the crowds, **feeling** very excited.* (While he looked down at the crowds, he felt …)
- give [2]__________ to explain an action or event.
  ***Learning** how to prepare ropes properly, Petit decided to try more ambitious walks.* (Because he learned …)
- talk about [3]__________ .
  ***Done** correctly, high-wire walking is not as dangerous as it looks.* (If you do it correctly, high-wire walking …)
- talk about [4]__________ .
  *Petit made the rope higher for each walk, gradually **allowing** him to **get used to** the heights.* (… as a consequence, this gradually allowed him to get used to the heights.)

We can introduce participle clauses with *before, after, while, by, since* and *on.*

We can only use a participle clause if the subject of the two clauses is [5]__________ .

*While white-water rafting, **Jenny** broke her leg.*

We use [6]__________ participles for active clauses and we use [7]__________ participles for passive clauses.

***Jumping** out of the plane, Emma felt exhilarated.*

***Carried** by the wind, she parachuted safely down to the ground.*

**2 Read these sentences taken from a leaflet about the Saltwater Croc Dive in Darwin, Australia. Transform the participle clauses to make longer sentences with *after* or *if*.**

*A sure way to become*

# A DAREDEVIL ...

*Saltwater crocodile watching*

0 Having opened its doors last year, Saltwater Croc Dive has become the best place to get a close look at the world's most dangerous reptiles. (After)

1 Having climbed into a glass cage, the thrilled and terrified tourists are lowered into the water with the crocodiles. (After)

2 Carried out correctly, the dive is completely safe. (If)

3 Having returned to the safety of the beach, you can look at the amazing pictures taken by our professional photographer. (After)

4 Sharing these photos with your friends, you will be the talk of the town. (If)

*After opening its doors last year, Saltwater Croc Dive has become the best place to get a close look at the world's most dangerous reptiles.*

**3 Use a participle clause to shorten each of the following sentence constructions.**

0 Because she'd noticed there was something wrong with her parachute, she didn't jump out of the helicopter.
*Having noticed that something was wrong with her parachute, she didn't jump out of the helicopter.*

1 If you do these exercises regularly, they'll help you to become extremely fit.

2 After they'd watched the stunt, most people were speechless.

3 While we were watching the people in their canoes, we decided to try it, too.

4 She's always been aware of the risks, and because of this, she's never had any serious accidents.

5 He learned how to climb from his father. He became passionate about climbing.

→ workbook page 46

## VOCABULARY
### Thrill seeking

**4 Match the sentence halves.**

1 The skydiver completed an epic *stunt* when ☐
2 Jumping from a plane without ☐
3 As Jenny walked on the narrow edge of the building, 75 metres above ground, ☐
4 She's a real *daredevil*. Have you ever seen ☐
5 We need to *assess the risk* of doing this climb ☐
6 This documentary explains why some people *get a real* ☐
7 She'd never do anything extreme ☐
8 Did you see the video of his *death-defying* ☐

a a parachute is extremely *audacious*.
b leap from the Statue of Liberty?
c *kick out of* doing extreme sports.
d without *minimising the risk* beforehand.
e she said she wasn't scared. She was a *risk-taker* by nature.
f videos of her insane extreme mountain skiing?
g she somersaulted from one glider to another at 180 km per hour.
h before making the decision to go.

**5 Complete the sentences with the correct form of the words and expressions in italics in Exercise 4.**

1 Jumping over ten buses on his motorbike, the ______________ performed another terrifying feat for the crowds.
2 She often climbs without a harness. She's a ______________ .
3 My sister gets a ______________ extreme mountain climbing. She loves it.
4 She ______________ of injury by wearing a helmet.
5 It was an ______________ thing to do. It showed the young hang-glider's skill, strength and lack of fear.
6 He's performed ______________ in many different films, but his most famous was in *Everest*.
7 You need to ______________ before you decide whether or not to climb the building.
8 He performed his ______________ jump from the top of the Eiffel Tower without a parachute.

→ workbook page 48

## SPEAKING

**6** ROLE PLAY **Work in pairs. Student A: Go to page 127. Student B: Go to page 128.**

## LISTENING

**7** SPEAKING **Work in pairs and look at the photo. In what way is this activity different from extreme sports, such as bungee jumping or base jumping? In what way is it similar?**

**8** 5.03 **Listen and compare your answers to what the expert says.**

**9** 5.03 **Listen again and complete these sentences with one or two words.**

1 According to the psychologist, risk-takers need the adrenalin rush they get from doing ______________ .
2 Going on a roller coaster isn't really dangerous, but it ______________ real danger.
3 Some people don't seek an adrenalin rush. They have no interest in ______________ their lives.
4 People who love taking risks are commonly described as ______________ .
5 Some people do dangerous activities to feel adrenalin levels rise in their ______________ .
6 Another theory is that they can forget their ______________ by doing dangerous activities.

## SPEAKING

**10 Rank the activities from 1 to 6 according to how risky they are (1 = not very risky; 6 = very risky).**

☐ riding a motorcycle without a helmet
☐ base jumping
☐ playing tennis
☐ walking in the countryside
☐ playing ice hockey
☐ swimming in the sea

**11 Now rank the activities from 1 to 6 according to how much they make people 'feel alive' (1 = not very alive; 6 = fully alive).**

**12** SPEAKING **Work in pairs. Compare your results with your partner.**

## READING

**1** **Read the statements and tick (✓) the ones you agree with.**

- I never sleep with the air conditioning on. ☐
- I prefer a cold winter to a hot summer. ☐
- I often take cold showers. ☐
- I often wear T-shirts and shorts when others are in long trousers and jumpers. ☐

**2** SPEAKING **Compare with a partner and discuss.**

**3** **Read the article below quickly. Find three of the world records that Wim Hof holds.**

**4** 5.04 **Read the article again and listen. Answer the questions.**

1. Why is the first minute in freezing water the most dangerous?
2. How long does Hof stay in the water?
3. How did Hof create his ability to survive freezing temperatures?
4. Why are scientists interested in Hof?
5. What event changed Hof's life?
6. What does Hof do these days?

**5** SPEAKING **Work in pairs and discuss the questions.**

1. Do you think anyone could learn the Wim Hof method? Why/Why not?
2. Would you be interested in learning the method? Why/Why not?

# WIM HOF: THE ICEMAN

A man sits cross-legged on top of a small mound of ice in Glacier View, Alaska. The temperature is -3°C. He is surrounded by nothing but ice and water. He feels the cold air blowing across his body. He is wearing only shorts and a headband to keep his long hair away from his face. He seems to be meditating. He gets up and walks towards the water's edge. At 2°C, it is just above freezing point. The man bends down and with cupped hands, he pours the water over his face. He feels the ice-cold water run down his face and then he slowly walks into the water and starts swimming. The first minute is the most dangerous – the freezing water is enough to send the human body into panic, causing a fatal heart attack. But a minute is nothing for this extraordinary man. He is in the water for 15 minutes. This would be more than long enough to kill most ordinary people, but one thing is for certain: Wim Hof is no ordinary person.

Wim Hof is a 60-year-old Dutchman who has the ability to endure extreme cold. He developed this ability through using particular breathing techniques. These techniques allow him to get into a mindset where he is able to convince his body that it is not bothered by the freezing temperatures. He has been studied by scientists to see exactly what it is that makes him so remarkable, although Hof himself claims there is no physiological difference. He believes that his techniques can be learned by anyone. Furthermore, he claims that his method brings about an improved immune system – something that the scientists are keen to explore further.

Hof's remarkable journey started with heartache when his wife died, leaving him with four young children to raise on his own. At first, he was unsure how he would cope and he looked for alternative ideas to help him overcome the grief. This led him to the discovery that through his relationship with coldness, he was able to control his breathing and begin to deal with the intense physical pain that he felt. This led him to more and more extreme adventures, which tested his body to its limits and allowed him to explore hidden depths within his mind. It was the start of a long healing process. These days, Hof tours the world, giving inspirational talks and offering courses. On these courses, students can learn the Wim Hof method to help them tune into the inner power of their body to help them cope with the everyday stresses of modern life. He has also made many appearances on TV in several countries to promote his ideas and talk about the successes he has enjoyed.

Unsurprisingly, Hof also holds several world records when it comes to enduring extreme cold; in fact, he holds 26. To break the record for staying in direct contact with ice for the longest time, he stood in a glass box which was filled up with ice cubes while officials watched. After 1 hour and 53 seconds, and to a huge cheer from the audience, the record was his. Other records he holds include running the fastest half marathon in bare feet, climbing Mount Kilimanjaro in only shorts, and swimming for the greatest distance under ice.

# GRAMMAR

## Verbs of perception with infinitive or gerund

**6 Read the sentences from the article. In which sentence is the sensation felt from when it starts to when it ends? Circle the correct options in the rule.**

1 He feels the cold air **blowing** across his body.
2 He feels the ice-cold water **run** down his face .

**RULE:** We use a verb of perception (*see, hear, feel*) plus a gerund to say we have experienced [1]*an entire action / part of an action*.
*I **saw** a man **painting** a house.*
*I **felt** my heart **beating** fast.*
*I **heard** someone **playing** the piano.*
We use a verb of perception plus an infinitive to say we have experienced [2]*an entire action / part of an action*.
*I **saw** a man **paint** a picture.*
*I **felt** her hand **touch** my shoulder.*
*I **heard** someone **close** the door.*

**7 Complete the sentences with the correct form of the verb in brackets.**

1 We heard somebody ______________ and then it was silent. (scream)
2 The noise was terrible and it went on for hours. We heard people ______________ drums and ______________ whistles loudly. (bang, blow)
3 When he woke up after the operation, he saw lots of people ______________ around his bed. (stand)
4 When we were driving home, I suddenly saw a deer ______________ across the road before it disappeared. (run)
5 I was lying in bed when I became aware of an insect ______________ on my face. I switched on the light, but couldn't see anything. (crawl)
6 The rain was beating down on the roof of the car, and I suddenly felt water ______________ down onto the back of my neck. (drip)

→ workbook page 47

# VOCABULARY

## Idioms with *hot* and *cold*

**8 Read the sentences. Complete the idioms with *hot* (x3) or *cold* (x3).**

1 It was only a joke. There's no need to *get so* ______________ *under the collar* about it.
2 I tried to talk to Ann, but she completely ignored me and *gave me the* ______________ *shoulder*.
3 When your dad finds out you've scratched his car, you'll *be in* ______________ *water*.
4 I don't mean to *pour* ______________ *water on* your idea but it really isn't very practical.
5 No one's told me anything. I've been completely *left out in the* ______________ .
6 Her interview is today and she's getting very ______________ *and bothered* about it. She just needs to relax.

**9 Use the idioms in Exercise 8 to complete the dialogues.**

1 A This is so annoying! I can't log in to my computer, but I'm sure this password is correct.
B OK. There's no point getting all ______________ about it. Try a different one.
2 A I saw Steve today and he completely gave me ______________ .
B Well, I'm not surprised after you ______________ on his ideas for his new website.
A Well, they were really silly. I don't know why he got so ______________ about what I said.
3 A Be careful when you see Sally. You're really in ______________ with her.
B Why? What did I do?
A I think she feels you left her ______________ when you booked the holiday without asking her. She isn't at all happy with you.

→ workbook page 48

# FUNCTIONS

## Giving and reacting to an opinion

**10** 5.05 **Listen to the dialogues and answer the questions.**

1 What opinions are expressed in dialogue 1? And in dialogue 2?
2 In each case, who do you agree with?

**11** 5.05 **Listen to the dialogues again and match the phrases with functions 1–4 below.**

1 giving an opinion
2 agreeing
3 disagreeing
4 conceding a point

- ☐ To my mind, that's …
- ☐ Yes, I suppose you're right.
- ☐ I don't accept that …
- ☐ The way I see it is …
- ☐ I hadn't thought of that.
- ☐ That's not how I see things.
- ☐ True.
- ☐ I'd go along with that.
- ☐ OK. Point taken.

**12** ROLE PLAY **Work in pairs. You're going to discuss extreme sports and try to convince your partner of your opinion. Student A: Go to page 127. Student B: Go to page 128. Use the phrases from Exercise 11 in your discussions.**

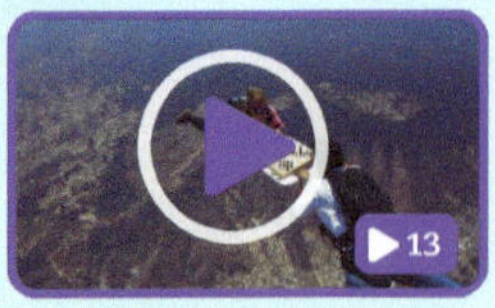

**TH!NK**

Extreme sports

# Culture

**1 Look at the photos and read the article quickly. Then answer the questions.**

1 Where are these places?

2 What do the activities have in common? What differences are there between them?

# GOING TO THE EXTREME

**We all have different interests, that's for sure, and extreme sports are certainly not for the faint-hearted. They're for those people who live on adrenalin and whose idea of hell is sitting at home watching TV. If you're looking for that ultimate thrill, no matter how brief, there are places you can go to get the most exhilarating experiences. Here are a few of them.**

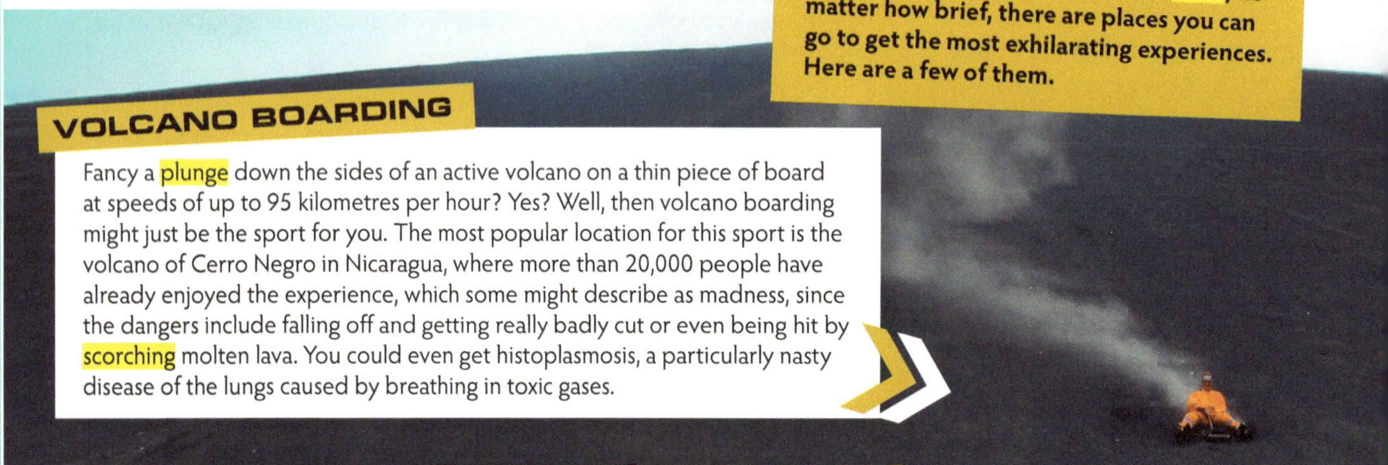

## VOLCANO BOARDING

Fancy a plunge down the sides of an active volcano on a thin piece of board at speeds of up to 95 kilometres per hour? Yes? Well, then volcano boarding might just be the sport for you. The most popular location for this sport is the volcano of Cerro Negro in Nicaragua, where more than 20,000 people have already enjoyed the experience, which some might describe as madness, since the dangers include falling off and getting really badly cut or even being hit by scorching molten lava. You could even get histoplasmosis, a particularly nasty disease of the lungs caused by breathing in toxic gases.

## CALCIO STORICO

If you ever find yourself going for a wander through the Piazza Santa Croce in the beautiful Italian city of Florence in late June, you may well come across an extraordinary sight: dozens of men dressed in historical costumes, chasing a ball and stopping at nothing to get to it. Calcio storico is a game you won't find anywhere else in the world. It's probably best described as a mixture of football and rugby with a lot of wrestling thrown in. Four teams of 27 players, representing each of the four districts of Florence, compete in semi-finals and a final to find that year's champion. The general idea is to score as many 'cacce' as you can by throwing the ball over marked-out goals around the pitch. Of course, you also need to stop your opponents doing the same thing and can use tactics such as punching, elbowing and head-butting to help you, although these days kicks to the head are no longer allowed.

## CLIFF DIVING

La Quebrada, Acapulco, is the site of the famous cliff divers' performance. Since 1934, this has been one of Mexico's top attractions. The divers leap from cliffs 41 metres above the Pacific, landing in water just over three metres deep. There are five performances daily, including four evening shows, performed by divers carrying torches – an unforgettable display.

Anyone who's watched Acapulco's cliff divers plunge into the rough sea may wonder how daring and tricky an act this is. Ramirez Vasquez, who comes from a family of cliff divers, says that timing is key. He explains that in order to hit the water when it's at its deepest and ultimately, safest, cliff divers have a five-second window during which the wave is high. It takes three seconds to reach the water, giving them a two-second margin of error.

In preparation for his twice-daily dive, Vasquez works out from 8 am to 10 am, five times a week. Meditation is also part of his routine. He still gets nervous before each and every dive, despite his vast experience. An average diver who starts their career at 17 and ends it at 45 will do 15,560 dives into the Quebrada. Many cliff divers have been involved in accidents, most caused by the impact of the water. Remarkably, no deaths have been recorded to date.

2 5.06 **Read the article again and listen. At which of the three places …**

1 could you see people dressed in clothes from the past?
2 could you be burned by hot rock?
3 are even experienced participants always scared before the activity?
4 can you see a sport that doesn't take place anywhere else?
5 will you see people wrestling in a public square?
6 will you see people leap from a 41-metre cliff into the sea below?
7 could you see a dangerous eruption?
8 could you see several people competing in a game?

3 VOCABULARY **Match the highlighted words in the article with the definitions.**

1 a casual walk
2 the people you play against in a sporting contest
3 fall or move down very quickly or with force
4 a length of time when it's possible to do something
5 not brave
6 a strong feeling of excitement, joy
7 force or action (created by one object hitting another)
8 very, very hot

4 SPEAKING **Work in pairs and discuss the questions.**

1 Which of these sports would you most like to try? Put them in order of preference.
2 Which of these sports would you most like to watch? Put them in order of preference.
3 What's your view on these and other extreme sports?

## WRITING
### A newspaper article

5 INPUT **Read the newspaper article. Why did the writer choose this title?**

# Eight and a half seconds I'll never remember

Had anyone asked me a year ago if I'd ever be standing in a small cabin, looking out over a 134-metre drop, preparing to launch myself towards the ground below, I'd have told them they were mad. But that's exactly where I found myself yesterday morning.

I've never been much of a daredevil. I've ridden a few of the smaller roller coasters at Alton Towers, but that's about it. So why was I now about to risk life and limb for the sake of a newspaper story?

The idea to 'do' the world's highest bungee jump came from my editor. When he requested a travel article on New Zealand, naturally I leapt at the chance. It was only while I was travelling to the airport that a text came from him suggesting I check out the Nevis bungee in Queensland. OK, I thought, there's no harm in that.

Thirty-six hours later, having checked into my simple but charming hotel in the heart of the city, I spent the evening talking with locals about my imminent jump. That's when I started to wonder if I'd completely taken leave of my senses. 'It's the highest in the world,' they told me. Had any of them done it? 'No.'

The beautiful drive out to the privately owned jump is worth an article of its own, but that isn't what my editor wants. He wants to know about the longest eight and a half seconds of my life as I free-fell through the air, with only a thin wire to save me from certain death. Well, I'm pretty sure it was the most frightening experience of my life – the only problem is, I don't really remember a single thing about it.

6 ANALYSE **Read the article again and put the information below in the order in which it is mentioned.**

- ☐ how high the jump was
- ☐ where the bungee jump was
- ☐ how long the jump lasted
- ☐ what the writer thought about the jump
- ☐ when the writer did the jump
- ☐ the journey to do the jump
- ☐ where the writer stayed
- ☐ when the writer realised how scary the jump might be

7 **Find an example of a participle clause in the article.**

8 PRODUCE **Write a newspaper article (200–250 words) about one of the other extreme sports you've read about in this unit.**

- Either imagine you did it or you saw someone else doing it.
- Think carefully about how to introduce the details of the experience. It doesn't need to be in chronological order.
- Present the facts throughout the article to maintain interest.
- Try and include at least two participle clauses.

# 6 FAMOUS LIVES

## Get THINKING

Watch the video and think: would you like a life of fame and fortune?

**OBJECTIVES**

**FUNCTIONS:** complaining

**GRAMMAR:** modals 1: *may, might, can, could, will, won't*; modals 2: *should, shouldn't, must, mustn't, can't*

**VOCABULARY:** admiration; fame

A

C

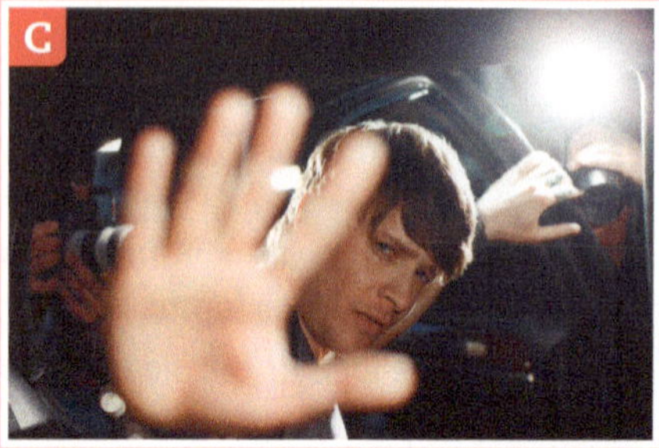

E

B

D

## READING

**1** SPEAKING **Work in pairs and discuss.**

1 Which celebrities are currently in the news or have been recently? Why are they in the news?
2 Do you think celebrities are in the news too much? Why?

**2 Look at the people in the photos (A–E). Match each one to the thoughts below.**

1 I can't believe I'm this close to him/her!
2 Can't wait to post this on Instagram!
3 Look this way! Smile for the camera.
4 'You really look like that famous actor.' 'I get that a lot.'
5 This is my downtime. I'm not at work now.

**3** SPEAKING **Compare with a partner. What other thoughts might the celebrities and their followers be having?**

**4 Read the magazine article quickly. How does the author feel about a celebrity's right to privacy?**

**5** 6.01 **Read the article again and listen. In which paragraph are each of these points made? Write 1–5 in the boxes below and underline the words and phrases in the article which helped you choose your answers.**

- [ ] It was the right decision not to tweet about the YouTuber.
- [ ] A celebrity's private life is his or her business and no one else's.
- [ ] Many celebrities are not keen to have a fan take a selfie with them.
- [ ] We think too much about the lives of celebrities.
- [ ] A celebrity's fame relies on followers commenting about them on social media.
- [ ] If you are going to tweet about a celebrity, tweet something positive.
- [ ] The author feels it would be uncomfortable to be the focus of attention on social media.
- [ ] People wrongly think of celebrities as friends because they recognise them.

**6** SPEAKING **Work in pairs and discuss the questions.**

1 Name the three most popular celebrities among people of your age. Why are they popular? Do you like them? Why/Why not?
2 Which famous people, if any, do you follow on Twitter or in the media?
3 Why do you think that some people find the lives of celebrities so interesting?
4 Would you like to be famous? Why/Why not?

# To tweet or not to tweet?

**1** When you buy your plane ticket, you never know who you will be sitting next to on the plane, and on this particular flight, I was sitting next to a famous YouTube star – an [1]*idol* of mine, in fact. Of course, my first thought was to ask him for a selfie, but then I asked myself: would that be intrusive? This was a private moment in his life and celebrities can become very upset when fans ask for selfies. Then I thought: he makes his living from being famous, so does he have a right to a private life? If people didn't tweet about him, he wouldn't be so famous, would he? I contemplated the issue of celebrity and privacy for a few moments more. His face was so familiar, I felt as though I knew him. In reality, he was a stranger and you wouldn't ask a complete stranger for a selfie, would you?

**2** Of course, you don't know who I'm talking about, do you? Here are some clues: he posts *Minecraft* videos on his YouTube channel and has 25 million subscribers who [2]*worship* him. He's got a vlog that I'm [3]*addicted* to. No? You still don't know who he is? I may just have to tweet about this. But then it could go viral. I could get a million likes, who knows. But would I be happy being [4]*the centre of attention*? I don't think so.

**3** It's then that I remember reading Alankrutha Giridhar's tweets. She was the 25-year-old who shared her story about sitting next to the Academy Award-nominated actor, Timothée Chalamet, on a three-hour flight. Just about the only thing she didn't share was where she flew to on that flight because she didn't want people to know Chalamet's location. That was sensible of her. She tweeted everything else in 21 social media posts. Was that a foolhardy thing to do? It might have been if she had said disagreeable things about him and he was shown in a negative light, but she only commented on how affable he was. It was great publicity for him, really. And as there was no harm done, you might forgive her. After all, he did give her permission to tweet after the flight had landed. Still, I won't tweet about the celebrity sitting next to me. It wouldn't be fair. This is his private life and despite everyone's [5]*fascination* with him, they don't need to know that he's just ordered a chocolate bar and a hot chocolate. Besides, he may be annoyed if I tweet about him and I don't want that. Our [6]*obsession* with finding out every little detail about the lives of celebrities is wrong.

**4** And so I don't tweet. I slip my phone into my bag, and I decide to talk to him instead. I tell him that I follow him on YouTube and that I'm a [7]*huge fan* of his vlog. He's interested to know what I think of it and I tell him. We chat and he's actually very amiable and sincere. We have a lot of similar interests and we have a fascinating conversation. I think about that, and I'm content that I chose not to invade his privacy. I will remember this flight for the rest of my life, but take my word for it, just a few friends and I will be the only ones who know who I sat next to that day.

**5** We are [8]*fixated* on finding out about the private lives of celebrities but I've come to the conclusion that their private lives should remain exactly that – private.

## Train to TH!NK

### Making logical conclusions (syllogisms)

*A syllogism is a system of logic where a conclusion is drawn from two propositions that are assumed to be true. It is often attributed to the Greek philosopher Aristotle, who used the following example:*

*All men are mortal. (proposition 1)*

*Socrates is a man. (proposition 2)*

*Therefore, Socrates is mortal. (conclusion)*

*Syllogisms can only work if both propositions are true, so before we accept any conclusion, we should consider whether each of the propositions on which it is based is indeed true.*

**7 Look carefully at these two syllogisms. Find the flaws in the logic of each conclusion.**

1 A lot of famous people love attention.
Timothée Chalamet is famous.
Therefore, he loves being tweeted about.

2 Celebrities enjoy being the centre of attention.
Chalamet is a celebrity.
Therefore, Chalamet enjoys being the centre of attention.

**8** WRITING **Work in pairs. Write a valid conclusion and an invalid conclusion for this syllogism.**

*Scorpion* is an album by Drake.
Lucy has all of Drake's albums.
Therefore, …

## GRAMMAR

Grammar video ▶15

### Modals 1: *may, might, can, could, will, won't*

1 **Underline the modal verbs in these sentences from the article on page 57 and then match each modal with the meanings they give to the sentences in the rule box.**

1 When you buy your plane ticket, you never know who you will be sitting next to on the plane.
2 But then it could go viral.
3 And as there was no harm done, you might forgive her.
4 I could get a million likes, who knows.
5 Celebrities can become very upset when fans ask for selfies.
6 Still, I won't tweet about the celebrity sitting next to me.
7 Besides, he may be annoyed if I tweet about him and I don't want that.
8 I will remember this flight for the rest of my life.

**RULE:**
a hypothesising: example ______ and ______
b talking about possibility: example ______
c talking about typical behaviour: example ______
d refusing: example ______
e making a concession: example ______
f a belief about the future: example ______
g theoretical possibility: example ______

2 SPEAKING **Work in pairs. Discuss the difference in meaning of the modal verb in a and b in each pair of sentences. Pay attention to any time references.**

1 a I may watch the film tonight – I'll see how I feel.
  b He may be rich and famous, but has his work taken over his life?
2 a It might rain later. I think I heard that on the weather forecast this morning.
  b They might be French. I think they said something about her parents living in Paris.
3 a Learning a new language can be difficult.
  b He can speak three languages.
4 a We could have a problem.
  b My grandfather could solve most problems.
5 a We'll be a bit late if we don't hurry.
  b Children will get restless if they've got nothing to do.
6 a He won't tell me. It's so annoying. I really want to know!
  b I really don't want to go to the party. I won't know anyone there.

→ workbook page 54

**PRONUNCIATION**
Modal stress and meaning Go to page 120.

## VOCABULARY

### Admiration

3 **Match the words in italics (1–8) in the article on page 57 with the meanings.**

a someone or something that everyone is focused on ☐
b having very strong habits that are hard to break ☐
c extreme interest in ☐
d something that you think about all the time ☐
e someone admired or adored by lots of people ☐
f a very big admirer ☐
g not take your eyes off something ☐
h to adore ☐

4 **Complete the text with words and phrases from the list.**

addicted | centre of attention
fascination | fixated | huge fan
idols | obsession | worshipped

When I was growing up, the TV was very much the [1] ______ in our house. Mum, Dad, me, my baby sister – we were all [2] ______ on that little box in the living room. It caused a lot of arguments, too.

Take Saturday mornings, for example. Lola wanted to watch her pop [3] ______ performing on children's TV. Dad wanted to watch the football preview programme to get the latest news on his football team. He [4] ______ Chelsea! Mum and I were [5] ______ to the cookery programmes. We couldn't get enough of them. Mum was a [6] ______ of one chef and she even wrote him a letter once.

The problem is these programmes were all on at the same time and we only had one TV. These days, people's [7] ______ with the TV seems to be much less pronounced. There's a new [8] ______ in most people's lives: their smartphone or social media.

→ workbook page 56

## LISTENING

**5** **Work in pairs. Make a list of the ways a sports team can become successful globally.**

**6** 🔊 6.03 **Listen to a radio programme about Liverpool F.C. and how the team is marketed around the world. Which of the ways you listed in Exercise 5 did you hear? Which other ways were mentioned?**

**7** 🔊 6.03 **Listen again and match the speaker (Steve, David or the presenter) with the sentences which paraphrase the ideas expressed. There are three sentences that don't correspond to any of the speakers.**

1. In my heart, I know it's wrong to support them.
2. Millions of supporters follow their football team online.
3. My family supports Liverpool and so do I.
4. Social media has played a large part in making the team popular around the world.
5. Campaigns don't all take place at the same time of year.
6. In Colombia, Liverpool fans meet up to watch a live broadcast of a match.
7. If a team loses a match, their merchandise still sells.
8. The weather can affect merchandise sales.
9. He probably won't go to watch a football match in the UK.
10. They can buy the Liverpool shorts and shirt in Colombia.
11. You will always be alone.
12. You will always have the support of other fans.

## SPEAKING

**8** **Discuss in small groups.**

1. What sports teams do you follow?
2. How do you feel when they lose?
3. How do you feel when they win?
4. What do these teams mean to you?
5. Are there any famous players from your country who play in overseas teams?
6. How do people in your country feel about this?

## TH!NK *values*

### Teamwork

**9** **Rank the following qualities in order of how important they are to be a good team player (1 = least important; 5 = most important).**

- ☐ being a good listener
- ☐ possessing strong leadership skills
- ☐ having a small ego
- ☐ liking your teammates
- ☐ respecting your teammates

**10** **Think of and note down other important qualities and decide on your final top five.**

**11** SPEAKING **Work in groups of four. Compare your ranking and agree on a new list of five.**

**12** SPEAKING **Discuss in pairs.**

1. How easy was it to come up with a group list?
2. Did your group work well as a team? Why/Why not?
3. What sports teams can you think of that are an example of
   - a good teamwork?
   - b bad teamwork?
4. What makes them good/bad?

## READING

1 SPEAKING **Work in pairs. Imagine you are a celebrity. What would be the advantages and disadvantages of your celebrity status?**

2 **Read the article quickly. Which of your ideas are mentioned?**

3 6.04 **Read the article again and listen. Answer the questions.**

1 What do you need to do in return for being given expensive clothes?
2 What do celebrities soon become tired of?
3 What kind of opportunities does fame bring?
4 What can celebrities find very hurtful?

## WordWise
## Expressions with *take*

→ workbook page 56

4 **Look at these sentences from the unit so far. Complete them with the phrases from the list.**

take […] personally | take it (that) | take my word for it | taken over his life | taking an interest in

1 He may be rich and famous, but has his work _____________ ?
2 Are people _____________ you because they like you or because you are famous?
3 But _____________ , just a few friends and I will be the only ones who know who I sat next to that day.
4 David, I _____________ you've never seen them play at Anfield.
5 It's almost impossible not to _____________ the comments _____________ .

5 **Choose the correct options.**

1 I told her I wasn't meaning to criticise. Why does she always take everything so *over / personally*?
2 It's always nice when someone else takes *my word / an interest* in you and your life.
3 You don't believe me? Well, don't take *my word for it / it personally*. Ask Mr Jones.
4 What a big smile! I *take it / take your word for it* you've had some good news!

# FAME – A BLESSING OR A CURSE?

**Being a celebrity has advantages and disadvantages. Read this article and decide for yourself whether the life of a celebrity is a blessing or a curse.**

## THE ADVANTAGES

**Getting special treatment** Luxurious homes and cars, luxury holidays and expensive clothes can all be yours; in fact, you shouldn't ever need to buy clothes again, as global brands will give them to you in return for you wearing their clothes and being photographed in them. Restaurants will seat you at their best table and give you star treatment. What's not to like?

**Being recognised** For up-and-coming celebrities, being recognised can be a giant ego-boost and they never grow tired of being in the limelight. Adoring fans wanting a selfie with you can be very flattering. However, for others the constant recognition can quickly become tiresome, so celebrities should perhaps be prepared for the initial charm to wear off.

**Adoring fans** Adoring fans can often develop a celebrity crush on their favourite actor or pop star. The fan mail that celebrities receive can be both inspiring and motivating, as well as very humbling. After all, who wouldn't like to have their own fans and followers?

**Business opportunities** Fame brings with it other opportunities for the popular celebrity. For example, Michael Jordan didn't only make a living from playing basketball; he was also the face of Nike and he promoted many other brands. Being famous can open other doors in life and celebrities often start up other businesses. For instance, female stars such as Kylie and Beyoncé have their own fashion labels and beauty brands.

## THE DISADVANTAGES

**No privacy** As an A-list celebrity, you can't lead a normal life. You can't have a quiet meal with friends in a restaurant; you can't just go to a beach and swim; you can't go shopping or do any of the things you like to do without the constant intrusion of fans and paparazzi.

Some celebrities have strategies to combat this invasion of their privacy. They will go to enormous lengths to keep a low profile and avoid appearing in newspapers and magazines. For five or six months, Daniel Radcliffe always ventured out wearing the same clothes. The paparazzi following him couldn't sell any photos of him because it looked like they were all taken on the same day.

**Attracting fake friends and stalkers** Are people taking an interest in you because they like you or because you are famous? You must constantly be on your guard and your celebrity status will attract envy, jealousy and gossip. There is also the danger of being harassed by stalkers. These are people who become obsessed by their idol and their obsession can potentially turn into threats and violence.

**Being judged** Celebrities should always watch what they wear and what they do, because the media is constantly judging them. Reading nasty and insulting comments and lies about yourself is a part and parcel of a celebrity's daily routine. It's almost impossible not to take the comments personally. How would you like to see unflattering photos of yourself and read derogatory comments about anything from your weight to your choice of clothes?

Is fame and the fortune it brings really worth it? What do you think?

# GRAMMAR

## Modals 2: *should, shouldn't, must, mustn't, can't*

**6 Complete the example sentences and check them in the article. Then match each modal with its function.**

1 Celebrities _______________ perhaps be prepared for the initial charm to wear off.

2 As an A-list celebrity, you _______________ lead a normal life.

3 You _______________ constantly be on your guard.

4 Celebrities _______________ always watch what they wear and what they do, because the media is constantly judging them.

RULE:
a what you'd expect (under normal circumstances): example ______
b strong advice: example ______
c it's reasonable: example ______
d advice: example______

**7 Read the sentences. In each one, who do you think is talking to whom? What do you think they are talking about?**

1 a You should think carefully about the offer.
b You should arrive on time if you leave now.

2 a You shouldn't stay up too late.
b You shouldn't be surprised if she says 'no'.

3 a They must be really happy about the news.
b You must watch this film.

4 a You mustn't tell anyone.
b You mustn't be too hopeful.

5 a You can't go to the party.
b She can't be very popular.

**8 SPEAKING Work in pairs. Look at the sentences in Exercise 7 and discuss the difference in meaning of the modal verb in a and b. Pay attention to the time reference in each case.**

**9 WRITING Choose two of the sentences in Exercise 7 and use them to write mini dialogues of four to six lines.**

A *You should think carefully about the offer.*
B *Really? I wasn't very impressed with it.*
A *You won't get a better one, I promise.*
B *That's where I disagree. I think I will.*
A *Well, I hope you don't end up regretting it.*
B *I won't.*

→ workbook page 55

# VOCABULARY

## Fame

**10 Match the sentence halves.**

1 She's enjoyed *being in the* ☐
2 He's an *up-and-* ☐
3 The *paparazzi* couldn't ☐
4 She doesn't like attention and tries ☐
5 She was followed everywhere ☐
6 My sister has a *celebrity* ☐
7 She is *the face* ☐
8 The party was amazing. All the *A-list* ☐

a *coming* comedian. He's going to be huge!
b *celebrities* were there.
c she went by a *stalker*.
d *crush* on Chris Hemsworth.
e *of* an expensive new perfume.
f take any photos of her because she hid her face.
g to *keep a low profile*.
h *limelight* since she was in the school play aged six.

**11 SPEAKING Complete the sentences with the missing words. Then work in pairs and discuss the questions.**

1 Which famous people can you think of who like to keep _______________ ?
2 Who are the A-_______________ celebrities in your country?
3 Do you enjoy being in the _______________ ? Why/Why not?
4 What punishment should a _______________ get for following a celebrity?
5 Is it normal to have a _______________ on an actor/actress?

→ workbook page 56

# WRITING

## An essay

**12 INPUT Read these essay titles.**

- Famous people have a right to privacy. Discuss.
- Some people will do anything for fame. Discuss.
- The media is too focused on celebrities. Discuss.

**13 PLAN Your class had a discussion on the third title. You made the notes below. How could you organise them into an essay structure?**

- Famous people sell newspapers.
- They're a distraction from all of the horrible things happening in the world right now.
- Our children are growing up wanting to be famous. There needs to be a balance.

**14 PRODUCE Your teacher has asked you to write one of the essays from Exercise 12. Write your essay in 220–260 words.**

# DEVELOPING SPEAKING

**1** 🔊 6.05 **Look at the photos. Who do you think the girl is talking to? Who is the tennis player? What's the connection between the girl and the tennis player? Read, listen and check your ideas.**

**Mum:** So, at the weekend, let's have a picnic in the park. I'm tired of always being indoors. I want to do something outside for a change. What do you think, Becky?

**Becky:** Sure, Mum. Whatever. Oh no! Seriously?

**Mum:** Becky? Just out of curiosity, what are you doing on your phone? No, let me guess. You're reading her feed on Instagram, aren't you?

**Becky:** Well, if by 'her' you mean Naomi Osaka – yes, I am. What's the big deal, Mum?

**Mum:** Tennis, tennis, tennis. It's always tennis. And always following Osaka on social media. But seriously, ... it's all you ever do.

**Becky:** Oh, come on, Mum. That's so not true.

**Mum:** It *is* true, Becky. I think it's great you like playing tennis, but constantly following players on your phone ... Haven't you got anything else to do with your time? I'm worried your schoolwork's suffering.

**Becky:** Oh, Mum, give me a break, please! I really don't need this right now.

**Mum:** Well, have you finished your project work, by any chance?

**Becky:** No, but I can do that this evening, after the match.

**Mum:** Match? What match?

**Becky:** Um, well, I'm playing mixed doubles with Steve this evening, at the club. Six o'clock.

**Mum:** Well you might have told me, Becky. And what about your dinner?

**Becky:** Sorry, Mum, I forgot. Don't worry, I'll be back by seven thirty.

**Mum:** Fat chance of that! You'll never finish a match and get back home in an hour and a half.

**Becky:** OK. I'll call off the tennis, do my project work and then have dinner. Happy now?

**Mum:** There's no need to be like that. And don't call off your match. It's just ... I think you should have other interests, that's all.

**2** 🔊 6.05 **Read and listen to the dialogue again. Answer the questions.**

1 What are Becky's mum's concerns about her?
2 What has Becky forgotten to do?
3 How does Becky's mum feel at the end of the conversation?

## Phrases for fluency

**3 Find these expressions in the dialogue. Who says them? How do you say them in your language?**

1 for a change
2 Just out of curiosity
3 Come on
4 ..., by any chance?
5 You might have told me
6 Fat chance

**4 Use the expressions in Exercise 3 to complete the dialogues.**

1 A Have you tidied your bedroom? I want that done before you go out.
B ____________, Dad, I haven't got time. I'll do it later.

2 A We always eat Italian. Why don't we try Japanese food ____________?
B But I don't really like Japanese food.

3 A Do you think we're going to win today?
B ____________. They're way better than we are.

4 A ____________, can I ask you why you're looking so happy?
B I've just had the most fantastic news!

5 A Joan? Listen, sorry, I can't make it tonight.
B What? ____________ earlier. I've just finished getting ready!

6 A Can you lend me ten pounds, ____________?
B Sorry, I haven't got ten pounds.

## FUNCTIONS
### Complaining

**5 Write the phrases in the correct column.**

But seriously, ... it's all you ever do. | ~~Give me a break ...~~
Haven't you got anything else to do with your time?
I really don't need this right now.
I really haven't got time for this now. | ~~It's always tennis~~

| Making a complaint | Responding to a complaint |
|---|---|
| *It's always (tennis)* | *Give me a break ...* |

**6** ROLE PLAY **Work in pairs. Student A plays the part of Jake. Student B plays the part of Jake's father. Use the expressions from Exercise 5 in your conversation. Then switch roles.**

Jake is mad about horses. He's about to go horse-riding. His dad thinks he spends too much time on his hobby.

# LIFE COMPETENCIES

**It's good to have an interest or a hobby that you really love, but you should be careful about becoming obsessed with one thing. Having a wide range of interests can bring advantages.**

1 ▶ 16 **Watch the vlog. Tick (✓) the hobbies that Will has had at some point in his life.**

- ☐ birdwatching
- ☐ computer gaming
- ☐ photography
- ☐ film-making
- ☐ acting
- ☐ vlogging
- ☐ politics
- ☐ writing

2 ▶ 16 **Watch the vlog again. Work in pairs. Discuss these questions using your answers to Exercise 1.**

1 How did Will go from being a birdwatcher to a vlogger?
2 How is Will's life story a good example of the vlog theme?

3 **Read the book review and answer the questions.**

1 What is Paul's obsession?
2 What problems has this caused him in his life?
3 When does he start to realise there are other things in life?

4 SPEAKING **Work in pairs and discuss the questions.**

1 What other things/interests do people sometimes become fanatical or obsessive about?
2 Do you know of any other characters in films or books or TV programmes who are obsessive?

5 **Choose one or two of the following areas of interest. Think how the interest could be expanded.**

films | literature | mobiles | music | sport

*music: singing / playing an instrument / listening to music / history of music / music photography / ...*

## *Fever Pitch* (1997)

The film *Fever Pitch* is based on the novel by Nick Hornby. The story is set in London and concerns Paul Ashworth, a schoolteacher who is obsessed with football and the team he supports, Arsenal. He has been obsessed since he was 11 years old, when his father took him to his first match. Paul eats, drinks and sleeps football (he is the coach of the school football team) and Arsenal. Paul's life revolves around Arsenal and their games – he goes to every home game. However, he starts a relationship with another teacher, Sarah, who knows nothing about football and cares about it even less.

As the film develops, we see the extent of Paul's obsession, for example, when he is interviewed for a more senior position at the school, he is asked about his interests and can only say 'football'. (He doesn't get the job.) He also has a strained relationship with his mother because of football. We also see how Sarah at first cannot understand Paul's passion for the game – at one point she leaves him because of it. However, she slowly begins to empathise with him and helps him to see that there's more to life than one thing. When she becomes pregnant, Paul gets excited about starting a new life as a father and husband and starts to behave a little differently. Sarah shares his happiness at the end when Arsenal win the championship.

The film is an interesting examination of fanaticism, and looks at the importance of having as many interests as possible in order to lead a fulfilling life.

## Me and my world

6 **Complete the lists for yourself.**

- My big hobbies:
- Things I have a bit of interest in:
- Things I'd like to know more about:

7 SPEAKING **Work in pairs. Use your lists to discuss your interests with your partner and to give advice about how they could expand their interests.**

## TIPS ON HAVING A WIDE RANGE OF INTERESTS

- **Think about people that you have something in common with. The things they are interested in might interest you as well.**
- **If most of your interests are to be found indoors, think of one or two outdoor pursuits you might like to try (and vice versa).**

## READING AND USE OF ENGLISH

### Part 7: Gapped text

→ workbook page 61

1 **You are going to read an extract from a magazine article. Six paragraphs have been removed from the extract. Choose from the paragraphs A–G the one which fits each gap (1–6). There is one extra paragraph that you do not need to use.**

**FAN BEHAVIOUR**

While it may seem understandable that an athlete becomes attached to teammates and to being part of a team, it's clear that sports spectators can also become extremely passionate about their team, to the point that it becomes part of their identity and can affect their well-being.

1 ☐

Team identification is the extent to which that fan feels a psychological connection to a team, and the team's performances are viewed as relevant on a personal level, according to Daniel Wann, Professor of Psychology at Murray State University.

2 ☐

As with these other aspects of identity, people are investing a lot of who they are in their identity as a fan of a team. As Professor Wann explains: 'A huge part of who they are, where they derive a lot of their positive and negative feelings, is from what their team is doing.' Perhaps the most basic question is why people follow sports so ardently. What is it about watching sports that makes people scream, obsess over statistics, and paint their faces, particularly when they know that there's a very good chance that their team won't achieve success?

3 ☐

In other words, it's a voluntary activity where a large proportion of consumers aren't going to like the product when they've finished consuming it. As Wann says: 'You wouldn't go see a movie if you thought there was a fifty-fifty chance you wouldn't like it.'

4 ☐

Perhaps no fans demonstrate what these must be better than followers of the Chicago Cubs. The Cubs haven't won the World Series for nearly 100 years, yet the team has a legendary community. Ask a Cubs fan why they like the team and they won't say because of the championships.

5 ☐

The senior vice president of Marketing for the Cubs agrees. 'We're marketing the experience more than other teams,' he says. 'Here, it's about the unique mystique of the Chicago Cubs. What resonates the loudest with the fanbase is the experience.'

6 ☐

'When we look at motivation for following a sports team, group affiliation is one of the top ones,' says Wann. 'Identifying strongly with a local team where other fans are around – that's a benefit to social-psychological well-being.'

**A** 'They'll say, "I love Wrigley Field – I love the community here," ' says Wann. So it's evident that identification is not simply a matter of results; it has far more to do with an experience.

**B** Fans who watched their team win, however, reported significantly higher estimates of the team's future performance, their own task performance and personal self-esteem than those who watched their team lose.

**C** A fan may be affected in this way because, watching the action, the individual does identify with the team, and for some fans, this becomes important for their sense of self.

**D** People report many reasons for following a favourite team, but social connectedness is one of the most frequently mentioned aspects of the experience, as Wann finds in his research on college and professional sports fans.

**E** Sports fan researchers acknowledge the irony in this: sporting events are competitions in which it's assumed that one team will generally lose, which means that around half of those watching won't see their desired result. In other activities, those odds might not seem like a worthwhile investment of one's time.

**F** The research he's carried out there has shown similarities between a fan's identification with a sports team and how people identify with their nationality, ethnicity, or even gender.

**G** So being a fan can't be all about a team's winning performance. 'Everyone is eventually going to lose,' says Wann. 'It's clear there have to be other benefits.'

# TEST YOURSELF UNITS 5 & 6

## VOCABULARY

**1 Complete the sentences with the words in the list. There are four extra words.**

A-list | cold | crush | daredevil | for | hot | in | kick | on | risk | shoulder | stunt | with | worshipped

1 He's fixated ____________ getting into the football team. He talks about nothing else.
2 I really get a ____________ out of travelling. I find going to new places so exciting.
3 I told him he was wrong and he got ____________ under the collar. He obviously didn't agree.
4 My sister's a bit of a ____________ . She isn't scared to try any kind of extreme sport.
5 He doesn't really like being ____________ the limelight and tries to keep away from the cameras.
6 My mum ____________ a group called ABBA when she was young. She still has all their albums.
7 My two-year-old has got a fascination ____________ wheels. He loves anything that moves.
8 She apologised to her friend, but all she got was the cold ____________ .
9 I think we should assess the ____________ before we attempt the jump.
10 I'm a huge fan of Selena Gomez. She's always been my celebrity ____________ .

/10

## GRAMMAR

**2 Complete the sentences with the words in the list. There are two extra words.**

can't | having | inspired | inspiring | might | should | take | taking

1 He's lying about the chocolates. I saw him ____________ the last one.
2 You ____________ take your children to see this film. They'll love it.
3 It ____________ be warm now, but it'll get cold later, so make sure you take a coat.
4 ____________ by the concert, I decided to start piano lessons.
5 His team haven't won all year. They ____________ be very good.
6 ____________ lived in a cold climate most of my life, I found Brazil extremely hot.

**3 Find and correct the mistake in each sentence.**

1 Walking all morning, we were extremely hungry when we arrived home.
2 I heard the telephone ringing three times before it stopped.
3 She's just had a baby. She can be very tired.
4 They must be very famous – I've never heard of them.
5 Leaving my office, the telephone rang.
6 I looked up and saw the bus crashing into the car.

/12

## FUNCTIONAL LANGUAGE

**4 Choose the correct options.**

1 A The way I *understand* / *see* it, we'll never get anywhere if we keep on disagreeing.
B OK. *Point* / *Idea* taken. Let's make some decisions.
2 A To my *opinion* / *mind*, we should spend less money on defence and more money on hospitals.
B I *suppose* / *agree* you're right, but defence is also very important.
3 A You're *always* / *only* watching TV. If you aren't watching it, you're talking about it.
B Give me a *rest* / *break*, Mum. I'm trying to watch my show.
4 A I don't *accept* / *admit* that young people are responsible for most of our crime.
B That's not how I *see* / *observe* things either. It's too easy to just blame them.

/8

**MY SCORE** /30

22–30 | 10–21 | 0–9

# 7 A THING OF BEAUTY?

**OBJECTIVES**

**FUNCTIONS:**
language of persuasion

**GRAMMAR:**
substitution (*the ones, so, that of, do*); ellipsis

**VOCABULARY:**
fads; emotional responses

**Get THINKING**

**Watch the video and think: what does beauty mean to you?**

A

B

C

## READING

1 SPEAKING **Work in pairs. Discuss the questions.**

1 Which of the people in the photographs
  a look really interesting?
  b would you like to meet and talk to?
2 What can you say about the people just by looking at them?

2 SPEAKING **Quickly scan the article on the next page. Choose the best title. Compare your ideas with a partner.**

a Inner beauty is just as important as physical beauty
b Why worry about beauty at all?
c Our confused notions of beauty
d How beauty has changed over the centuries

3 7.01 **Read the article again and listen. Answer the questions below.**

1 What did the writer discover by searching for 'beauty' online?
2 What does she say about changing ideas of beauty?
3 What is her opinion of the current beauty industry?
4 What does she say about the connection between appearance and personality?
5 What examples does she give of what 'inner beauty' involves?
6 Why does she disagree that 'beauty fades'?

4 SPEAKING **Work in pairs and discuss the following questions.**

1 The writer lists some examples of what people these days do to improve their physical appearance. What do you think about these examples?
2 Note something the writer says that you agree with and something you disagree with.
3 To what extent, in your country, do you think that there is a concentration on physical beauty rather than personality?

**Train to THINK**

### Understanding irony

*Irony is a technique used in speaking and writing to create a contradiction between what people say and what they mean. Ironic remarks can sound humorous, but can also sound sarcastic or unkind.*

*Here's an example from the article:* Isn't it a wonderful world?

*Explanation: This is an ironic remark. It's clear from everything else the writer says that she doesn't think it's a wonderful world at all.*

## Gemma Stanley wonders if we've got our priorities straight.

**Try this: pick a search engine (it doesn't matter which one) and type in the word 'beauty'. I guarantee that the first 20 hits will be to do with women's beauty salons, hair, cosmetics, and so on. This is true even if you live, as I do, in a country where the first language isn't English. After that, click on 'Images'. Guess what the first hundred images will be of? You probably don't even need me to tell you that it will be the faces of women, mostly western, who conform to the current idea of what a beautiful woman looks like (and who are frequently photographed to promote a 'beauty' product of some kind).**

Our society's concentration on beauty as physical appearance is nothing new, of course. And there has always been a 'beauty industry' tagged on to this. Our idea of what constitutes beauty is quite different from that of our grandparents, let alone our great-grandparents or people in the Middle Ages. But our age of magazines, Hollywood and social media seems to have resulted in what I consider to be a rather depressing state of affairs. Now, we have plastic surgery; we have facial makeovers; we have hair transplants; we have stomach reductions; and a whole lot more. There are endless numbers of must-have clothes or accessories, and trendy fads and treatments, urging people (women and girls in particular) to spend money they perhaps don't have on things that, deep down, they don't really need. Isn't it a wonderful world?

This all leads me to ask: why are we so obsessed with appearance and with gender ideals as defined by the media and beauty industry? Why are we taken in by these messages? Haven't we got everything upside down?

Not long ago I saw something on social media about a famous person (no names) who had made some derogatory comments about another person's appearance. But that same person, who is very beautiful facially, apparently had a website all about how we should focus on people's inner beauty. How twisted is that?

In my life, I've met all kinds of people, some of whom are outwardly stunning. As we all know, though, that has nothing to do with what a person is truly like. I know physically lovely people who I like, and several that I don't. And I know many physically ordinary people who are kind, funny, generous and compassionate. They're the ones I want to spend time with. Don't get me wrong. I like to look good, too, or as good as I can anyway. I like elegant clothes, I use make-up, I try to look after my hair, I'm flattered if someone says I look cool. But that can't compare to knowing that someone enjoys my company, or that they turn to me for advice, or that they like being with me because I'm interesting to be with.

Some people say that beauty fades, but I don't think so; physical beauty simply changes over time. But more importantly, inner beauty remains. If you can achieve any level of inner beauty, it's likely to stay with you throughout your life. Instead of worrying how your hair looks or if you could be slimmer, think about how you can be more kind-hearted, more compassionate. So, to my kids, my friends, my readers, I'd like to say: Try to be less concerned about how you look. Pay attention to who you are. Think about how to be as positive a presence as possible in the world. As Khalil Gibran said, 'Beauty is not in the face; beauty is a light in the heart.'

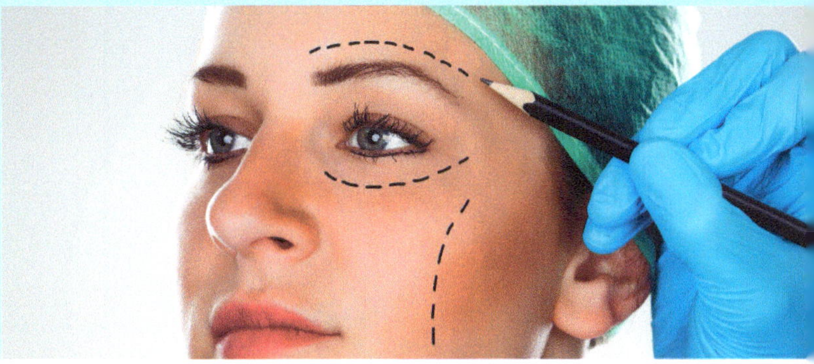

**5 Match the situations 1–3 with the ironic remarks a–c below.**

1 Mr Brown is in a hurry and has been patiently queuing up in a bank. Just as it's his turn, the assistant asks if he'd mind if she made a phone call before serving him. He says: ☐

2 It's Monday morning. Joanne leaves the house and gets her bike out of the shed to ride it to school, but then notices it's got a flat tyre. She says: ☐

3 Ken drives a brand new sports car. He notices a little stain on the front window and complains about it. His friend Carol drives an old car. She says: ☐

a 'Brilliant. Today couldn't have started any better!'

b 'My goodness! How can you ever think of getting into that filthy car again?'

c 'Sure. Why on earth would you think I'd mind?'

**6 SPEAKING Work in pairs. Think of an ironic remark people might make in each of the following situations.**

1 It's a beautiful Sunday morning. Sally and her friend have decided to go to the beach. Ten minutes after the girls arrive at the beach, it starts raining heavily. Sally says: …

2 Nick always leaves home early. He hates being late. One day, he arrives at the station half an hour before the train leaves. He sits down on a bench and starts reading a book. He loves the story so much that he completely forgets about the train and misses it. When he notices the train has gone, he says: …

3 Mr Miller has had his new suit cleaned. When he puts it back into the wardrobe, he notices that there are several stains that weren't there before. He says: …

**7 WRITING Now, in pairs, write down two more situations and think of ironic remarks that you could make about them.**

## GRAMMAR

Grammar video ▶18

### Substitution (*the ones, so, that of, do*)

**1 Read the sentences from the article on page 67. Complete them with *that, ones, so, do*. Then choose the correct options in the rule.**

1 This is true even if you live, as I _____________, in a country where the first language isn't English.

2 Our idea of what constitutes beauty is quite different from _____________ of our grandparents.

3 They're the _____________ I want to spend time with.

4 Some people say that beauty fades, but I don't think _____________ .

> **RULE:** We use substitution to avoid repetition.
> *The cosmetic industry today is a lot stronger than **that of (the cosmetic industry)** 100 years ago.*
> *Your new hairstyle is much nicer than **the one (the hairstyle)** you had before.*
> *Many people say beauty is skin-deep, and I **think so (think it's skin-deep)**, too.*
> *Will those new clothes make me feel good? – I certainly **hope so (hope they make me feel good)**.*
> *I don't like him very much and **neither do my friends (my friends also don't like him very much)**.*
>
> - The words *that of/those of* tend to be more [1]*formal / informal*.
> - The words *the one/the ones* tend to be more [2]*formal / informal*.
> - The words *so* and *do/did* replace a [3]*word / phrase*.
> - The words *so/neither/nor* include the meaning 'also'. Here, we invert the subject and [4]*auxiliary / main* verb.

**2 Rewrite the sentences, substituting the underlined words. Sometimes more than one correct answer is possible.**

1 Today's idea of beauty is very different from <u>the idea of beauty of</u> 200 years ago.

2 A Are you going to try that beauty treatment?
B No, I don't think <u>I'm going to try that beauty treatment</u>.

3 I don't think the clothes shops in this city are as good as <u>the clothes shops</u> in my previous town.

4 A I really like his new hairstyle.
B I <u>like his new hairstyle</u>, too.

5 My brother doesn't like my new glasses, and <u>my best friend doesn't like my new glasses either</u>.

6 I'm keen on doing a course about make-up, and <u>my sister is keen on it, too</u>.

**3 Read the dialogue and underline the repetitive sections. Then rewrite the dialogue using substitution to replace these sections.**

A Have you heard of Tough Mudder?
B Yes, I have. It sounds too tough for me, though. I wouldn't want to run a mile waist-deep in mud.
A And I wouldn't want to run a mile waist-deep in mud.
B The good thing is there aren't any winners of Tough Mudder and there aren't any losers of Tough Mudder. You have to work as a team and help each other. I think that's a great idea.
A I also think that's a great idea. And the company sounds really cool. I've heard their employees can take as much holiday as they like.
B That's good from a company perspective, too. Apparently, studies have found that high-performing employees take more holiday than employees who aren't performing so well.

→ workbook page 64

## VOCABULARY

### Fads

**4 Match the sentence halves.**

1 The retro look ☐
2 The latest smartphone quickly ☐
3 We have seen many rather *short-lived* ☐
4 The pilates class was full, ☐
5 Can you remember when ☐
6 Long hair for men was ☐
7 I don't think jeans ☐

a fitness crazes over the years.
b ripped jeans became *a thing*?
c so I'm doing yoga, which is *the next best thing*.
d will ever *go out of fashion*.
e *really in* in the '70s.
f established itself as the new *must-have* device.
g is *bang on trend* at the moment.

**5 Choose the correct words to complete the sentences.**

1 Wide-legged trousers are *really in / short-lived*.
2 Everybody's got a selfie stick nowadays. It's a *really in / must-have* device.
3 You can't always take your guitar with you. The Pocket Strings is *a thing / the next best thing*.
4 Cafés with odd chairs and tables were *bang on trend / must-have* in London in 2019.
5 It was *a thing / short-lived* in 2019 to drink out of jam jars.
6 Do you think gyms will ever *be the next best thing / go out of fashion*?

→ workbook page 66

# LISTENING

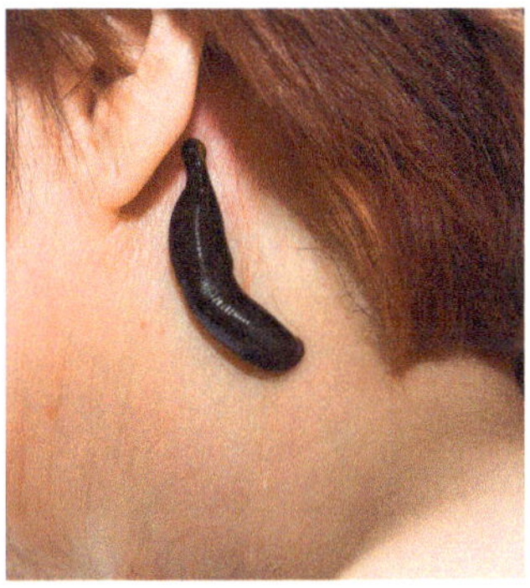

6 7.02 **Look at the photos. How do you think these things relate to beauty? Listen and check your answers.**

7 7.02 **Listen again. Mark the statements T (true) or F (false) according to what the historian says. Correct the false statements.**

1 An American actor is reported to use the venom from a snake to purify his blood. ☐
2 People are prepared to spend money on beauty treatments which lack scientific corroboration. ☐
3 Media stories make us think that we can buy beauty. ☐
4 Certain ingredients used in facemasks in Ancient Rome and Egypt were difficult to find. ☐
5 Japanese women rubbed nuts against their teeth to make them black. ☐
6 Having black teeth in 19th-century Japan signalled that you wanted to get married. ☐

8 **Read the list of things people do to improve or change their looks. Check the meaning of the words and phrases. Can you add two more things?**

- have plastic surgery, for example a tummy tuck or a face lift
- dye their hair
- buy expensive cosmetics
- have a facial treatment
- cut down on sugar
- have a teeth-whitening treatment
- take steroids
- take up bodybuilding and/or exercise regularly
- ______________________
- ______________________

9 SPEAKING **Work in pairs. What do you think about each of the things listed in Exercise 8?**

*It's a safe way to change your looks.*
*It can be fun.*
*It poses a serious health threat.*
*It's ridiculously expensive.*
*It doesn't have any long-lasting effects.*
*It may be worth trying.*

# GRAMMAR
## Ellipsis

10 **Read these sentences (1–6) from the listening. Match them with the omitted words (a–f). Then complete the rule with *subject*, *informal* and *verbs*.**

1 Not heard that one before. ☐
2 Want to hear another example? ☐
3 Fancy trying any of these yourself? ☐
4 Unbelievable! ☐
5 Why black teeth? ☐
6 Some examples? ☐

a That's
b did they want
c Would you
d Can you give
e I have
f Do you

**RULE:** We often leave words out, especially in [1]______________ spoken English. This is known as 'ellipsis'. We can omit [2]______________ pronouns, articles, auxiliary [3]______________ or, in fact, any verb when it's clear from the context what the verb is.
*Would you like more ice cream?* ➜ *More ice cream?*
*I would love some.* ➜ *Love some.*

11 7.03 **Read the three dialogues and underline the words that can be omitted. Then listen and check your answers.**

1 **Peter** Do you fancy another game, Matt?
**Matt** I would love one.
**Peter** What about you, Jamie?
**Jamie** Sorry, there is not enough time. I have got to be home by five.
**Peter** See you at the same time tomorrow, then?
**Jamie** That would be great.

2 **Helen** Have you got a minute? I need to talk to you.
**Mike** No, I'm sorry, I'm busy now. Maybe we can talk later.
**Helen** That is no problem.

3 **Emma** Do you want a coffee?
**Jake** I'd love one.

→ workbook page 65

## READING

1 **Make a list of five things that you find beautiful.**

2 SPEAKING **Work in pairs. Look at the photos. Where is the 'beauty' in each one? Discuss.**

*I think this shows the beauty that's there in nature.*

A

D

B

E

C

F

3 7.04 **Read and listen to the blog. Match each photo with a post.**

**PRONUNCIATION**
Connected speech feature: assimilation
Go to page 121.

## SPEAKING

4 **Work in pairs and discuss the questions.**

1 What did the blog ask readers to do?
2 Which of your ideas in Exercise 1, if any, were mentioned?
3 Underline some of the positive words and expressions used in the posts (that you liked).
4 Read each post again and give it a score from 0 to 5 according to how much you liked it. Then discuss your scores in pairs.

*I didn't like number 5. I thought it was pretentious.*

*My favourite is number 3. I'd never thought that it was possible to find mathematics beautiful.*

# What's beautiful for you?

**We asked you to tell us, in no more than 60 words, about something you think is beautiful. And we got a great range of answers. Here are some that we really liked. Which one do you like the best? Write and let us know.**

**1** In 1932, my great-grandfather bought a camera. My grandfather had it, then my mother, now it's mine. It sits on a shelf in my office, a bit battered but still working and still lovely – a beautiful piece of old technology, and part of my family history. I look at it and it brings a smile to my face.

**2** A bird flying is already a lovely thing. But sometimes, in the evening, thousands of starlings come together and make an immense cloud of birds, a cloud that swirls and dances in the air. I saw it once and it set my heart racing. It's beautiful to watch and has a beautiful name: a 'murmuration'.

**3** People are always surprised when I say I'm a mathematician. They're even more surprised when I talk about the beauty of mathematics. But I agree with the man who said, 'mathematics, rightly viewed, possesses not only truth, but supreme beauty'. Equations, mathematical shapes – they're like music to me, or art. It's the beauty of understanding, perhaps.

**4** The most wonderful thing in my world is to watch professional ballet dancers. My dream was always to dance, but illness prevented me. The music, the grace, the seemingly effortless movement. Doing pirouettes and standing on tiptoe, spinning and swirling. It makes my heart soar and do pirouettes when I watch!

**5** The right leg moves across the left, knees bent, perfect balance, eye on the ball. The racket swings back. The crowd gasps as he hits the ball, his right arm finishing high over his right shoulder. Federer's backhand is a wonderful shot to watch, perhaps the best ever. It sends shivers down my spine to think of it.

**6** Last year, we took a winter cruise on the coast of Norway, up to the Arctic Circle, to see the aurora borealis. Our second night there, it happened – those magical waves of green and blue light, flashing in the sky. It gave me goosebumps all down my arms. Unfortunately, we didn't see it again on the cruise.

**7** When he comes home and smiles and I look into his eyes, I always think of that Peter Gabriel song: 'In your eyes, the light, the heat. In your eyes, I am complete.' That describes perfectly how I feel about my husband's beautiful, smiling eyes. He's older now, but the light is still there.

**8** When our little girl was born, my husband said we should take her to the local swimming pool. It's what his parents did with him when he was a baby. I could not believe it as she splashed happily in the water, with his hand under her tummy. It brought tears to my eyes!

## VOCABULARY
### Emotional responses

5 What does *It* refer to in each of these sentences from the posts on page 70? Complete the sentences with the missing parts of the body. Then read and check.

1 *It* set my ______________ racing.
2 *It* sends shivers down my ______________ to think of it.
3 *It* brought tears to my ______________ !
4 *It* brings a smile to my ______________ .
5 *It* makes my ______________ soar and do pirouettes when I watch!
6 *It* gave me goosebumps all down my ______________ .

6 SPEAKING Work in pairs. Discuss what gives you the feelings described in each of the sentences in Exercise 5. Then make a list and share your ideas with another pair.

7 WRITING Now choose one of the ideas and write your own post about something you find beautiful for the blog.

→ workbook page 66

## TH!NK values
### Valuing the beauty around us

8 SPEAKING Work in pairs. Look at the photos and discuss.

1 In what ways are the photos similar?
2 How are they different?
3 Do sights like these bother you? How do they make you feel?

9 SPEAKING Work in groups. Make a list of four things you could do to tackle the environmental problem shown in one of the photos.

10 SPEAKING Work in pairs. Make a list of four 'ugly' sights in the town where you live and complete the table.

| Place | Issue | Cause | Solution |
|---|---|---|---|
| | | | |

11 Choose one of the sights and talk about the advantages and disadvantages of using each of the different media below to raise awareness about the problem. Decide on the best one and, using your notes from Exercise 10, plan a campaign.

- a video
- banners
- social media

## FUNCTIONS
### Language of persuasion

12 Match 1–8 with a–h to complete the expressions.

1 *I strongly* ☐
2 *Try* our brand ☐
3 *This revolutionary new* ☐
4 *This offer* ☐
5 *Have you always* ☐
6 Five million *people* worldwide ☐
7 *We understand that* ☐
8 *Imagine* ☐

a *is limited.*
b *have already discovered* Nutrawheat.
c your health is important.
d *recommend* trying this treatment.
e having perfect sight again.
f new product.
g *dreamed of* owning a sports car?
h system is easy to use.

13 What is the aim of the expressions above?

14 7.06 Now complete the advert with six of the expressions in italics in Exercise 12. Then listen and check your answers.

**Smile and the world smiles with you – or does it?**

[1] ______________ having a perfect smile? Well, now you can. If you want a confident smile, try our brand new, almost invisible tooth-straightening device. [2] ______________ device is easy and comfortable to wear, and it fits perfectly. 'I always tried to hide my teeth when I smiled, but now I show them,' said Karen. 'If you feel the same way, [3] ______________ trying Smile-Align.' '[4] ______________ being able to smile for a photo again,' says Max. 'After using Smile-Align, I can do that.' [5] ______________ the price is important, so we have a great offer for you today. The process usually costs £2,000, but we're offering it to you for just £1,500. But hurry, [6] ______________ and must end soon.

15 WRITING Now create your own advert for a beauty gadget or piece of exercise equipment. Then present your advert to the class.

# Literature

1 7.07 **Read and listen to the extracts from three poems. Which one:**

a talks about how someone's beauty will never die? ☐

b talks about remembering beauty and a love that was not fulfilled? ☐

c talks about seeing someone beautiful for the first time? ☐

2 **Look at the first extract. Match these sentences to lines 5–10.**

[8] And when I take her hand, my poor hand will be very fortunate.

☐ A white bird looks like this when it walks in the middle of a group of black birds.

☐ Have I ever been in love before? My eyes say no!

☐ How this woman stands out amongst the other women.

☐ Tonight is the first time I've ever seen someone really beautiful.

☐ When the dancing finishes, I'll watch where she stands.

3 VOCABULARY **Look at the second extract. Match the highlighted words with their definitions.**

1 walked backwards and forwards while feeling nervous
2 sadness, unhappiness
3 producing a warm light
4 above (your head)
5 someone who makes a long and difficult journey to a special place
6 speak or say something quietly
7 falling asleep
8 ran away

1

## Romeo and Juliet

*William Shakespeare*

Romeo:
O, she doth teach the torches to burn bright!
It seems she hangs upon the cheek of night
Like a rich jewel in an Ethiope's ear;
Beauty too rich for use, for earth too dear!
So shows a snowy dove trooping with crows,
As yonder lady o'er her fellows shows.
The measure done, I'll watch her place of stand,
And, touching hers, make blessed my rude hand.
Did my heart love till now? forswear it, sight!
For I ne'er saw true beauty till this night.

2

## When you are old

*William Butler Yeats*

When you are old and grey and full of sleep,
And **nodding** by the fire, take down this book,
And slowly read, and dream of the soft look
Your eyes had once, and of their shadows deep;
How many loved your moments of glad grace,
And loved your beauty with love false or true,
But one man loved the **pilgrim** Soul in you,
And loved the **sorrows** of your changing face;
And bending down beside the **glowing** bars,
**Murmur**, a little sadly, how Love **fled**
And **paced** upon the mountains **overhead**.

3

## Sonnet 18

*William Shakespeare*

Shall I compare thee to a summer's day?
Thou art more lovely and more temperate.
Rough winds do shake the darling buds of May,
And summer's lease hath all too short a date.
Sometime too hot the eye of heaven shines,
And often is his gold complexion dimmed;
And every fair from fair sometime declines,
By chance, or nature's changing course, untrimmed;
But thy eternal summer shall not fade,
Nor lose possession of that fair thou ow'st,
Nor shall death brag thou wand'rest in his shade,
When in eternal lines to Time thou grow'st.
So long as men can breathe, or eyes can see,
So long lives this, and this gives life to thee.

4 **Look at the third extract. Match these phrases to the lines which mean:**

- [4] summer does not last very long
- [ ] as long as there are people in the world
- [ ] everything that is beautiful loses its beauty at some time
- [ ] this poem will live on, and will keep you alive
- [ ] you will not die
- [ ] you will not lose the beauty that you have now

5 SPEAKING **Work in pairs and discuss the questions.**

1 Which of the three poems do you like most? Why?
2 Which poem was easiest to understand, and which was the most difficult? Why?
3 Do you know any poems or songs, in English or in your own language, about beauty? Tell the class about it/them.

## WRITING
### A formal letter

6 INPUT **Read the letter. What two issues is Clara upset about and how does she hope the newspaper will respond?**

7 **Complete the letter by choosing the best option for each adverb.**

8 **Complete the sentences with your own ideas.**

1 Although she has made several great films, her latest is arguably …
2 I have to admit I found the book thoroughly …
3 He's a talented singer, but he's an equally …
4 The last chapter of the book is especially …
5 Not being a football fan, I wasn't remotely …

9 ANALYSE **Match the paragraphs (1–4) with their functions.**

- [ ] This paragraph outlines the issue (what is wrong).
- [ ] This paragraph gives the background information.
- [ ] This paragraph proposes a solution.
- [ ] This paragraph explains why this situation is wrong.

10 PLAN **While reading a fashion magazine, you noticed that several of the models have been photoshopped to make them look perfect. You decide to write a letter about this. Use the structure of Clara's letter to help you organise your ideas.**

11 PRODUCE **Write a letter to the magazine complaining about this issue. Use your notes to help you.**

Dear Madam,

1 Being a student in my final year at the London School of Fashion, I was [1]*equally / especially* looking forward to the special fashion edition of your newspaper's weekend magazine. At first glance, I was not disappointed. The clothes that you featured were as original as they were exciting.

2 However, while I was [2]*arguably / thoroughly* enjoying the featured fashion, something did not feel quite right. I was trying to work out what it was when suddenly it dawned on me. Of the 12 different models you used for your shoot, ten were white, one was Asian and one was black – hardly reflective of the multicultural society in which we live. Furthermore, all of the models were what the media like to refer to as size zero. None of them were even [3]*remotely / thoroughly* approaching the shape or size of the majority of your female readership.

3 I have to say that I was particularly disappointed that your paper, which normally prides itself on its forward-thinking articles, should fall into the trap that less progressive magazines are keen to promote, i.e. that women should aspire to unreasonable, and [4]*arguably / especially* unhealthy, body sizes. I was [5]*remotely / equally* upset that you did not take the opportunity to portray a fair representation of the women who actually inhabit this world.

4 I do not imagine that you will consider making amends by offering us another fashion special in the next few weeks which features more diverse models. However, I do hope you will take note of my comments and observations, and make sure that in the future you present us with a fashion edition I know you are capable of producing.

Yours faithfully,

Clara Bowen

# 8 CRACKING THE CODE

**OBJECTIVES**

**FUNCTIONS:**
saying that you don't understand or didn't fully hear

**GRAMMAR:**
relative clauses with determiners and prepositions; *however, wherever, whatever*, etc.

**VOCABULARY:**
language and communication; personality (2)

**Get THINKING**

**Watch the video and think: how many different codes do you know?**

A

B

C

## READING

1 SPEAKING **Work in pairs. Look at the photos. Tell your partner what you can see in them.**

2 **Read the article quickly. What three languages appeared on the Rosetta Stone?**

3 8.01 **Read the article again. Match the headings to the paragraphs 1–6 in the article. There are two you won't use. Then listen and check.**

a Time to reconsider
b A language lost forever?
c Changing times
d A key to the past
e The story it told
f A chance discovery
g The final breakthrough
h First steps

4 SPEAKING **Work in pairs. Discuss your answers to the questions.**

1 What other important objects do you know of that people have discovered and used to learn about the past?
2 Imagine you were burying a piece of text for civilisations in the far future to discover and learn about your language. What text would you bury and why?

**PRONUNCIATION**
Stress in multi-syllable words Go to page 121.

**Train to THINK**

### Making logical deductions about unknown words

*When reading, we may sometimes come across words with which we are not familiar. If we look carefully at the context, we can often make logical deductions to help us understand the meaning of these words.*

# THE ROSETTA STONE

1 ☐ In 1798, the French emperor Napoleon Bonaparte invaded Egypt. Napoleon was particularly interested in art and education, and one of his missions in Egypt was to take anything that might be of cultural importance. In 1799, a group of French soldiers, one of whom was called Pierre-François Bouchard, was rebuilding a fort near a town called Rosetta. While digging in the sands, Bouchard came across an unusual slab of black rock. It was about 120 cm long and 75 cm wide. On closer inspection of the rock, he could see that it was inscribed with ancient writing. Knowing about his emperor's interest in such things, he took it back to show him.

2 ☐ As soon as the scholars looked at the stone, they knew they were looking at something very important. The Rosetta Stone, as it became known, had three layers, and on each layer there was a different language inscribed. The top layer contained ancient Egyptian hieroglyphics and the second layer was written in the later Egyptian Demotic script, neither of which anyone knew how to read. Luckily, the third layer was written in Ancient Greek, a language which was familiar to many of the scholars.

3 ☐ For many years, scholars had been baffled by the inscriptions they had found on the walls of Ancient Egyptian buildings. They knew these series of repeating images were a kind of language, in which case they must be saying something, but what? There were clearly pictures of birds, beetles and body parts, among many other things, but what did they mean? This ancient language, which they called 'hieroglyphics', had not been used for over 1,600 years and it seemed there was no way of ever being able to interpret it. The Rosetta Stone was about to change all that.

4 ☐ The first thing the scholars did was to translate the Ancient Greek passage on the stone, all of which they learned had been written by a group of priests in 196 BC to praise a pharaoh called Ptolemy V, who ruled over Egypt at that time. The passage contained a list of all the great things the pharaoh had done for his country. It also said that there should be a statue of the leader in every temple in the land, along with a copy of the text written on the Rosetta Stone. The passage in Greek was easy; the difficult part was what was written in the other two unknown scripts.

5 ☐ The first breakthrough came when scholars realised that all three passages said the same thing. Using the Greek translation, they now had the tools to start working on deciphering the hieroglyphics. Over the years, language experts, many of whom came from the world's most famous universities, studied the Rosetta Stone to try and crack its code, but it proved to be really difficult. It wasn't until 1822, when a Frenchman called Jean-François Champollion started studying the stone, that progress really started to happen.

6 ☐ Champollion had been fascinated with the Rosetta Stone since the age of 12. He became a scholar of languages and set about learning Latin, Greek, Hebrew, Arabic, Syriac, Persian, Aramaic and, most usefully of all, Coptic, which was a later form of the Egyptian language. But hieroglyphics was to prove his greatest challenge. It was a language compared to which all the others he knew seemed easy. However, slowly he was able to identify seven signs that the Coptic script shared with the Demotic script (that was also on the stone) and identify their meanings. He used this to start working out what several individual hieroglyphics meant. He was then able to make educated guesses about other signs and slowly the code began to unravel, unlocking stories and secrets from one of the world's most fascinating ancient cultures.

**5 Look at the sentence from the article and answer questions about the underlined word.**

*Using the Greek translation, the scholars now had the tools to start working on deciphering the hieroglyphics.*

1 Who is doing the deciphering?
2 What are they using to do the deciphering?
3 What are they deciphering?
4 What do they hope to achieve by deciphering?

**6 Use your answers in Exercise 5 to write a definition for *decipher*, and then compare with a partner.**

**7 Find the following underlined words in the article and write questions that will help you arrive at a logical definition for each one.**

1 baffled 2 breakthrough 3 unravel

## GRAMMAR

Grammar video ▶ 20

### Relative clauses with determiners and prepositions

**1 Complete the sentences from the article on page 75 using the phrases in the list. Then complete the rule by choosing the correct options.**

all of which | compared to which | in which case
many of whom | neither of which | one of whom

1 A group of French soldiers, ____________________ was called Pierre-François Bouchard, was rebuilding a fort.

2 The top layer contained ancient Egyptian hieroglyphics and the second layer was written in the later Egyptian Demotic script, ____________________ anyone knew how to read.

3 They knew these series of repeating images were a kind of language, ____________________ they must be saying something, but what?

4 The first thing the scholars did was to translate the Ancient Greek passage on the stone, ____________________ they learned had been written by a group of priests.

5 Over the years, language experts, ____________________ came from the world's most famous universities, studied the Rosetta Stone.

6 It was a language ____________________ all the others he knew seemed easy.

**RULE:** Typically, prepositions go at the [1]*beginning / end* of a clause, for example 'Egyptian hieroglyphics, Egyptian Demotic and ancient Greek were the languages (which) the Rosetta Stone was inscribed with.'

In writing or in very formal spoken contexts, we can put the preposition at the [2]*beginning / end* of a relative clause, for example 'Egyptian hieroglyphics, Egyptian Demotic and ancient Greek were the languages with which the Rosetta Stone was inscribed.'

In this case, the relative pronoun is always [3]*that / whom* for people.

Sometimes the relative clause [4]*begins / ends* with a determiner, for example *all, some* or *none*.

**2 Rewrite the sentences in more formal language.**

0 Coptic is a language that few people are familiar with.
*Coptic is a language with which few people are familiar.*

1 Grammar is something that I know nothing about.

2 She is a woman that I have never spoken to.

3 Language is something we all give great importance to.

4 Translation is the profession that he has dedicated his life to.

5 He's a friend that I almost never hear from.

→ workbook page 72

## VOCABULARY

### Language and communication

**3 Read the paragraphs. Which one isn't about spoken language?**

**A** When I'm in France I like to try to practise my language skills. However, my **broken French** is so poor that sometimes I **can't make myself understood** and so it ends in a complete **communication breakdown**. I do my best to **pronounce** things clearly, but of course I'm not a **native speaker** or anywhere approaching that level, so people often **misunderstand** me.

**B** The other day, I met someone from another part of the country who had such a **strong accent** that at times I found him virtually **incomprehensible**. It was hard to believe that we shared the same **first language**, to be honest. And it wasn't just the accent – he was actually speaking a different **dialect** and using slang words that meant I just couldn't **follow** him. We had to get someone to **interpret** for us!

**C** When you travel, there's sometimes a **language barrier** that makes communication difficult. But I've found that **body language**, while obviously not exactly the same around the world, is sufficiently universal to mean that we can 'talk' to other people. **Gestures** and **facial expressions** allow you to show people that you don't understand, that you want a particular thing, or whatever.

**4** SPEAKING **Work in pairs. Discuss the meaning of the words and phrases in bold. Use a dictionary to help you.**

**5 Use expressions from Exercise 3 to complete the text.**

I'll always remember the first time I went to the north-east of England. People there speak with a really [1]____________________ and there are some vocabulary differences, too, which means it's really a different [2]____________________ of English. More than once, people said things to me and I just couldn't [3]____________________ them. And sometimes they [4]____________________ me, too. It's strange when there seems to be a [5]____________________ between people who share the same [6]____________________!

→ workbook page 74

## SPEAKING

**6 Work in pairs. Give examples of:**

1 a time when you couldn't make yourself understood.
2 a slang expression in English.
3 a dialect that someone in your family speaks.
4 mistakes people often make when writing your language.
5 someone you know who speaks with a strong accent.

# FUNCTIONS

## Saying that you don't understand or didn't fully hear

**7 Match the beginnings (1–6) with the correct endings (a–f).**

1 Sorry, there was a bus going past. ☐
2 He was using all sorts of technical jargon, ☐
3 His argument isn't very clear. ☐
4 She hasn't explained it very clearly. ☐
5 That was a bit of a complicated explanation! ☐
6 The teacher said that I needed to 'use some elbow grease', ☐

a so I **didn't quite get** what he said.
b but I wasn't **familiar with** that expression.
c I **didn't catch** what you said with all the noise.
d I'm afraid **you've lost me**. Can you explain it more simply?
e I **don't quite see** what she means.
f I **don't follow** him at all.

**8 How do you say the expressions in bold in your language?**

**9 Answer the questions about the expressions in Exercise 7.**

1 Which one(s) do you like most?
2 Which one(s), if any, do you not like at all?
3 Which one(s), if any, could you see yourself using?
4 Which one(s), if any, would you not feel very comfortable using?

# LISTENING

## Codes

**10** SPEAKING **Work in pairs. Discuss the question.**

What famous codes can you think of?

**11** 8.03 **Listen to the radio programme. Who was the Somerton Man?**

**12** 8.03 **Listen again and answer the questions.**

1 How long had the man been on the beach when he was found?
2 Why did the police think he wasn't local?
3 Why were they not able to find out his identity?
4 What did they find in his pocket?
5 How did the case develop from this discovery?
6 What two things were odd about the book?
7 How successful have experts been in solving the code?
8 Why can't the book be used to solve the code now?

# GRAMMAR

## *however, wherever, whatever, etc.*

**13 Match the beginnings and endings of the sentences from the listening. Then choose the correct options to complete the rule.**

1 However hard they tried,
2 Whoever the police asked,
3 Whatever he'd been doing on the beach

a would remain a mystery.
b no one seemed to know who he was.
c the experts could not crack it.

> **RULE:** We can add *-ever* to *how* and [1]*all / some wh-* words: *however/whatever/whoever/wherever/whenever/whichever.*
> We use *whatever/wherever/however,* etc. to mean it isn't [2]*important / necessary* what/where/how because the result is always the same.
> The word order is *-ever* word + (adjective) subject + verb.

**14 Rewrite these sentences. Start each one with an *-ever* word.**

0 It doesn't matter when you arrive – we'll be here.
*Whenever you arrive, we'll be here.*
1 It doesn't matter what you say – he won't like it.
2 It doesn't matter when we leave – the roads are always full of traffic.
3 It isn't important which way you say it – it means the same thing.
4 It doesn't matter how strong your accent is – everyone will understand you.

**15** SPEAKING **Complete the sentences, and then compare with a partner.**

1 Whatever I decide to do after I leave school, …
2 Whenever I have free time, …
3 Wherever I go to university/on holiday … , …
4 However expensive it … , …

→ workbook page 73

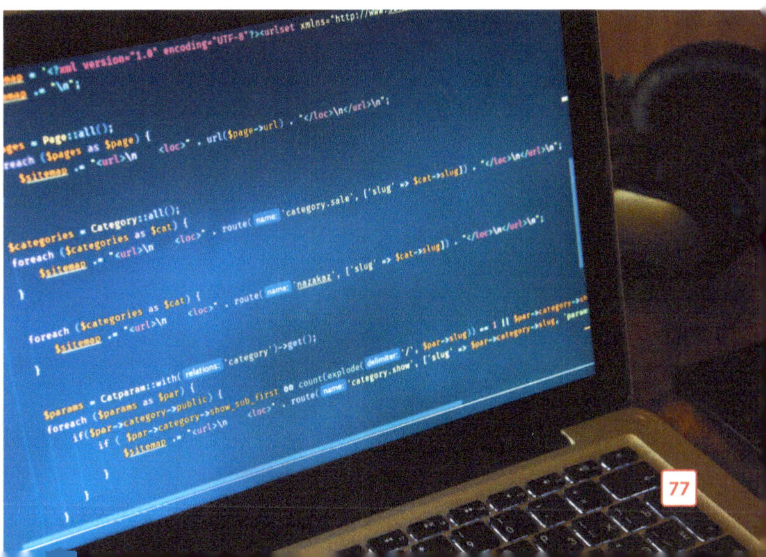

# Multilinguals have multiple personalities

Between 2001 and 2003, linguists Jean-Marc Dewaele and Aneta Pavlenko asked over a thousand bilinguals whether they 'feel like a different person' when they speak different languages. [A]

Susan Ervin, a sociolinguist at the University of California, Berkeley, set out to explore the differences in how bilinguals represent the same stories in different languages. She recruited 64 French adults who lived in the US and were fluent in both French and English. On average, they had spent 12 years living in the US; 40 were married to an American. On two separate occasions, six weeks apart, Ervin showed her subjects a series of illustrations [B]. In one session, the volunteer and experimenter spoke only in French, [C].

One of the illustrations Ervin used in her first experiment

Ervin then analysed the stories, and she identified some significant topical differences. The English stories more often featured female achievement, physical aggression, verbal aggression towards parents, and attempts to escape blame, while the French stories were more likely to include domination by elders, guilt, and verbal aggression toward peers.

[D] This time, Ervin looked at Japanese women living in the San Francisco area. Ervin had a bilingual interviewer give the women various verbal tasks in both Japanese and in English, and found – as she expected – important differences.

For instance, when the women were asked to complete the following sentences, their answers differed depending on the language in which the question was asked:

**1 When my wishes conflict with my family …**
*(Japanese)* it is a time of great unhappiness.
*(English)* I do what I want.

**2 I will probably become …**
*(Japanese)* a housewife.
*(English)* a teacher.

## READING
### Multilingual people

1 SPEAKING **Do you know anyone who is multilingual? Tell your partner about them.**

2 **Look at the title of the article. What do you think it is going to say about multilingual people? Read it quickly to check your ideas.**

3 8.04 **Read and listen to the article again. Put these sentences/phrases into the correct place in the article, A–E. There is one that you won't use.**

1 And their own personas changed, too.
2 In 1968, Ervin designed another experiment to further explore her hypothesis that the content of bilinguals' speech would change along with the language.
3 Nearly two-thirds said they did.
4 while the other session was conducted entirely in English
5 She believed that the content of bilinguals' speech would change along with the language.
6 and asked them to make up a three-minute story to accompany each scene

4 SPEAKING **Work in groups. Discuss the questions.**

1 To what extent do you feel 'different' when you speak English (or another language that isn't your first language)?
2 In what other way(s) could you test the effect that language has on someone's personality?

Scholars have also used more qualitative methods to try to understand language's impact on personality. In 1998, Michele Koven spent a year and a half carrying out ethnographic research with bilingual Parisian adults whose parents had immigrated from Portugal. All of her subjects were fluent in both French and Portuguese, and most maintained close ties to Portugal while living in France. Koven focused specifically on how her subjects represented themselves in narratives of personal experience, which she elicited by asking them to recount various life events in both languages. Koven saw that her subjects emphasised different traits in their characters, depending on which language they were speaking. For instance, the women in the French stories were more likely to stand up for themselves, whereas the female characters in the Portuguese narratives tended to cede to others' demands. [E] One girl, Koven writes, sounded like 'an angry, hip suburbanite' when she spoke French, and a 'frustrated, but patient, well-mannered bank customer who does not want attention drawn to the fact that she is an émigré' when she spoke Portuguese. Whether that's due to the different context in which she learned French and Portuguese, an inherent difference between the two languages, or some combination of the two, researchers have yet to figure out.

## VOCABULARY
### Personality (2)

5 **Look back at the article on page 78 and find two words to describe personality.**

6 SPEAKING **Here are some people talking about language and personality. Work in pairs. Discuss the meaning of the words in bold. Use the context to help you.**

1 I tend to be a bit afraid to say what I think in a foreign language. I can be a lot more **assertive** and **forceful** in my own language.
2 I feel really **self-conscious** if I speak another language, like everyone is listening and thinking I'm not very good at it, so I often don't even try.
3 I love speaking other languages – I feel much more **expressive** than I do in my own language and my true personality comes out.
4 I'm usually a **modest** person, but when I speak another language I feel like I get a bit **conceited** and start to behave as if I think quite highly of myself!
5 I've got a friend who's more **impulsive** when he isn't speaking his native language – he just says whatever he's thinking!
6 Maybe speaking more than one language helps you become more confident and **self-assured**?

7 **Use a word from Exercise 6 in each space. There may be more than one possibility.**

1 He thinks he's wonderful – he's so ______________ !
2 She often acts without thinking – she's really quite ______________ .
3 It's difficult for me to talk to new people – I always feel a bit ______________ .
4 Don't let other people tell you what to do! You have to be a bit more ______________ .
5 He's a very well-mannered and ______________ child. He never boasts about his achievements.
6 It's captivating watching her tell a story. Her facial expressions are amazing. She's so ______________ .

8 **Which (if any) of the statements in Exercise 6 do you identify with? Think of examples and make notes. Compare ideas with a partner.**

9 SPEAKING **Work in pairs and discuss the questions.**

1 What's your favourite word in any language other than your own? Why do you like it?
2 What other languages have you heard people speak? How would you describe how they sound? Do you think that they suggest a certain kind of personality?
3 What gestures do native speakers of your language use to help them communicate more expressively? What gestures have you noticed speakers of other languages use?
4 Do you feel different in any way when you speak English compared to when you speak your first language?
5 What do you think are the advantages and disadvantages of being able to speak more than one language?

→ workbook page 74

## TH!NK values
### Learning another language

10 **Tick (✓) the statements that reflect how you feel. You can tick as many as you like.**

A good reason to learn another language is to …

- be able to communicate when travelling; ☐
- learn about another culture; ☐
- improve my job prospects; ☐
- be able to talk to foreigners in my country; ☐
- be able to read books, magazines and newspapers in another language; ☐
- develop myself personally. ☐

11 SPEAKING **Work in a group of six to eight. Find out from the other students which statements they ticked. Did anyone tick the same statements as you?**

12 **Make a graph or chart like the one below to show how your group feels.**

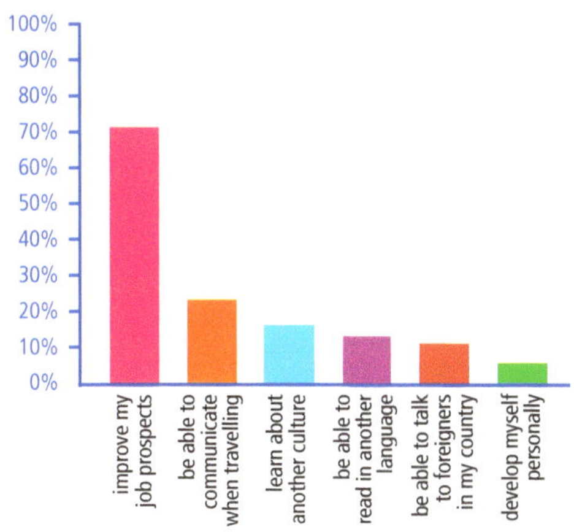

THINK

Language extinction

# Culture

1 Look at the photos. What do you think these languages have in common?

2 8.05 Read and listen to the article and check your ideas. Which of the languages does not have an accompanying photo? Why is this?

# Extinct languages – or are they?

**Languages are dying out all the time. There are currently approximately 7,000 languages spoken across the world and that's fewer than there were two years ago. Here are five languages that were once widely spoken but these days are classified as 'dead' languages.**

## Middle English

Middle English was spoken in England between the 12th and 15th centuries and is very different to the English we use these days. In the past, England, along with Scotland and Wales, was a country that had been invaded by several different nations, and this was reflected in its language, which was highly influenced by Norman French and Old Norse. Middle English also included a lot of Germanic vocabulary. There are very few **manuscripts** in Middle English as it was much more fashionable in those days to write in French. Perhaps the most famous document that has survived is *The Canterbury Tales* (or *Tales of Canterbury*, as it was originally known), which was written between 1387 and 1400 by the poet Geoffrey Chaucer. Middle English gave way to early modern English, which is popularly associated with Shakespeare.

## Ancient Greek

More than 4,000 years ago, the Greeks displayed great knowledge in philosophy, maths, literature and politics. They also spoke a very **sophisticated** language known today as Ancient Greek, and developed the first alphabet to contain vowels. Indeed, the English word 'alphabet' is taken from the first two letters of the Greek alphabet: *alpha* and *beta*. The ancient Greeks wrote a lot of historical accounts and philosophical essays. They also wrote many plays which are considered to be the forerunners of modern theatre. Although the language is no longer spoken anywhere, it continues to be studied by scholars around the world and, along with Latin, is regarded as one of the most important languages of all time.

## Old Norse

Old Norse was spoken and written by the Vikings from the northern countries of Europe from about the 7th century. It belongs to the Germanic group of languages and was used in countries as far apart as Iceland and parts of Russia. It used a complex system of characters known as runes to depict individual letters and sounds. Much of our knowledge of Norse mythology comes from stories written down in runes. The Vikings were also famous for their **raids** on neighbouring countries, and so it is not surprising that Old Norse had an influence on the languages of the places they raided, including English. For example, English words such as 'egg', 'gift', 'anger', 'want', 'trust' and 'score' are all **derived from** Old Norse. Although it is no longer spoken, it is still possible to learn runes.

## Latin

Back in 5 BC, there were many different languages spoken in Italy. In an area called Latium, which included Rome, the people spoke Latin, so as Rome became more and more important, Latin spread throughout the country until it became the principal language. But Rome's influence did not stop in Italy. As the Roman Empire spread across Europe, it took its language with it and gradually Latin became the **lingua franca** for much of the continent. Latin was spoken mainly by the noblemen and **aristocrats**, but there was another form of the language known as Vulgar Latin which was used by ordinary people. When the Roman Empire collapsed in the 5th century, it took Latin with it. However, its huge influence can still be found in many modern European languages, including French, Italian, Portuguese, Spanish and English.

## Hunnir

Hunnir is the most mysterious of the languages on our list, because it is the one that the least is known about, as no documentation of the language exists. The Huns were a **tribal** community that spread across much of eastern Europe in the 4th and 5th centuries. The most famous of the Huns was Attila, a warrior famous for his raids in western Europe. Despite the Huns' success in expanding their **empire**, their language was never written down, which is why we have very little knowledge of it today. The few words that are known are mainly names, which are similar to names used in modern Turkey and Mongolia. Apart from these, only three words are known: *medos*, *kamos* (both types of drinks) and *strava* (a feast served at funerals).

**3** **Match the statements and the languages according to the information in the article.**

1 Hardly any words have survived from this language. ☐
2 Many educational documents were written in this language. ☐
3 There were two forms of this language. ☐
4 It's the most 'modern' language on the list. ☐
5 It used a system of signs called runes. ☐

a Middle English
b Hunnir
c Ancient Greek
d Latin
e Old Norse

**4** VOCABULARY **Match the highlighted words or phrases in the article to the definitions.**

1 people of a higher social class
2 belonging to a group of people
3 intelligent or designed in a complicated way
4 attacks or invasions
5 comes or develops from
6 many countries controlled by one ruler
7 written documents
8 the common, shared language

**5** SPEAKING **Work in pairs and discuss the questions.**

1 Why do you think languages die out?
2 Do you think it's important to save these dying languages? Why/Why not?
3 What do you think can be done to help save dying languages?

## WRITING
### A report from a graph

**6** INPUT **Read the report and complete the empty spaces in the graph.**

**1** A lot of people around the world are keen to gain some level of proficiency in another language. Many people start their learning motivated to succeed but then experience numerous difficulties along the way which can hamper their enthusiasm. A recent study was carried out in the US among adult and teenage learners who were taking a foreign-language course outside of their normal school to find out what difficulties they had encountered.

**2** By far the most widely cited difficulty was a lack of time, which 24% of respondents reported as their main obstacle – especially (but not exclusively) the adults. Of those surveyed, 16% stated that an inability to maintain motivation was their main problem, while 15% claimed that it was not being able to meet and converse with native speakers.

**3** Other problems encountered included budgetary constraints impeding their ability to continue their course, which 11% of learners put forward as a reason for giving up. Finally, a meagre 5% of respondents, especially those who were learning less frequently studied languages, such as Bulgarian or Farsi, stated that they had either no or limited access to good learning materials. Various other difficulties were mentioned by 18% of people.

**4** It seems, then, that difficulties are far from rare among language learners. However, of the respondents, only 17% said that the difficulties had made, or might make, them give up, since the benefits of doing a foreign language course far outweighed the drawbacks.

**Difficulties in learning another language**

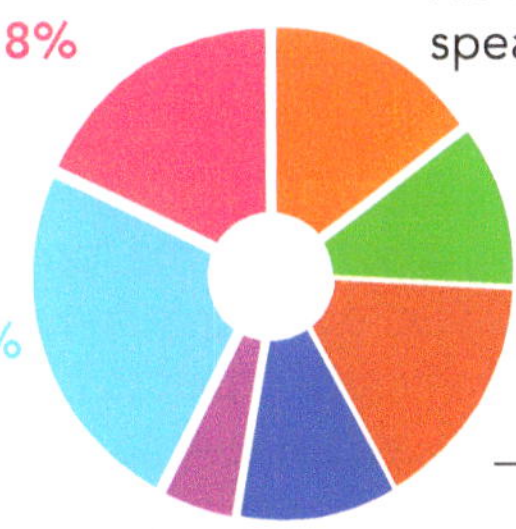


**7** ANALYSE **Which paragraph of the report:**

a starts the presentation of the data? ☐
b introduces the subject of the information in the graph? ☐
c pulls the ideas together and adds a concluding comment? ☐
d adds further data? ☐

**8** **Read the report again. Find different words which the writer uses to refer to what people said.**

*said, claimed,* ___________
___________ ___________

**9** PLAN **You are going to work with the data you gathered in the Values activity on page 79. Look at it again and:**

- remind yourself of the topic and the information you gathered.
- think about how you can introduce the topic.
- decide in what order to present the main findings.
- decide how you might draw the report to a close and any final comments you might make.

**10** PRODUCE **Write a report from the graph you drew (180–220 words).**

## READING AND USE OF ENGLISH

### Part 6: Cross-text multiple matching

→ workbook page 79

1 **You are going to read four extracts from reviews of a book on the subject of cosmetic surgery. For questions 1–4, choose from the reviewers A–D. The reviewers may be chosen more than once.**

# Cosmetic Surgery by Sean Calston

**Reviewer A**

In his book on the supposed misuses of cosmetic surgery, Calston makes the point that it meets the needs of a certain sector of society in which people are so obsessed with their appearance that this obsession could be considered a form of illness. Although he is rightly critical of those in the medical profession who make enormous profits from the trade in plastic surgery, and he has a point when he says the industry should be more tightly regulated, I don't go along with his main thesis. He dismisses the view that such surgery could actually help to alleviate mental-health problems, but frustratingly he doesn't really explain why. Calston's book has attracted a lot of media attention, but it's hardly a gripping read. I'd got the point by chapter two after which the same ideas just get recycled with tedious examples.

**Reviewer B**

A vital part of being human is the ability to express yourself freely and fearlessly, and I, for one, wouldn't want to live in a society where freedom of expression was limited or legislated against, which is what Calston seems to be suggesting when he calls for laws to control what he sees as the 'misuses' of plastic surgery. Sure, cosmetic surgery is big business, but that in itself doesn't make it wrong. Calston's book isn't exactly an engaging read, although he does illustrate his points with some relevant examples – my problem is that I just don't agree with his main arguments. One point where I thought it fell down badly, however, was when he disagrees with those who claim that cosmetic surgery can be a therapy in the treatment of depression. I wanted to know more about the rationale behind that view, but we don't get one.

**Reviewer C**

Sean Calston seems to be a writer who can turn his hand to any subject and he's never shy about giving us an opinion. His latest book on cosmetic surgery is no exception. His direct journalistic style makes the subject very accessible and readable – and the wealth of fascinating examples is it's real strength. Calston gives us quite a negative view of those who make a living out of cosmetic surgery, and he does seem to have a point. He's also quite justified in questioning the rather dubious notion that cosmetic surgery is actually therapeutic for people with some forms of mental illness. He makes a convincing case why this isn't a serious proposition. Less convincing, however, is his idea that the cosmetic surgery industry needs to be more strictly governed by legislation – to my mind what he's suggesting would be a step too far.

**Reviewer D**

I found it quite difficult to get through Sean Calston's book on cosmetic surgery. Much as I like his style, I got rather bogged down in all the long-winded anecdotes and examples. I think I got the main points he was making, but it was a struggle to keep going to the end. It's difficult to argue, however, with what he says about the commercial aspects of cosmetic surgery – there is certainly money to be made from the vulnerable and this may be open to abuse. Calston is right, therefore, to suggest that it might well be time for us to introduce laws to control the abuse of what remains a medical procedure. He also deals sensitively and thoroughly with the issue of whether such surgery could help mental-health patients, although he clearly doesn't agree with it.

Which reviewer ...

1 has a different opinion to Reviewer A regarding Calston's attitude to the business side of cosmetic surgery. ☐

2 shares Reviewer B's opinion of how well Calston deals with the question of whether cosmetic surgery could be used to treat mental illness. ☐

3 has a different view to the others regarding how easy Calston's book is to read. ☐

4 shares reviewer D's opinion of Calston's suggestion that there should be more laws regulating cosmetic surgery? ☐

## VOCABULARY

**1 Complete the sentences with the words in the list. There are four extra words.**

arms | broken | communication | conceited | forceful | heart
impulsive | in | modest | must-get | must-have | short | slang | spine

1 He's quite ______ . He's certainly not shy when it comes to putting himself forward if it means getting what he wants.
2 Loom bands were really ______ a few years ago.
3 That scene at the end of the film sent shivers down my ______ .
4 I think we've got a ______ breakdown here. We're really not understanding each other.
5 He's a bit ______ and often acts without really thinking first.
6 Are you cold? You've got goosebumps all down your ______ .
7 I make lots of mistakes, but I can just about get by in Brazil with my ______ Portuguese.
8 Are smartwatches really going to be the next ______ item?
9 She thinks she's better than everyone else. She's so ______ .
10 Nobody knows this band anymore – their fame was rather ______-lived.

/10

## GRAMMAR

**2 Complete the sentences with the words/phrases in the list. There are two extra words/phrases.**

all of which | hope so | however | in which case | most of whom | think so | whatever | wherever

1 ______ hard I try, I never really understand what he says.
2 I have a lot of friends on social media sites, ______ I rarely see in person.
3 Many people think this film will win an Oscar, but I don't ______ .
4 ______ he goes, people recognise him.
5 Do you think it'll be sunny this weekend? I ______ because I'm planning to go to the beach.
6 She has two jobs and three children to bring up on her own, ______ means she never has any time to herself.

**3 Find and correct the mistake in each sentence.**

1 Some people say it's a dangerous sport, but I don't hope so.
2 I have three brothers, one of who lives in Argentina.
3 Whatever do you, don't say anything.
4 She has three phones, both of which are broken.
5 I'll follow you whatever you go.
6 I'm not sure we'll win, but I hope.

/12

## FUNCTIONAL LANGUAGE

**4 Choose the correct options.**

A Have you always [1]*dreamed / hoped* of an easier life?
B I'm sorry? I don't quite [2]*follow / catch* you.
A An easier life. If you try our [3]*brand / known* new product, you'll save hours every week.
B I'm afraid you've [4]*got / lost* me. What product are you talking about?
A Lush 2.0. It's on offer. But only for a [5]*narrow / limited* time.
B I'm sorry, but I'm not [6]*known / familiar* with Lush 2.0. What is it exactly?
A Lush 2.0 – our most advanced washing powder yet. I [7]*powerfully / strongly* recommend you give it a go.
B Washing powder?! I don't quite [8]*see / follow* why I'd be interested in washing powder. I'm only 13 years old.

/8

**MY SCORE** /30

22–30 | 10–21 | 0–9

# 9 FAIRNESS MATTERS

## OBJECTIVES

**FUNCTIONS:**
talking imprecisely about numbers

**GRAMMAR:**
negative inversion; spoken discourse markers

**VOCABULARY:**
court cases; fairness and equality

**Get THINKING**

**Watch the video and think: how do you decide what's fair?**

## READING

1 SPEAKING **Work in pairs. Discuss your answers with a partner.**

1 What do you think a *miscarriage of justice* is?
2 Can you think of any famous miscarriages of justice?

2 **Look at the photos, read the headline and introduction on page 85 and check your answers to Exercise 1 question 1.**

3 **Work in groups of three. Read your text and the questions, and note down your answers.**

**Student A:** read text 1
**Student B:** read text 2
**Student C:** read text 3

1 What was the person/were the people convicted of?
2 What was the evidence that was used to convict them?
3 How were they set free, and after how long?
4 What happened to them after their release from prison?

4 9.01 SPEAKING **Tell your group what you learned. Use your notes to help you. Then listen and read the texts to check.**

5 SPEAKING **Work in pairs and discuss the questions.**

1 Which of the three cases do you think describes the worst miscarriage of justice? Why?
2 In your country, what kind of punishment is given for:
   - shoplifting?
   - dangerous driving?
   - fraud? (getting money by deceiving people)
   - murder?
3 Which of the crimes in question 2 do you think a person should go to prison for? Why?
4 What other crimes should a person go to prison for? Why?

**PRONUNCIATION**

Unstressed syllables and words: the /l/ phoneme.

Go to page 121.

# Miscarriages of JUSTICE

**Imagine – one day, out of the blue, you are arrested, accused of a crime that you didn't commit, found guilty and sent to prison. Even in the best legal systems, innocent people can find themselves convicted by judge and jury and sentenced to years behind bars.**

## 1 Sally Clark (UK)

Sally Clark was a lawyer and mother of two. Her first son was born healthy in 1996, but died suddenly when he was just three months old. In 1998 she had another son, but he too died aged just two months and in the same circumstances. At this point, social services intervened and Mrs Clark was subsequently put on trial for murder.

The prosecutors based their evidence on the findings of a medical expert, who claimed that the chances of two babies from the same family dying a natural death in identical circumstances were virtually nil. Despite protesting her innocence, Clark was found guilty on the basis of that evidence and sentenced to life imprisonment. She appealed the verdict and after three years in jail, she was released when it emerged that evidence proving that one of the children had died from natural causes had been withheld from her defence lawyers. Furthermore, the statistical evidence on which the prosecution was based was shown to be invalid. One doctor commented that rarely had statistical evidence been so misused in a trial. Sally Clark never fully recovered from her ordeal and she died in 2007, aged only 43.

## 2 Rubin 'Hurricane' Carter (US)

Rubin Carter was born in 1937 in New Jersey. He was convicted of several crimes before he became a professional boxer in 1961. Nicknamed 'Hurricane' because of his lightning-fast fists, he was a promising boxer who was on the way to winning the middleweight world championship. But in 1966, Carter and his friend John Artis were arrested and prosecuted for the murder of three people in a bar. The evidence was weak – two witnesses said they'd seen Carter and Artis running away from the crime but later they changed their story. Not only did Carter and Artis have no motive, but they also had alibis. Moreover, it was never proven that their guns were the ones used in the murders. Nor were any fingerprints taken at the crime scene. Despite all of this, both Carter and Artis were convicted in 1967 and given life sentences. Throughout his incarceration, Carter campaigned for his release, always protesting his innocence. Various people campaigned on his behalf and singer Bob Dylan even wrote a song about his case. Finally, in November 1985, the case was thrown out of court and Rubin Carter was finally released after having spent 18 years behind bars. Artis had already been released four years earlier. Carter died in 2014 at the age of 76. His story was made into an Oscar-nominated film, *Hurricane*, in 1999, starring Denzel Washington.

## 3 The Guildford Four (UK)

In the 1970s, the Irish Republican Army (IRA) ran a bombing campaign in the UK to protest against British military presence in Northern Ireland. One bomb, in 1974 in a town called Guildford, killed several soldiers and their girlfriends. No sooner had the bombing taken place than four young people – Gerry Conlon, Patrick Armstrong, Carol Richardson and Paul Hill – were arrested and charged. All four of them confessed under police interrogation, but they later retracted their confessions. In 1975, they were sent to prison for life. None of the four had the typical profile of a bomber and furthermore, the prosecution withheld evidence that proved that Conlon had been in London at the time of the bombing. Later, the IRA itself stated clearly that none of the four had been involved in the Guildford bombings. Nevertheless, it took until 1989 for them to be released, fifteen years after their arrest. Conlon went on to become a campaigner against miscarriages of justice both in the UK and abroad. He died in 2014. A film, *In the Name of the Father*, was made about him in 1993, starring Daniel Day-Lewis.

## Train to TH!NK

### The *ad hominem* fallacy

*'Ad hominem' means 'against the man'. The* ad hominem *fallacy describes a situation where instead of using logic or evidence to argue against an opinion, claim or point of view, you attack an opponent's character. Often the* ad hominem *fallacy uses stereotypes and encourages prejudice. For example, a man complains to the police about his noisy neighbours. The neighbours defend themselves saying that they aren't surprised about the complaint since he's a really grumpy man and is always complaining about things. Their comments about his personality don't necessarily mean that his complaint isn't valid.*

6 **Look at the texts again. Which of the victims do these remarks refer to?**

1 They're young. They must be guilty.
2 He's a violent man. He must have done it.
3 I don't trust lawyers so I'm sure she's guilty.

7 SPEAKING **Work in pairs. What examples can you come up with of people (individuals or groups) who often unfairly find themselves victims of the *ad hominem* fallacy?**

# GRAMMAR
## Negative inversion

**1 Complete the sentences from the texts on page 85.**

1 One doctor commented that ________________ had statistical evidence been so misused in a trial.
2 ________________ did Carter and Artis have no motive, but they also had alibis.
3 ________________ had the bombing taken place than four young people [...] were arrested and charged.

**2 Here are the same ideas written in a more usual form. What differences do you notice? Think about meaning and form. Then choose the correct options in the rule.**

1 One doctor commented that statistical evidence had never been so misused in a trial.
2 Carter and Artis not only didn't have a motive, but they also had alibis.
3 The bombing took place and immediately afterwards, four young people were arrested and charged.

> **RULE:** We can bring [1]*positive / negative* and limiting adverbs and adverbial phrases, such as *rarely, little, not only ... but (also), no sooner ... than, never, under no circumstances, on no account* to the [2]*beginning / end* of a sentence to make it [3]*more / less* emphatic. The rest of the sentence follows the pattern of a [4]*normal statement / question.*
> In present and past tense forms of non-modal verbs, we use the auxiliary *do* or *did* and invert the auxiliary and the subject. With other verb tenses or modals, we use the auxiliary that's already there (for example *is, are, have, can, will*).
> We use this structure much more often in [5]*written / spoken* English. We can use it in speech when we want to add dramatic effect.

**3 Choose the correct options.**

1 *Never have I / Never I've* read about such disturbing cases.
2 *Not only they were / Not only were they* innocent, but they weren't even at the scene of the crime.
3 No sooner *the case had finished / had the case finished* than the judge set them free.
4 Under no circumstances *could they / they could* be the criminals.

**4 Rewrite the sentences. Use the word(s) in brackets at the start of the new sentence.**

0 The film finished and we immediately left. (No sooner ... than)
*No sooner had the film finished than we left.*
1 We should not discuss this in front of other people. (On no account)
2 I've never read such an appalling story. (Never)
3 He was innocent and so were the others. (Not only ... but)
4 Innocent people are not often released from prison following a miscarriage of justice. (Rarely)

→ workbook page 82

# VOCABULARY
## Court cases

**5 Match the words with the definitions.**

1 to be found guilty/innocent ☐
2 to appeal a verdict ☐
3 a witness ☐
4 to make a confession ☐
5 to retract a confession ☐
6 the defence ☐
7 the prosecution ☐
8 to give evidence ☐
9 to withhold evidence ☐
10 to be sentenced to life imprisonment ☐

a to say that you committed a crime
b to not give information that is important in a trial
c the lawyers who try to prove that someone is guilty
d to have a court say that you did/didn't commit a crime
e to be told that you will spend the rest of your life in prison
f to give information in a court
g someone who says in court what they know or saw
h to ask to go to a higher court for another trial
i to say that the confession you made before wasn't true
j the lawyer(s) who try to prove that someone is innocent

**6 Complete the text using words and phrases from Exercise 5 in the correct form.**

> The woman was arrested for murder and she made [1]________________ , but three days later, she [2]________________ it. However, the case went to court.
> During the trial, about 20 people [3]________________ evidence. A witness for [4]________________ said he had seen the woman at the scene of the crime. But the lawyer for [5]________________ claimed that that wasn't possible. In the end, she was [6]________________ and she was [7]________________ to life imprisonment.
> The defence [8]________________ the verdict and, in the subsequent retrial, it was shown that the prosecution had withheld [9]________________ . The woman was [10]________________ and released.

→ workbook page 84

# LISTENING

7 SPEAKING **Look at the cartoons. What do you think is happening in each one? Discuss with your partner.**

8 9.03 **Listen to a radio programme about how two fathers, Daniel and Chris, discipline their teenagers and choose the correct answers.**

1 How do you think Daniel's three sons feel when Daniel uses his punishment?
  a embarrassed
  b proud
  c disappointed
  d furious

2 What does Daniel do to cause this reaction?
  a tell the boys to sing a song
  b act out a scene from a play
  c do a dance routine from a famous musical
  d perform a song from a musical

3 What had Chris' children done to upset him?
  a They hadn't tidied their rooms when he asked them to.
  b They had gone into his study and left it untidy.
  c They had taken something from his desk.
  d They had hidden their doors.

4 What did Chris decide to do?
  a He didn't let them go to sleep.
  b He took away the doors to their bedrooms.
  c He didn't give them their mobile phones or laptops for a week.
  d He made them swap bedrooms.

9 **Who do you think might say these things later – Daniel's or Chris' children? Why? Compare your ideas with a partner.**

1 'It made me feel very insecure. I hated it.'
2 'It feels really strange going to sleep without it.'
3 'We need to make sure we don't have any arguments in the supermarket again.'
4 'If we're good and we don't act up, he'll keep quiet.'

10 SPEAKING **Work in pairs and discuss the questions.**

1 In your opinion, which parent's punishment is the most effective– Daniel's or Chris'? Discuss and give your reasons for your choice.
2 What is the most effective punishment that you have ever received from your parents? Tell your partner.

## WordWise
## Expressions with *on*

11 **Look at these sentences from the unit so far. Complete them with the phrases from the list.**

on good terms | on his behalf
on the basis | on the way | on trial

1 She was put ________________ for murder.
2 He was a promising boxer who was ________________ to winning the middleweight world championship.
3 My three sons are usually ________________ with each other.
4 Various people campaigned ________________ and singer Bob Dylan even wrote a song about his case.
5 She was found guilty ________________ of that evidence.

12 **Choose the correct options.**

1 It must be awful to be put *on the way / on trial* for something you didn't do.
2 I'm saving up and I'm well *on the way / on the basis* to having enough money for a new tablet.
3 He isn't my best friend, but I'm on quite *good terms / behalf* with him.
4 She couldn't be at the ceremony, so her husband accepted the award on her *behalf / basis*.
5 You'll be given marks on the *basis / behalf* of the progress you make.

→ workbook page 84

# WRITING
## An essay

13 PLAN **Note down three arguments in favour of the statement below, and three arguments against it. (You can use your own ideas or any from the unit.)**

*Prisons should be decent, comfortable places for prisoners.*

| For | Against |
| --- | --- |
| 1 ____________ | 1 ____________ |
| 2 ____________ | 2 ____________ |
| 3 ____________ | 3 ____________ |

14 **Compare your ideas with a partner.**

15 PRODUCE **Use your notes to write an essay of around 150–200 words.**

## READING

1 **Which of these statements do you agree with?**

A huge gap between the earnings of rich and poor people in society leads to …

1 more crime.
2 people being unhappier.
3 people having shorter and unhealthier lives.

2 **Read the book review quickly. Which of these is the best summary of the review? The book …**

1 is about ways to increase wealth and happiness in society.
2 is about ways to prevent violent crime in society.
3 shows that inequality is the cause of most problems we face in society.

3 9.04 **Read the review again and listen. Answer the questions.**

1 Which countries are the happiest and healthiest?
2 What examples does the writer give of things that inequality leads to?
3 What would every country benefit from?
4 What does Peter Saunders question in his report on the book?

## SPEAKING

4 **Work in small groups. Discuss your responses to the statements. Are there any that you all agree or disagree with?**

1 'I believe that I will have a better life in Sweden than in the US.'
2 'There is more crime in countries where there is a bigger gap between the incomes of the richest and the poorest.'
3 'Poverty is the only cause of ill health.'
4 'People with a higher income live longer.'

BOOK REVIEW

# *The Spirit Level*

### by Richard Wilkinson and Kate Pickett (2010)

A few months before his election as British Prime Minister, David Cameron said: 'Research by Richard Wilkinson and Kate Pickett has shown that among the richest countries, it's the more unequal ones that do worse according to almost every quality of life indicator.'

The then Labour leader Ed Miliband also seemed to make a reference to *The Spirit Level* when he proclaimed that, 'The gap between rich and poor does matter. It doesn't just harm the poor; it harms all of us.'

These political leaders are just two of many people across the world who have been influenced by *The Spirit Level*, the surprise bestseller which has sold over 200,000 copies.

*The Spirit Level* claims that income inequality is bad not only for the poorest in society, but also for the wealthiest, and that an equal society benefits both the rich and the poor. And let's face it, inequality causes shorter, unhealthier and unhappier lives. The authors' claims are based on statistical evidence, which they say shows that more unequal countries (and within the US, more unequal states) suffer from higher crime rates, a lower than average life expectancy, increased infant mortality rates and less social mobility. In fact, almost every social problem from obesity to crime has one root cause: inequality. Because of this, their conclusion is that we would all benefit from a more equal distribution of income, and to be honest, I agree with them. *The Spirit Level* was praised by politicians on both the left and the right, and it seemed the book was proof that economic inequality leads to chronic health and social problems for everyone, including the rich.

I found the book so interesting that I then did some more research and came across Peter Saunders' report, *Beware False Prophets*. It looks again at the arguments made in *The Spirit Level* and finds that only one of the 20 statistical claims (the association internationally between infant deaths and income inequality) truly supports their theory. For example, Saunders points out in his report that the claim that a country's murder rate is linked to its level of income inequality depends entirely on the high murder rate in the US, while the claim that average life expectancy is linked to income inequality rests entirely on the long lives of the Japanese. Across the other 22 countries analysed, there was simply no association.

I strongly recommend reading both the book and the report and coming to your own conclusions.

### COMMENTS

**James Inkworth**
I went to a talk given by Richard Wilkinson and I can assure you that he is as convincing in a lecture theatre as he is in this book. Inequality and widening inequality is dangerous for every level of society – not just the worst-off. This book should be on everyone's bookshelf.

**Margaret Baker**
An extremely interesting read. I highly recommend this book. To tell you the truth, it shows how almost everything – from life expectancy to mental illness, violence to illiteracy – is affected not by how wealthy a society is, but how equal it is.

**Martin Wiseman**
In general, it is an excellent read. However, I would recommend skipping the first 12 chapters and reading the last few chapters for their brilliant conclusion and excellent recommendations.

**Gemma Hunter**
A thorough and brilliant evidence-based analysis of the many reasons why it would be wise for us to look to Scandinavia and not to the US as our role model for how to build a healthier and happier society.

**Kim Fletcher**
The more unequal our world becomes, the more problems we face, and if you ask me, this book provides the evidence to confirm this. That said, it is not impossible to believe, especially in the age of AI, that a universal income could be introduced and we could have equality. I give it six stars.

# VOCABULARY
## Fairness and equality

**5** SPEAKING **Work in pairs. Read the sentences below. Discuss and check the meaning of the words and phrases in bold.**

1. We live in an **unfair** society with a widening gap between the richest and the poorest.
2. It is **evident** that poverty does, in some cases, lead to crime.
3. Cases of **violent** crimes using knives and guns are on the increase.
4. Poverty can lead to **social** problems such as bad health and unhappiness.
5. The authors of *The Spirit Level* have medical rather than **political** motives for writing the book.
6. People are not born **equal**. Some people have greater opportunities than others.
7. In **general**, people are happier and healthier in Japan than in the US.
8. People are **obese** because they cannot afford to buy healthy food.

**6** SPEAKING **Work in pairs or small groups. Think of examples of:**

1. how society is unfair.
2. violent crimes being committed in your country.
3. people who have a political motive for doing something.
4. people who aren't born equal into society.

**7 Complete the noun related to the adjectives in Exercise 5.**

0 evid*e n c e*
1 viol__ __ __ __
2 soc__ __ __ __
3 polit__ __ __
4 equal__ __ __
5 general__ __ __ __ __ __ __
6 obes__ __ __

**8 Write the correct form of the word in brackets in each space.**

1. There were no __________ confrontations at the protest today. (VIOLENCE)
2. I hope that one day we will see __________ for everyone. (EQUAL)
3. I think it is a __________ to say poverty causes crime. (GENERAL)
4. The number of __________ children in developed countries has been on the rise in the last decade. (OBESITY)
5. It was __________ from the meeting that many politicians want to stop climate change. (EVIDENCE)
6. Every __________ needs a fair justice system. (SOCIAL)

→ workbook page 84

# GRAMMAR
## Spoken discourse markers

Grammar video ▶23

**9 Complete the sentences from the book review and comments on page 88 and then complete the rule with the correct sentence numbers.**

1. __________ , it is not impossible to believe, especially in the age of AI, that a universal income could be introduced and we could have equality.
2. Almost every social problem from obesity to crime has one root cause: inequality. __________ , their conclusion is that we would all benefit from a more equal distribution of income.
3. __________ , inequality causes shorter, unhealthier and unhappier lives.
4. In general, it is an excellent read. __________ , I would recommend skipping the first 12 chapters.

**RULE:** We use discourse markers to:
- talk about a result. Example sentence [a]__________
- show the writer's opinion. Example sentence [b]__________
- introduce a concession. Example sentence [c]__________
- introduce a contrast. Example sentence [d]__________

**10 Write the discourse markers in the correct column in the table below. Some may go in more than one column.**

actually | anyway | as a result of | at the end of the day | ~~because of~~
by the way | for a start | however | if you ask me | let's face it
mind you | ~~nevertheless~~ | on the other hand | ~~personally~~ | that said
the thing is | to be honest | to tell you the truth | ~~while~~

| Cause and result | Contrast | Opinion | Topic change | Concession |
|---|---|---|---|---|
| *because of* | *nevertheless* | *personally* | *anyway* | *while* |

**11 Rewrite each sentence. Remove the word in bold and use a discourse marker from Exercise 10 to replace it. (There are several possibilities.)**

0 I knew it was wrong. **So** I didn't do it.
*I knew it was wrong. Because of this, I didn't do it.*
1 They all knew it was unethical. **But** they went ahead and did it.
2 I left in the middle of the film. **I thought** it was awful.
3 The company director resigned. **There were** accusations of corruption.
4 I'll listen to your thoughts. But **finally** it's my decision.
5 It wasn't at all good. **I think** it was the worst idea ever.

→ workbook page 83

# DEVELOPING SPEAKING

**Company Director gets five years**

**Employees wait to learn about pensions**

**1** 🔊 9.05 **Look at the photos. What do you think Steve is angry about? What do you understand from the newspaper headlines? Read, listen and check your ideas.**

**Steve:** This makes me really angry. It's just so completely unfair! Only five years?! After what he did!

**Michelle:** What are you talking about? Let me see. Oh, that guy. He's the one who took the money from his company's pension plan, if I'm not mistaken.

**Steve:** 'Took'?! Stole! And he's been found guilty. But he only got a five-year jail sentence. Apparently, it could be only three years or so if he gets time off for good behaviour.

**Michelle:** That's news to me. And it certainly doesn't sound like a strong enough sentence.

**Steve:** It absolutely isn't. I'd have thought around 20 years would have been more appropriate. I mean, he's left over 100 people with no pension in the future. It's two crimes, in a way: not just stealing money, but stealing people's futures.

**Michelle:** Well, when you put it like that, it does seem really bad.

**Steve:** It's worse! Do you know, as the boss of the company, he was earning roughly 300 times more than his average employee?

**Michelle:** Seriously? And he isn't so old, is he? Only 40ish, by the look of it.

**Steve:** More to the point, if you're making that kind of money, why do you need to steal from the pension plan?

**Michelle:** Yes. And you know, I think maybe he didn't get a more severe sentence because he's rich and could afford a really expensive lawyer. That's how it works a lot of the time.

**Steve:** One law for the rich, another for the poor. And that makes me angry, too!

**2** 🔊 9.05 **Read and listen to the dialogue again. Answer the questions.**

1 What was the company director found guilty of, and what was his sentence?
2 What do we learn about the director's salary, and about his employees' futures?
3 How does Michelle explain the reason for the 'light' jail sentence?

## Phrases for fluency

**3 Find these expressions in the dialogue. Who says them? How do you say them in your language?**

1 ..., if I'm not mistaken.
2 Apparently, ...
3 That's news to me.
4 I'd have thought ...
5 ... when you put it like that, ...
6 More to the point, ...

**4 Use the expressions in Exercise 3 to complete the dialogues.**

1 A This music's horrendous!
B I'm surprised. ______________ you'd like it.

2 A John hasn't turned up yet. Where is he?
B He isn't coming. ______________, he's very busy or something.

3 A What time does the match start, Sir?
B Eight thirty, ______________.

4 A We've run out of milk, I think.
B Yes, you're right. But ______________, who left the empty bottle in the fridge?

5 A Paul Graham's taking on the role of Student Representative. Did you know?
B No. ______________.

6 A Let's not go out. It's miserable outside.
B Well, ______________, perhaps a walk really isn't a good idea.

## FUNCTIONS

### Talking imprecisely about numbers

**5 Complete the sentences from the dialogue.**

1 It could be only three years ______________ if he gets time off for good behaviour.
2 I'd have thought ______________ 20 years would have been more appropriate.
3 He was earning ______________ 300 times more than his average employee.
4 Only 40______________, by the look of it.

**6 What are the imprecise expressions in these sentences? Do the numbers come before or after each expression?**

1 It cost around $120.
2 It took something like three years to build.
3 Fifty people turned up, give or take.
4 In the region of 10,000 people live here.

**7 Answer the questions using an imprecise expression.**

1 How many students are there at your school?
2 How much does a bottle of water cost where you live?
3 How far is it from your house to the town/city centre?
4 How long does it take you to get to school every day?

# LIFE COMPETENCIES

**Most of us will feel strongly about certain issues throughout our lives. But it isn't always easy to stand up and let others know how you feel. Taking the right kind of action is a skill that will lead you to feeling more satisfied and like you can make a difference.**

1 ▶ 24 **Watch the vlog. What did Annie protest against? Was the protest successful?**

2 ▶ 24 **Watch the vlog again and answer the questions.**

1 Which of her heroes does Annie talk about?
2 What did Annie do on her protest outside the town hall?
3 What happened to Annie when she met the mayor?

3 **Read the article and answer the questions.**

1 What did Jenny decide was wrong?
2 What two things has she managed to do?
3 Who helped her?

4 SPEAKING **Work in groups. Read through the mini-scenarios. Rank them in order of how strongly you feel about each one (1 = least strong; 4 = most strong).**

- ☐ Your town council is planning to sell off the local park to a building company who are going to turn it into a shopping centre.
- ☐ The headmaster of your school has decided to ban all mobile phones from the school buildings.
- ☐ The government wants to introduce a tax of £500 for anyone who owns a dog.
- ☐ Your local hospital is going to close because the local authorities say it is too expensive.

## Me and my world

5 SPEAKING **In your groups, think about something you feel strongly about and organise a campaign. Discuss the following questions:**

- What do you want to say?
- Who do you want to say it to?
- How you are going to say it?
- What change do you hope for?

### TIPS ON STANDING UP FOR YOUR BELIEFS

- **If you feel strongly that something is wrong, you should try to find the courage to speak out against it, although this is not always so easy.**
- **Think carefully about why you feel strongly, what it is you would like to see changed and the best way to achieve it.**
- **Try to keep a calm head. Aggression rarely achieves anything.**

## Teen brings Christmas cheer to elderly

Over 50 elderly people who live alone in the local area are going to get a visit over Christmas, thanks to 15-year-old Jenny Stainsby. Jenny was determined to do something to ensure that the elderly people wouldn't be entirely alone.

'Many old people either have no relatives at all, or else their relatives live too far away to visit them,' said Jenny. 'No one should be alone over Christmas – that's miserable – so we've tried to do something about it.'

'We' means Jenny and around 20 of her co-pupils at the high school. Jenny created a page on social media, asking for the names of elderly people living alone in the area. Then she called on her friends at school to help her to do two things: firstly, to draw up an agenda of visits (i.e. which of them would go and visit who, and when) over the Christmas period; and secondly, to start a campaign amongst the school pupils, staff and parents to collect small presents that they could take to the elderly people. Their campaign was generously responded to, and they will now be able to not only call in on the 50 elderly folk, but also take each of them two small gifts (for example a book, an item of clothing, a small cake).

Jenny said: 'It was my idea at first, but all my friends and their parents have been brilliant. I'm so happy we can do this, and if it's successful, I hope we can repeat the idea every year.'

# 10 LEARNING FOR LIFE

**OBJECTIVES**

**FUNCTIONS:**
reacting to news

**GRAMMAR:**
reported verb patterns (review); passive report structures; hedging

**VOCABULARY:**
higher education; life after school

**Get THINKING**

Watch the video and think:
how important is it to learn new things?

## READING

1 SPEAKING **Work in pairs and look at the photos. What might the people be learning from doing these activities? How might they be feeling? In which of the situations would you most enjoy learning? Why?**

2 **Think of a memorable teacher you had in primary school. What made him/her memorable? Write down your ideas. Then compare them with a partner.**

3 **Read the notice and answer the questions.**

1 What kind of meeting is this?
2 Is it the kind of meeting you'd go to? Why/Why not?
3 What do you think the 'school crisis' might be?

> St Jonathan School, Greenway
> Tuesday 12th April
>
> **Meeting with school governors and staff**
>
> *Parents and children are invited to attend this meeting to discuss the current school crisis.*

4 10.01 **Read and listen to the summary of the meeting written by a pupil and the comments which follow. What issue was being debated and what question was being answered by the people who commented?**

5 **Read the comments again. Which of the people who commented on the summary do you think might say the following things?**

1 'The 1979 elections were a turning point for the country.'
2 'I learned so much from playing the part of Biff.'
3 'Now I know what 'blue notes' are, and why they're so common in jazz.'
4 'It's crazy that you spent eight years at school, and you still don't know about phishing.'
5 'I can see why people learning the language might get this wrong, but there's no excuse for native speakers.'
6 'Who was it who said that if you don't remember the past, you'll just repeat the same mistakes?'
7 'I couldn't possibly stand in front of people and act, but I love helping the people who do.'
8 'The worst thing is that when everyone starts making the same grammar mistake, it starts to become OK.'

6 SPEAKING **Work in pairs and discuss the questions.**

1 Should less academic subjects such as Food Technology, Art and Dance be taught in schools? Why/Why not?
2 List the subjects you study at school. Then put them in order from most to least important. Compare your list with your partner, giving reasons for your choices. Then agree together on a final ranking.
3 Imagine one of your subjects was going to be cut from the timetable. Agree on which subject that should be.

Home About New reports Community

## What to drop?

Last night at our school, there was a meeting of the school governors, and they invited any interested parents to come along. My parents went and I tagged along. The place was packed – governors, teachers, parents, kids – because everyone knew the main topic for the meeting was the school's financial problems. The chair of the governors thanked everyone for coming and confessed that they had to find a way of making savings. Our headteacher, Mrs Grimmond, insisted that the school was doing everything it could, and blamed government spending cuts for putting the school in a bad position. Then the chair of governors said that the only thing left to do was to remove at least one subject from the school curriculum, in order to save on staff salaries. Mrs Grimmond promised to keep working towards making the school more financially viable but, very reluctantly, she agreed that something had to be cut. Then, of course, the discussion moved on to which subject that could be. Mrs Grimmond said that she would not make any suggestions because she had to remain impartial. One parent accused her of being indecisive, but most people agreed with her decision. Then someone suggested cutting Art because it wasn't a life skill for kids. Someone else said, 'Well, if that's true, then you could also cut Music, and maybe PE.' As you might expect, there were arguments for and against every subject put forward, and in the end, the governors decided to organise an online vote. And I was thinking, I know which subject I would *never* cut. But before I tell you what it is, why don't you tell me which school subject you would never, ever leave out of the curriculum?

**Comments** 5 20 9

I would never leave out History. How can we understand where we are at the present moment – and why – if we don't know how we got here? I think it's vital that children learn the history of not only their own country (incredibly important), but also that of other countries, at least over, say, the last 50 years. And I don't mean just learning historical facts and figures – I mean analysing what's happened and why. Truly important, to my mind.

*JoBolton*

For me, the most important thing in the school curriculum is English. I don't mean literature – I mean good grammar, spelling, punctuation and so on. I'm horrified when I meet people who don't know when to write 'its' or 'it's', or the difference between 'there', 'their' and they're'. Everyone should learn to write and speak their own language properly. Then you've immediately got an advantage.

*Ali_Burke*

I know a lot of people will think I'm crazy, but for me it's Drama. Not just because I love it, but because I see how being on stage and acting a role gives so many kids confidence and a better understanding of themselves and other people's lives. Drama also involves teamwork, and this is a big plus in an age when we spend so much time working alone on computers, and so on.

*Nancy421*

I really don't like IT and computing much, but in this day and age it's vital, and it has to be on the curriculum. I think we're going to see (if we aren't seeing it already) a world where anyone who isn't up to speed with what's going on in IT is going to be left behind.

*RedmanOfYork*

I would keep Music. Learning to play a musical instrument is fantastic for anyone who does it, so I think everyone should do it! It's creative, stimulating and something that you can enjoy for the rest of your life – I don't think you can say that about a lot of other subjects! Even if you don't learn to play, you can start to understand and appreciate music more – what's not to love about that?

*GrantG*

## Train to TH!NK

### Doing something for the 'right' reasons

*Before taking a particular course of action, we should make sure that any decision we make is based on valid and logical reasons. We must be careful not to be influenced by reasoning that isn't relevant. For example, Mandy says she wants to study Physics next year because the teacher doesn't give much homework. James wants to study Physics next year because he's interested in studying Medicine at university. Whose reasoning is the most valid?*

7 SPEAKING **Work in pairs. Read the reasons people give for wanting to go to university. Who has a valid reason? Whose reasoning is flawed? Why?**

**I want to go to university after leaving school because …**

I can't think what else to do. *Kevin*

All my brothers and sisters went. *Susan*

I want to be in the university football team. *James*

I want to be a lawyer. *Diana*

8 SPEAKING **Work in pairs. Complete this sentence with two valid and two invalid reasons.**

I want to get married before I'm 25 because …

## GRAMMAR
### Reported verb patterns (review)

**1** **Read the sentences from the summary on page 93 and complete them with the correct form of the verbs in brackets. Then complete the rule with the reporting verbs (in bold in sentences 1–4).**

1 Our headteacher **insisted** that the school ______________ everything it could. (do)
2 Mrs Grimmond **promised** ______________ working towards making the school more financially viable. (keep)
3 One parent **accused** her ______________ indecisive. (be)
4 They **invited** any interested parents ______________ along. (come)

**RULE:** Instead of using *say* and *tell*, we can use other verbs to report what someone said more accurately.

| Pattern | Reporting verbs |
|---|---|
| + (person) + preposition + gerund | blame/apologise/confess/congratulate/ [1]______________ <br>*She* ***blamed government spending cuts for putting*** *the school in a bad position.* |
| + *to* + infinitive/ *that* clause | decide/[2]______________ <br>*They* ***decided to organise*** *an online vote.* |
| + gerund or *that* clause | recommend/admit (to)/regret/suggest/ deny/[3]______________ <br>*Then someone* ***suggested cutting*** *Art.* |
| + (person) + (*not*) *to* + infinitive | warn/[4]______________ <br>*They* ***warned us not to take*** *that route.* |

**2** **Rewrite the sentences, using the reporting verbs in the list.**

~~apologise~~ | confess | congratulate | deny | suggest

0 'We're sorry that we didn't invite Nick to the party.'
They *apologised for not inviting Nick to the party.*
1 'We hacked into his account and stole his identity.'
The men ______________.
2 'I didn't have any idea that the Prime Minister was planning to reduce the number of English lessons.'
The education minister ______________.
3 'Well done, Valerie! You've got a place at the top university!'
The headmaster ______________.
4 'Let's discuss this more before making a decision.'
The project leader ______________.

**3** ROLE PLAY **Work in groups of four (A, B, C, D). Students A & C: go to page 127. Students B & D: go to page 128. You have five minutes to reach a decision on what the government should invest in. Then work in pairs and summarise the discussion using reporting verbs.**

*Marcus suggested that …*

*Max convinced Marcus that …*

→ workbook page 90

## VOCABULARY
### Higher education

**4** SPEAKING **Match the sentence halves. Then discuss the meaning of the expressions and words in italics with a partner.**

1 Margaret *sailed through her* end-of-school ☐
2 She *took a gap year* in India before *starting her undergraduate degree* ☐
3 She *did her master's degree* ☐
4 She *wrote her dissertation* on 20th-century ☐
5 After graduating, she *got* ☐
6 She went to work in Africa ☐

a *full-time* over the course of a year.
b *a scholarship* to do a postgrad course in Toronto.
c economic policy.
d *exams* when she was 18.
e as a *fully qualified* economist.
f *in* Economics at Newcastle University.

**5** **Complete the sentences using the words and phrases in italics in Exercise 4.**

1 She's a ______________ doctor now. She starts work at her local hospital next month.
2 He graduates today. He ______________ and got a first.
3 She ______________ on molecular biology. It's a tough read!
4 He didn't go straight to university after school. He ______________ volunteering in Laos.
5 She ______________ in English Literature this year.
6 After graduating, I ______________ to do a postgrad course at Columbia University.
7 He doesn't want to do his master's part-time. He wants to do it ______________ and finish within a year.
8 After her undergraduate degree, she went on to ______________ in Art History at the Sorbonne.

→ workbook page 92

## SPEAKING

**6** **Choose four of the phrases in italics in Exercise 4 and use them to write three true sentences and one false one about you.**

**7** **In small groups, take turns to read out your sentences. Ask follow-up questions to try to work out which sentence isn't true.**

# LISTENING AND VOCABULARY

## Life after school

**8** SPEAKING **Work in pairs and discuss which of these things are typical choices for school-leavers.**

- travel
- do military service
- get a full-time job
- go to university
- take a gap year
- do an apprenticeship

**9** 10.02 **Listen to Joanna, Harry and Tanya talking about life after school and complete the table.**

| | Joanna | Harry | Tanya |
|---|---|---|---|
| 1 Did they go to university? If not, what are they now doing? | | | |
| 2 What factors helped them make their decision? | | | |
| 3 How do they feel now about the decision they made? | | | |

**10** 10.02 **Listen again. Which of the three people would you most like to talk to? Why?**

*It would be interesting to hear about Joanna's travels.*

*I disagree. She sounds a bit selfish. I'd rather talk to Harry. He seems the most normal.*

**11** 10.03 **Listen to a headteacher giving his opinion. Answer the questions. Use your answers from Exercise 9 to help you.**

1 Which two things does he say his answer depends on?
2 What would he think about what Joanna did?
3 Do you think he'd approve of Harry's decision? Or Tanya's?
4 What does he say about current trends in gap years?

**12** SPEAKING **Work in pairs and discuss the questions.**

1 Are gap years common in your country at the moment? Have they ever been common?
2 Which of the headteacher's views do you agree with? Which do you disagree with? Why?
3 Would you consider taking a gap year? Why/Why not?
4 How would you spend it? How would you finance it?

**13** **Choose the correct option to complete the sentences.**

1 I'm glad I *took* / *went* a gap year before starting my degree course.
2 I've graduated and I now *have* / *do* a large loan to pay off.
3 I was very lucky that I *went* / *got* a scholarship to *do* / *have* my master's degree.
4 I'm *going to* / *doing* university next year, but I'd like to *take* / *have* a year out first.
5 I'm *having* / *doing* a course in French at the moment and I'm really enjoying it.
6 Lots of young working people live with their parents. This means they *have* / *afford* a reasonably high disposable income.
7 I *went* / *got* a part-time job to help finance my university degree.
8 I need to *do* / *have* the right qualifications for the job.

**14** **Match the verbs in Column A with the words and phrases in Column B.**

| A | B |
|---|---|
| 1 earn | a gap year |
| 2 get into | straight to university |
| 3 afford | money |
| 4 go | a loan |
| 5 sit | tuition fees |
| 6 pay off | debt |
| 7 pay | an exam |

→ workbook page 92

**PRONUNCIATION**
Lexical and non-lexical fillers
Go to page 121.

# SPEAKING

**15** **Work in pairs. Choose one of the statements below and try to convince your partner of your opinion. Student A: you agree with the statement. Student B: you disagree with the statement.**

- Being an honest person is more important than being highly educated.
- If more people had access to higher education, fewer people would believe everything they heard and read on the news.

**16** **Now discuss your real opinion on the statement with your partner.**

## READING

1 **Look at the photo and the title of the article. Which of these summaries do you think is best for the article?**

a The guitar is the best musical instrument to learn.

b There are several benefits to learning to play music.

c Playing a musical instrument helps children with problems.

2 **Read the article quickly and check your ideas.**

3 10.05 **Read the article again and listen. Answer the questions.**

1 What effect does cortisol have on people?

2 What effect does dopamine have on people?

3 What can be improved by learning to play a musical instrument?

4 What evidence is given that not only young people can benefit from learning an instrument?

# Pick up your guitar and (learn to) PLAY

**George Howard looks at music and learning to play an instrument.**

It has been known for quite a long time that listening to music is good for you. Why do people get home from work and put music on, or listen to music while they're going to and from work? Stress reduction, that's why. People working in the area of music therapy have gathered lots of evidence to show that listening to the music you love brings down the amount of cortisol in your body – and it's cortisol that's responsible for most of the stress we feel.

There are other good reasons to listen to music. Listening to classical music (or any soothing music, in fact) for 30 minutes or so before going to bed could help you sleep significantly better. Runners listen to music too, and it seems that doing so improves their performance. And it helps to improve your mood as well – people who listen to music regularly have been shown to be calmer, more patient and more sociable.

But that's just *listening* to music. Great though it is, listening to music is nothing compared to actually *playing* it. If you already play an instrument, well, you probably know already how it can make you feel. But if you don't – well, think hard about learning to play an instrument, because the benefits are fantastic.

First of all, listening to and playing music have something in common, which is the release of dopamine into the brain. Dopamine is a chemical that gets released when we do things we like – eating good food, having fun with friends, getting to the next level in a game like Candy Crush. It's now understood that dopamine also plays an important role with regard to the brain. It stimulates things like motivation and memory, focus and attention, learning and creativity. It improves your mood. And learning to play music gives people a dopamine rush.

So much is involved in playing an instrument such as the guitar – there are motor functions (controlling your fingers), visual functions (reading the music), auditory functions (listening to the sounds you make and judging them), and of course there's the emotional response – hopefully pleasurable – to the music you're making. This is all excellent for the human brain, and helps to reduce the effects that ageing naturally brings. Learning to play an instrument improves things like memory (remembering a sequence of chords, for example) and abstract reasoning skills (understanding what the relationship is between this chord and another one), and this can lead to improved academic achievement, for both children and older people. It is believed to improve language skills, too. In one UK study, kids learning an instrument were found to be far more likely to score well on verbal skills.

Are there other benefits from learning to play an instrument? There probably are. Like anything else, the early stages of learning can be frustrating: it requires some dedication and commitment, and loads of patience. One music company reckons that anyone starting out needs to practise for a year before any clear improvements come. Does that sound terrible? Maybe. But there's a pay-off when you make the breakthrough and become more accomplished at playing. Satisfaction guaranteed – all that effort brings a reward.

So, if you don't already play, get learning. And it's never too late: I know someone who started to learn the guitar at the age of 60, and he loves everything about it – it's me.

## FUNCTIONS
### Reacting to news

4 🔊 10.06 **Listen to two people talking about the news. Number the headlines 1–4 in the order you hear them.**

☐ Cuts to education budget
☐ Tests for the very young
☐ Pupils get greener learning
☐ Government announces job losses in education

5 🔊 10.06 **Listen again and number the functions in the order you hear them. Then mark the expressions ✓ (= expressing agreement/satisfaction) or ✗ (= expressing disbelief/protest).**

☐ That's outrageous! ______
☐ I'm glad to hear it. ______
1 Finally, someone's taking things seriously. ✓
☐ They've got to be joking. ______
☐ They can't do that. ______
☐ What will they think of next? ______
☐ That's the best news I've heard in ages. ______
☐ It's about time they did something about it. ______

6 ROLE PLAY **Work in pairs. Student A: Go to page 127. Student B: Go to page 128.**

## GRAMMAR

Grammar video ▶26

### Passive report structures

7 **Read the sentences from the article. Then complete the rule.**

1 **It has been known** for quite a long time that listening to music is good for you.
2 Kids learning an instrument **were found** to be far more likely to score well on verbal skills.

**RULE:** We use passive report structures in more [1]*formal / informal* contexts to report information when the agent is [2]*not important / very important*. We use passive report structures with verbs such as *say, think, believe, know, find* and *consider*.

Compare these two pairs of sentences.

A *They say that music has a positive influence on humans.*
B *Music is said to have a positive influence on humans.*
A *In a UK study, they thought that learning an instrument improved children's verbal skills.*
B *In a UK study, learning an instrument was thought to have improved children's verbal skills.*

In the passive reporting structure (B), the underlined words are the [3]*subject / object* of the sentence. The word order is:

Present: subject + *be* + [4]______________ + *to* infinitive

Past: subject + *be* + past participle + *to* + [5]______________ + past participle

8 **Rewrite the following sentences, using passive report structures.**

0 Experts think a lot more research is needed into the effects of music on humans.
*A lot more research into the effects of music on humans is thought to be needed.*
1 Scientists believe music has beneficial effects on a number of illnesses.
2 Experts have found that some animals react strongly to certain types of music.
3 They say lots of experiments have been done.
4 Scientists think that the experiments were an important breakthrough.

### Hedging

9 **Which option in each sentence expresses uncertainty? Choose the correct words to complete the examples of hedging from the article on page 96. Then complete the rule.**

1 It *is believed to improve / improves* language skills, too.
2 Runners listen to music too, and *it seems that doing so / doing so* improves their performance.
3 Listening to classical music for 30 minutes or so before going to bed *could help you / helps you* sleep significantly better.
4 Are there other benefits from learning to play an instrument? *There are. / There probably are.*

**RULE:** Hedging refers to cautious or vague language used when a writer [1]*doesn't want / wants* to state something as fact.
We use verb phrases such as: *seems to/that, is thought/believed to be, could be, might be, is said/thought to have been* and adverbs such as: *probably, perhaps* and *possibly*.

10 **Replace the underlined verb in each sentence with the hedging expressions in the list.**

are thought to have been | could help
~~is believed to make~~ | is said to have been
seems to improve

0 Listening to music makes you learn better.
*Listening to music is believed to make you learn better.*
1 Playing music in hospital waiting rooms improves patients' moods.
2 My uncle was the best pianist in the country.
3 Early claims about playing music to very young children were exaggerated.
4 Music helps people become better human beings and overcome emotional difficulties.

→ workbook page 91

# Literature

1 **Think of the many different ways that we can communicate with other people. Which are the most common and what might be the advantages of some over others? Why are some of the ways we can communicate not so popular now?**

2 10.07 **Read and listen to the extract. Think about these questions:**

1 Do you think Jerusha enjoys writing her letters to Daddy-Long-Legs? Why/Why not?

2 What do we learn about the ways in which Jerusha is different from the other girls at the college?

## Daddy-Long-Legs

*by Jean Webster*

***Daddy-Long-Legs*** **is an American novel published in 1912. Jerusha Abbot is a freshman at college (someone in their first year.) She grew up in a home for children who have no parents, but someone offered to pay for her education. His identity is a secret, but Jerusha has to write him a letter every month, so she invents a name for him – Daddy-Long-Legs.**

October 1st.

Dear Daddy-Long-Legs,

I love college and I love you for sending me—I'm very, very happy, and so excited every moment of the time that I can scarcely sleep. You can't imagine how different it is from the John Grier Home. I never dreamed there was such a place in the world. I'm feeling sorry for everybody who isn't a girl and who can't come here; I am sure the college you attended when you were a boy couldn't have been so nice.

My room is up in a tower that used to be the infirmary. There are three other girls on the same floor of the tower—a senior who wears glasses and is always asking us please to be a little more quiet, and two freshmen named Sallie McBride and Julia Rutledge Pendleton. Sallie has red hair and a turn-up nose and is quite friendly; Julia comes from one of the first families in New York and hasn't noticed me yet. They room together and the senior and I have singles. Usually freshmen can't get singles as there aren't many of them, but I got one without even asking. I suppose the registrar didn't think it would be right to ask a properly brought-up girl to room with a foundling. You see there are advantages!

My room is on the northwest corner with two windows and a view. After you've lived in a dormitory for eighteen years with twenty room-mates, it is restful to be alone. This is the first chance I've ever had to get to know Jerusha Abbott. I think I'm going to like her.

Do you think you are?

Tuesday.

They are organizing the freshman basket-ball team and there's just a chance that I shall make it. I'm little of course, but terribly quick and wiry and tough. While the others are hopping about in the air, I can get under their feet and grab the ball. It's loads of fun practising—out in the athletic field in the afternoon with the trees all red and yellow and the air full of the smell of burning leaves, and everybody laughing and shouting. These are the happiest girls I ever saw—and I am the happiest of all!

I meant to write a long letter and tell you all the things I'm learning but the bell has just rung, and in ten minutes I'm due at the athletic field in gymnasium clothes. Don't you hope I'll make the team?

Yours always,

Jerusha Abbott.

October 10th.

Dear Daddy-Long-Legs,

Did you ever hear of Michael Angelo? He was a famous artist who lived in Italy in the Middle Ages. Everybody in English Literature class seemed to know about him and the whole class laughed because I thought he was an angel. He sounds like an angel, doesn't he? The trouble with college is that you are expected to know such a lot of things you've never learned. It's very embarrassing at times. But now, when the girls talk about things that I never heard of, I just keep still and look them up in the encyclopedia.

I made an awful mistake the first day. Somebody mentioned Maurice Maeterlinck*, and I asked if she was a freshman. That joke has gone all over college. But anyway, I'm just as bright in class as any of the others—and brighter than some of them!

[…]

(Dinner bell, goodbye)

Jerusha Abbot.

* A well-known Belgian writer at the time

3 **Read the extract again. Answer the questions.**

1 What impression do you get of Jerusha's personality? Which words or phrases give you this impression?

2 Can you find examples in the letters of words/expressions that are repeated? Why do you think Jerusha repeats these words?

3 What does the text suggest about how Jerusha's social background influences her life at the college?

4 Do you think Jerusha is going to be a popular person with the other students? Why/why not?

4 VOCABULARY **Match the highlighted words in the extract with the definitions.**

1 a large room containing many beds, for example in a boarding school
2 a young child who is left by its parents and then found and cared for by someone else
3 a room in a school, prison, etc. where people go when they are sick
4 someone whose job is to keep official records, of students at a university, for example.
5 only just/very limited
6 thin but strong, and often able to bend easily

5 SPEAKING **Work with a partner and discuss the questions.**

1 What kinds of challenges are there when you start at a new school or college?
2 Why do you think people become friends? What is it that makes some people want to be friends with others?
3 Nowadays not many people write letters. How would you feel if you received letters from a friend instead of texts or emails?
4 Imagine you had the opportunity to help someone go to college. How would you choose that person?

## WRITING
### An essay

6 INPUT **Read the essay and tick (✓) the correct option.**

The writer ...
- ☐ slightly agrees with the assertion.
- ☐ strongly agrees with the assertion.
- ☐ is undecided.
- ☐ slightly disagrees with the assertion.
- ☐ strongly disagrees with the assertion.

7 ANALYSE **Find expressions in the essay which have the same meanings as the underlined ones below.**

1 ... the most important of which is ...
2 For example, it is expensive.
3 Although it's true that education is expensive, it is also a fundamental right ...
4 With reference to the argument about salaries ...
5 As I see it, there are too many people going to university ...
6 Apart from my personal interest ...

8 **Read the essay again. Give a short summary of what the writer does in paragraph ...**

A ______________________
B ______________________
C ______________________
D ______________________

9 PLAN **Read the essay title and note down your ideas for and against the statement.**

No one should go to university before they are 25.

10 PRODUCE **Write your essay in 200–250 words giving both sides of the argument before presenting your position.**

**Further education should be provided free to all who want it**

A When my parents went to university in the early 1990s, neither of them had to pay their tuition fees. Sadly this is no longer the case. In a few years, I will probably choose to do a degree knowing that I am likely to leave with debts of around £30,000. It has made deciding to go to university a huge responsibility.

B My own personal interest aside, I can think of a number of reasons why further education should be free for all and none more persuasive than it means that it really is open to all, irrespective of family wealth. Obviously, the government will argue that there are schemes to help those from poorer backgrounds with funding, but clearly those from rich families will never have to take financial factors into consideration when deciding whether to go to university or not.

C Of course there are arguments that refute the assertion that further education should be free for all, namely, that it is costly and that those who go on to graduate are likely to earn higher salaries than those who start working at 18. Each of these will be discussed in turn. While education may be expensive, it is also a fundamental right for citizens of any society. It is an important investment in our country's future and without it our ability to compete on the world stage would diminish. As for the idea that having a degree enhances your earning prospects, this is unfortunately no longer always the case. A rise in the number of people going to university means that competition for high paid jobs is fierce and many graduates are struggling to secure the employment they believed having a degree would assure them.

D To my mind, too many people are currently going to university, and as a result the value of further education is falling. University entrance should be made harder for all and those who are successful should not have to pay tuition fees. But of course, to make things fair, the government should also be looking at how to provide those who leave school at 18 with opportunities to get ahead in the working world.

# C1 Advanced

## LISTENING

### Part 4: Multiple matching

→ workbook page 97

**1** 10.08 **You will hear five short extracts in which people are talking about an evening class that they attended.**

Task One

**For questions 1–5, choose from the list (A–H) each speaker's main reason for choosing the class.**

**A** to get better at something I'd always enjoyed
**B** to meet new people
**C** a love of languages
**D** to learn the basics of how to make things out of wood
**E** to fulfil a long-standing desire to learn something
**F** to improve an existing skill
**G** a desire to travel
**H** to be able to better enjoy something else

1 Speaker 1 ☐
2 Speaker 2 ☐
3 Speaker 3 ☐
4 Speaker 4 ☐
5 Speaker 5 ☐

Task Two

**For questions 6–10, choose from the list (A–H) what each speaker disliked about the class they chose.**

**A** There was insufficient time to practise.
**B** There were too many students in the class.
**C** Some students asked really difficult questions.
**D** The teacher's language level was poor.
**E** The teacher had a tendency to talk too much.
**F** The teacher's methods were poor.
**G** It revealed my lack of ability in the subject.
**H** Some students were not quick learners.

1 Speaker 1 ☐
2 Speaker 2 ☐
3 Speaker 3 ☐
4 Speaker 4 ☐
5 Speaker 5 ☐

## WRITING

### Part 1: An essay

**2** **You have been to a discussion on which levels of education should receive the most government funding. You have made the notes below:**

**Which levels of education should receive the most government funding?**

- primary education (4–10 years)
- secondary education (11–17 years)
- college/university education (18 years and older)

Some opinions expressed in the discussion:

'Primary schools are the basis for everything that comes later.'

'Secondary schools are important for training young people to get useful jobs in the real world.'

'Universities shouldn't get much money because they're for the privileged few.'

**Write an essay of around 220–260 words discussing two of the levels in your notes. You should explain which level you think is more important for the government to give money to, giving reasons in support of your answer.**

**You may, if you wish, make use of the opinions expressed in the discussion, but you should use your own words as far as possible.**

# TEST YOURSELF UNITS 9 & 10

## VOCABULARY

**1 Complete the sentences with the words in the list. There are four extra words.**

evidence | evident | fare | fees | gap | judge | jury
made | sailed | sit | undergraduate | unfair | witness | wrote

1 He did an ________________ degree at the University of Liverpool.
2 I wanted to go to university, but I couldn't afford the tuition ________________ .
3 The ________________ sentenced the thief to six months in prison. We were surprised by the harshness of her sentence.
4 The ________________ took two days to find him guilty.
5 It is ________________ that obesity is a growing problem in modern-day society.
6 He ________________ his dissertation on nineteenth-century American poetry.
7 I really wish I'd taken a ________________ year before I went to university.
8 It's ________________ to keep a bird in a cage, isn't it?
9 No witnesses were found to give ________________ , so the police had to drop the case.
10 He ________________ through his exams. They were no problem at all.

/10

## GRAMMAR

**2 Complete the sentences with the words/phrases in the list. There are two extra words/phrases.**

have left | have never | leave | meeting
never have | on passing | rarely | rarely does

1 The criminals are thought to ________________ the country.
2 ________________ I heard such a terrible story.
3 She congratulated me ________________ the exam.
4 He recommended ________________ a few hours earlier so that we'd have plenty of time to get to the airport.
5 I ________________ actually met him.
6 ________________ he give an interview.

**3 Find and correct the mistake in each sentence.**

1 Nevertheless I really like football, my brother prefers rugby.
2 The thieves are thought to steal more than $2 million.
3 No sooner had I got home the phone rang.
4 He's considered to being the finest guitarist ever.
5 He insisted about paying for dinner.
6 Because of it raining, we stayed in all day.

/12

## FUNCTIONAL LANGUAGE

**4 Choose the correct options.**

1 A It took *something* / *anything* like 500 men more than ten years to build it.
B And *around* / *area* how much did it cost to build?
2 A We've got half an hour give or *get* / *take* to get to the station.
B That's fine. I reckon it'll take us *around* / *least* ten minutes to walk there.
3 A Finally, someone is *taking* / *doing* things seriously.
B Yes, it's the best *news* / *report* I've heard in ages.
4 A A flying car?! What will they think of *soon* / *next*?
B Really? You've got to be *serious* / *joking*.

/8

MY SCORE /30

22–30 | 10–21 | 0–9

# 11 THE MODERN WORLD

**OBJECTIVES**

**FUNCTIONS**
telling someone to keep calm

**GRAMMAR:**
more on the passive; causative *have* (review); modal passives (review)

**VOCABULARY:**
(not) getting angry; *-isms*

## Get THINKING

**Watch the video and think: what makes life today stressful?**

A

B

## READING

1 SPEAKING **Work in pairs. Look at the cartoons on this page. How do the people feel in each one and why do you think they feel this way? Then make a list of things that make you angry about the internet and social media.**

2 **Read the article quickly. What's the author's final solution for dealing with anger on the internet?**

3 11.01 **Read the article again. Complete it with these missing extracts. Then listen and check.**

a on social media
b get criticised
c or ideally altogether
d and not always good for us
e and forget it
f being a doctor
g for a start
h the level of
i one thing is for sure
j don't be afraid to

4 SPEAKING **Work in pairs and discuss the following questions.**

1 What do you do when you come across angry people online?
2 What do you think can be done to make the internet a friendlier place?

## Train to THINK

### Do as I say, not as I do

*When someone says or does something which contradicts what they say they believe, we often find this hypocritical and we can dismiss their advice all too easily as a result. It's important to consider people's advice as separate from their actions. For example, a father who tells his children not to use their phones at the dinner table, even though he may occasionally check his, is still passing on very valid advice.*

5 SPEAKING **Work in pairs. Consider these situations. Why is the advice given still valid?**

1 My mother says I shouldn't spend too much time on social media, even though she often uses it.
2 My dad says I shouldn't get angry with my computer, even though I often see him shouting at his.

6 SPEAKING **Think of two situations in which you've been given hypocritical advice, but then on reflection, that advice has proven to be valid. These could be real or imaginary. Tell your partner about them.**

# INTERNET RAGE

Whether it's moaning about the government and injustices in society, losing your temper with cyclists or simply getting worked up about what someone said or didn't say about your favourite soap actor, [1]______ : there's plenty of anger on the internet. Just take a look through the comments after any online news story – for every positive reaction, there are many more negative comments. Let me give you a quick example. A doctor friend of mine was featured in the online version of her local newspaper. Her twin daughters had got sent to different high schools because there weren't enough places at their local one. For every comment offering sympathy for their situation, there were at least three saying that she should stop crying about the situation and that [2]______ , she was rich enough to send her children to a private school – and these were just the polite ones. It seemed the general public – complete strangers to my friend – had very little time or compassion for her.

So why exactly is there so much anger on the web? Well, [3]______ , anger is a strong emotion – it gets attention. Studies have shown that an angry post is more likely to get shared than a happy one, for example. The message seems to be that if you want to get noticed, get angry.

And then, of course, the internet is a great place for letting off steam, and because we can do it anonymously, we are often tempted to exaggerate [4]______ our feelings more than we might do if we knew the comments could be traced back to us.

Not all such displays of anger are done hiding behind an alias. There are plenty of examples of famous people having a go at other celebrities [5]______ , and the media is more than happy to publicise these feuds further – after all, they help sell newspapers.

Is all this anger good for us? Of course it isn't. For many of us, the internet is somewhere we go to get informed or meet like-minded people; we aren't looking for hatred and prejudice. Social media is a way of keeping in touch with family and friends and not a place to [6]______ or get our heads bitten off by those who might not agree with us.

So what should we do? Well, it starts with ourselves. Before you post anything, ask yourself if there's any chance it might upset someone somewhere; if there is, then ask yourself, 'Do I really need to write this?' Following the golden rule of 'If you haven't got anything nice to say, then don't say anything at all.' is a pretty good place to start. And if something has really annoyed you, bite your tongue [7]______ .

That takes care of the 'anger' in your online content, but what about that from others? Well, the simplest thing to do perhaps is to develop a thick skin and stay calm. That, though, may be easier said than done [8]______ – if something upsets you, it isn't always healthy to pretend it doesn't.

Perhaps the most effective way of avoiding the stress that internet anger can cause is to try to avoid it as much as possible [9]______ . Do you really need to read the comments section after news stories when you know that they'll only make your blood boil? Such behaviour can become addictive and you need to find a way of breaking that addiction. Avoid the sites that attract the most negative comments.
Your life won't suffer.

When it comes to social media, be careful who you choose to include on your friends list and [10]______ block those who write unkind comments. You're better off without them in your life anyway.

And if none of this works then there is one easy answer: switch it off.

# GRAMMAR
## More on the passive

**1 Complete each sentence from the article on page 103 with one word. Then complete the rule by choosing the correct options.**

1 An angry post is more likely to __________ shared than a happy one.
2 Her twin daughters had __________ sent to different high schools.
3 The internet is somewhere we go to __________ informed.

**RULE:**
- We can use the verb *get* instead of *be* in passive constructions. This is more common in [1]*formal / informal* English.
- We only use *get* with [2]*state / dynamic* verbs. We don't say *he got believed to be guilty* or *he got loved by his parents.*
- We often use *get* when there is a clear good or bad effect or when something happens unexpectedly or accidentally, for example *he got mugged* or *several things got lost when we moved house.*
- Sometimes *get* is used rather than *be* to make it clear that [3]*a state / an action* is involved, for example *the window was broken* could be a state or an action, but *the window got broken* has to be an action.

**2 Use the prompts to write sentences, using the correct past form of the passive with *get*.**

0 While / we / be / on holiday / we / rob / .
*While we were on holiday, we got robbed.*
1 While / she / cross / the road / she / hit / by a car / .
2 The man / take / hospital / by ambulance / .
3 My bike / damage / when / I / I / hit / by a car / .
4 I / shout at / for cycling / on the pavement / .
5 My jeans / ruin / when / I / I / fall off / my bike / .
6 We / not hurt / in the accident / .

→ workbook page 100

# VOCABULARY
## (not) getting angry

**3 Read the three passages. Which expressions in bold are about getting angry? Which are about *not* getting angry? Which involve someone *saying* something?**

A Yesterday I was late for work and my boss really **had a go at** me. She **shouted at** me really loudly. I wasn't surprised – she's someone who **loses her temper** quite easily and she **gets** really **worked up** if things don't go her way.

B My mum is great at **keeping her cool**. She always **stays calm**, even when someone else is **letting off steam**. If someone criticises her, she manages to **keep the peace** and not argue back.

C Alex is having a bad day. I asked him to lend me something and he just **bit my head off**, saying I always borrow things and never give them back! I didn't say anything – I just **bit my tongue**.

**4 Complete each space with one word from the expressions in Exercise 3 in the correct form.**

0 If I say something she doesn't like, she *bites* my head *off* .
1 When he shouted at me, I __________ my __________ and smiled at him!
2 My aunt's so calm – she never __________ her __________ .
3 He's really good at __________ __________ peace when an argument starts.
4 It's fine – don't __________ __________ up over it!
5 When you're angry, it's good to bite your __________ and say nothing.
6 When I'm stressed, I run – it's how I __________ __________ steam.

**5 SPEAKING Work in pairs. Answer the questions.**

1 Who do you know who always manages to keep the peace when tensions rise in your family?
2 When was the last time you lost your temper and shouted at someone? What was it that made you cross?
3 What do you think is the best way to let off steam, apart from shouting at the person who's upset you?
4 Who was the last person to have a go at you about something? How did you react? How did you feel?

→ workbook page 102

# FUNCTIONS
## Telling someone to keep calm

**6 11.02 Listen to two conversations. Why is the boy angry in situation one? Why is the girl angry in situation two?**

**7 11.02 Match 1–5 with a–e to make expressions for helping someone who's stressed. Then listen again and check.**

| | |
|---|---|
| 1 Chill | a easy. |
| 2 Take it | b getting worked up about. |
| 3 Don't let it | c get under your skin. |
| 4 He's not worth | d out. |
| 5 Don't let him | e get to you. |

**8 ROLE PLAY Work in pairs. Student A: Go to page 127. Student B: Go to page 128.**

## LISTENING
### Stresses and strains of modern life

9 **SPEAKING Work in pairs. What's happening in each of the pictures? How are the people feeling? Discuss with your partner.**

10 **11.03 Listen to the radio phone-in. Number the pictures in the order you hear about them.**

11 **11.03 Listen again. Mark the statements T (true) or F (false).**

1 Matt, the radio host, does a lot of online shopping. ☐
2 He can't choose the time of the deliveries. ☐
3 Daisy finds it difficult to remember any of her passwords. ☐
4 Matt only has one password. ☐
5 Matt doesn't understand what 'flex' means. ☐
6 Ryan's friend was disappointed with his exam results. ☐
7 Andy usually takes the train to work. ☐
8 Andy complains about the uncomfortable train seats. ☐

## SPEAKING

12 **The radio host talks about modern problems, i.e. things that your grandparents, for example, would not have had to face. Make a list of these.**

13 **Work in pairs. Compare lists and agree together on a ranking from most to least serious problems.**

**PRONUNCIATION**
Intonation: mean what you say Go to page 121.

## GRAMMAR Grammar video ▶28
### Causative *have* (review)

14 **Read the three sentences from the listening. Which sentence talks about something the person wanted another person to do? Then complete the rule.**

1 I try to have it delivered when I know I'll be in.
2 A friend of mine had her social media account hacked.
3 My car got broken into the other day.

**RULE:** This structure is formed with the verb [1]__________ + object + the [2]__________ of the main verb.
We can use it:
- when we ask or pay someone to do something for us (example sentence 1).
- when someone (often not known) does something unpleasant to us (example sentences 2 and 3).

We can also use *get* instead of *have*. This is more informal but doesn't change the meaning: *We got the car fixed last week.*

15 **Complete each sentence using causative *have*.**

0 Last week, I *had my phone stolen* on the bus. (phone, steal)
1 This afternoon at 3.00, I'll be in town __________. (hair, cut)
2 They didn't like the colour of the house, so they __________. (it, repaint)
3 Next week, I __________. I can take the bus until then. (motorbike, fix)
4 __________ you ever __________? (something valuable, steal)
5 Tomorrow I'm going to the clinic __________. (blood pressure, check)

16 **Which sentences in Exercise 15 talk about unwanted events?**

17 **SPEAKING Work in pairs. Make a list of as many examples as you can of:**
- something you/someone in your family often have done (intentionally).
- something you/someone in your family once had done to you.

18 **SPEAKING Work in groups. Compare lists and ask each other follow-up questions.**

→ workbook page 100

## READING

1 SPEAKING **Work in pairs. Look at the photos. How do you think these things relate to veganism? What else do you know about veganism?**

2 **Read the article quickly and check your ideas.**

3 11.05 **Read the article again and listen. Answer the questions.**

1 What food can a vegan not eat?
2 What evidence is there that veganism is becoming more popular?
3 What three reasons are given to suggest why people become vegans?
4 What health benefits have been linked to veganism?
5 What health issues might veganism cause?
6 Why is it easier to be a vegan these days?
7 What other things, apart from not consuming animal products, do true vegans do?

4 SPEAKING **Do you think you could be a vegan? Discuss in pairs and give your reasons.**

# EXPLAINING THE MODERN WORLD: VEGANISM

### What is veganism?

Veganism is the avoidance of eating any animal or animal products, such as eggs, honey and cheese. Vegans eat only plant-based foods. They don't wear any clothing that has come from animals and they also refuse to use any product that might have been tested on animals.

### Is it new?

Not at all. The Vegan Society was formed back in 1944. In recent years, however, veganism has grown more and more popular. According to one poll in the US, there has been a 600% rise in the number of vegans over the last three years, taking the percentage of US citizens who claim to be vegan from 1% to 6%. But it isn't just in the US; there has been a worldwide increase in the number of vegans. In the UK, for example, 7% of the population identifies as being vegan. The country with the highest percentage of vegans is India with a total of 27% of the population.

### So why is it so popular?

To answer this, we need to look at the reasons why people are choosing to become vegan. For many people, animal welfare is their biggest concern. They believe that animals shouldn't be killed for our consumption. It's as simple as that. There are also many people who are worried about the impact that raising farm animals has upon the environment. It is well known that producing red meat, in particular, is one of the biggest causes of global warming. There are also many people who believe that a vegan diet is healthier than one that includes meat, and so they are making the change for health reasons. Red meat has long been connected with health issues such as diabetes and heart disease, while chicken can cause salmonella and fish mercury poisoning.

### Is a vegan diet really healthier?

That will probably depend on who you ask. A lot of research has been done to look into this exact question and the general opinion is that a vegan diet can certainly help reduce the risk of heart disease and some forms of cancer. It's also believed to bring down stress levels and it has proven to be an effective way of losing weight for many people who have tried it. However, there is a downside, too: a true vegan diet is often lacking in important nutrients such as zinc, calcium, iron and, perhaps most importantly, vitamin B12 (commonly found in eggs, meat and fish), which supports healthy cell production. These minerals can easily be taken as supplements, though, as many dieticians would recommend.

### Avoiding meat – that sounds like a lot of hard work?

It is much easier to be a vegan these days and ready-made vegan food can be found in most large supermarkets. Rather oddly, this food is often versions of the meat cuts they are substituting, such as vegan bacon, vegan chicken fillets and even a vegan burger that 'bleeds' when you bite into it (the blood effect comes from beetroot juice). You can also find vegan restaurants in most reasonably sized towns and many other restaurants will also include vegan options on their menus.

### Is there anything else I should know?

To be a true vegan, you should also boycott any form of entertainment that exploits animals. This includes trips to zoos, aquariums or circuses that use animals as part of their show (although this has already been banned in many countries). You should also not get involved in any sport that uses animals, such as horse-racing or dog-racing.

### But can I have a pet?

Of course! So long as you are committed to looking after its welfare. In fact, the national vegan society encourages its members to visit and support animal sanctuaries that provide a safe home for animals that have been rescued.

## GRAMMAR
### Modal passives (review)

5 Read the sentences from the article. Complete them with the words in the list.

found | killed | taken | tested

1 They refuse to use any product that might have been ______________ on animals.
2 These minerals can easily be ______________ as supplements.
3 Ready-made vegan food can be ______________ in most large supermarkets.
4 They believe that animals shouldn't be ______________ for our consumption.

6 Answer the questions about the sentences in Exercise 5 and then complete the rule with *have been* and *be*.

1 Which sentence refers to a past situation?
2 Which sentences refer to the present?
3 Who performed each of the actions?

**RULE:** We can use modals in the passive voice by using these structures:
Present: modal verb + [1]______________ (infinitive) + past participle
Past: modal verb + [2]______________ + past participle

7 Write sentences using the passive. Do not include the agent.

0 Someone must know the answer.
*The answer must be known.*
1 People can find more information on our website.
2 Someone might think up new ideas.
3 People should re-use these things.
4 Someone could have hurt you.
5 Someone must have stolen your bike.
6 Someone may have put it here on purpose.

→ workbook page 101

## VOCABULARY
### -isms

8 SPEAKING Work in pairs. Match the *-isms* with their definitions. Then write the adjective form of each *-ism*.

1 capitalism ☐ *capitalist*
2 pessimism ☐ ______________
3 optimism ☐ ______________
4 socialism ☐ ______________
5 ageism ☐ ______________

a the tendency to see the worst in situations
b the belief that people should work together for the good of society
c prejudice against older people
d the belief that privately owned companies should control the economy
e the tendency to see the best in situations

9 Use the adjectives from Exercise 8 to describe these people.

1 'You can't have the job because you're too old.'
2 'I'm sure my train would arrive on time if it was owned by a company rather than the government!'
3 'If we all work together, we'll make the world a better place for everyone.'
4 'Why bother applying for the job? I'll never get it. I never get anything I want.'
5 'I have a really good feeling about this game. I'm pretty sure we're going to win.'

10 SPEAKING Work in pairs. Discuss the questions.

1 Are you more of an optimist or a pessimist? Why do you think that?
2 What examples of ageism have you seen?
3 What do you think are the problems of capitalism and socialism?

→ workbook page 102

## TH!NK *values*
### Modern life

11 Read the questions and tick (✓) your answer: a or b.

1 When something I own breaks, I …
a ☐ throw it away and get another one.
b ☐ get it fixed.
2 When a new model of my phone comes out, I …
a ☐ buy it immediately.
b ☐ wait until I need a new one.
3 I think that the internet …
a ☐ makes us lazy.
b ☐ is the most useful resource ever.

12 SPEAKING Work in pairs. Compare your answers with a partner.

13 SPEAKING How do you think your grandparents would answer the questions in Exercise 11? Would they answer them in the same way as you or differently?

THINK

Living in the past

# Culture

# BACK IN TIME

1 SPEAKING Work in pairs. Why are people interested in the past? Write down as many reasons as possible.

2 How might people explore a period of history they are interested in?

3 11.06 Read and listen to the article. Which of your ideas are mentioned?

**Whether it is enjoying hearing our grandparents talk about how life was when they were young or finding History the most fascinating subject at school, most of us have at least a little interest in the past. But how far would you take this? Would you be willing to give up all the comforts of modern life to live in the world that your ancestors would have recognised? Meet three people who have made that very decision.**

When Gabriel Chrisman goes out for a bike ride around his hometown of Port Townsend in Washington, he's always sure to turn a few heads – after all, it isn't every day you get to see someone riding high up on a penny-farthing. With his wife Sarah riding alongside him, both of them dressed in clothes their great-grandparents might have worn, the pair are affectionately known locally as 'the Victorian couple'. As a young girl, writer Sarah dreamed of living in the late 1800s, and when she met like-minded Gabriel, they set about making this dream a reality. Their house is decorated and furnished with items from the era, they make and wear their own clothes based on those from Victorian times, and they even cook and eat the same food their distant relatives would have eaten. They do have electricity for the lighting, which is something that came in at the end of the 19th century, but they usually only use this when they have visitors; normally, they will just light their oil lamps when it gets dark. All appliances in the house are manual and they don't miss their modern gadgets at all. The couple was drawn to the Victorian age because it was a time of immense change and optimism. Great inventions were constantly being unveiled to the public and people really believed they could make the world a better place. It is a spirit that the couple would like to see more of in the modern world. And do they mind when people stop and stare at them in the street? Not at all! They just hope they can be an inspiration to anyone who has a dream they'd like to make come true, even if it might make them stand out a little from the crowd.

Across the Atlantic Ocean, in Cambridgeshire in the UK, 35-year-old Brit, Ben Sansum, shares this passion for living in the past, albeit in a somewhat more modern era than that of the Chrismans. Ben earns his living working as cabin crew for an international airline, but when his shift is over, he swaps his temporary homes in the hotels of New York and Sydney for a life in 1946 rural Britain. Ben had been interested in the post-war years since he was at school, when his fascination with the cars, fashion and music of the times began. Ben always dreamed of living in the past as a way of making sure life in the olden days is not forgotten.

When he left home, started working and bought his own house, he set about transforming it into a living monument to the 1940s. Much of his furniture is even older, with some pieces (including his outdoor mangle and the range in his kitchen) dating back to the Victorian times. He does, though, have a modern fridge, which he keeps hidden behind a cloth curtain. For Ben, keeping his food fresh is the one sacrifice he will make!

Ben is no great fan of the modern world and feels that everything these days moves far too fast. He believes that our addiction to technology, such as mobile phones, has made us become detached from real life. He hopes that by surrounding himself with reminders of when life was simpler, he'll be able to reconnect with the more important things in life. The view from his bedroom is of the local church and graveyard – a view that hasn't changed for over a hundred years. It's just a shame that when he looks down at the road below, he is brought swiftly back to reality with his neighbours in their modern cars all fighting for somewhere to park.

4 **According to the article:**

1 why might people stop and stare at the Chrismans?
2 how do the Chrismans light their house?
3 what attracts them most to the Victorian era?
4 why is Ben keen to live in the 1940s?
5 what does he dislike about modern life?
6 what can he see from his bedroom window and what spoils the view?

5 VOCABULARY **Match the highlighted words in the article to the definitions.**

1 objects in a house such as a washing machine, TV, dishwasher, etc.
2 the people who ensure the passengers on a plane are safe and looked after
3 a building specially built to remember someone or some event from the past
4 your relatives from the past
5 a place where people are buried
6 to show something for the first time
7 to think the same way as someone else
8 the period of time when you work

6 SPEAKING **Work in pairs. Discuss the questions.**

1 If you could meet Gabriel, Sarah or Ben, what would you like to ask them?
2 What time in history interests you most and why?
3 Would you like to live in that time? Explain your answer.

## WRITING
### A blog post

7 INPUT **Sam has a blog and in her latest post, she imagines life in 1966, when her grandparents were teenagers. Read the blog post and look at the photos. Tick (✓) the things she mentions.**

8 **What other differences do you think Sam might notice in 1966?**

9 ANALYSE **Which of the underlined adverbs means:**

1 intently, without moving?
2 in a way that requires a lot of effort?
3 without really wanting to?
4 in an unpleasantly loud way?
5 quickly and willingly?
6 in an extremely worried way?

10 **None of the underlined adverbs is completely necessary in the blog. Why do you think Sam uses them?**

11 PLAN **You're going to write a blog post, imagining that you're in the year 2036. Make notes on the following:**

1 What different technology exists?
2 What everyday things have been replaced by technology?
3 How do you feel about all of this technology? Is there any technology from your normal life that you miss?

12 PRODUCE **Use your ideas to write a blog post (200–250 words). Use adverbs to make it as interesting and involving as possible.**

## Sam's blog: imagine 1966!!

Here I am. It's 1966, and I'm spending a day hanging out here just to see what things are like and how different everyday life is.

First of all, I wake up to a bell ringing shrilly – it's an alarm clock, not my smartphone. After my shower, I head off for breakfast. I'd like to find out what's been happening in the world, and hunt around a bit desperately for my tablet. No, I have to get my news from a newspaper.

I need to get in touch with my friend Alex, so I pick up the phone and dial his number – and I mean – I have to laboriously dial his number, using my index finger in those holes on the front of the telephone. Since it's the weekend, Alex suggests we go into Manchester for the day and I readily agree. He says to meet him at the corner of Argyle Street. OK, so all I have to do is buy a train ticket online – whoops, no, I'll have to do that at the station. I'd use my credit card, but I haven't got one and neither have my parents. Anyway, Dad reluctantly gives me five pounds and off I go to the station.

On the train I'm thinking: 'Argyle Street? Where's that?' I'd normally check it on the GPS on my phone, but naturally I can't, so when I get off the train I ask someone where it is. It's quite nice, actually – talking to someone rather than just staring fixedly at my screen.

more – click for page 2

A ☐

B ☐

C ☐

# 12 CELEBRATING HEROES

**OBJECTIVES**

**FUNCTIONS:** expressing anticipation

**GRAMMAR:** future perfect; future continuous (review); future in the past

**VOCABULARY:** awards; success and failure

**Get THINKING**

**Watch the video and think: what makes someone a hero?**

A

B

C

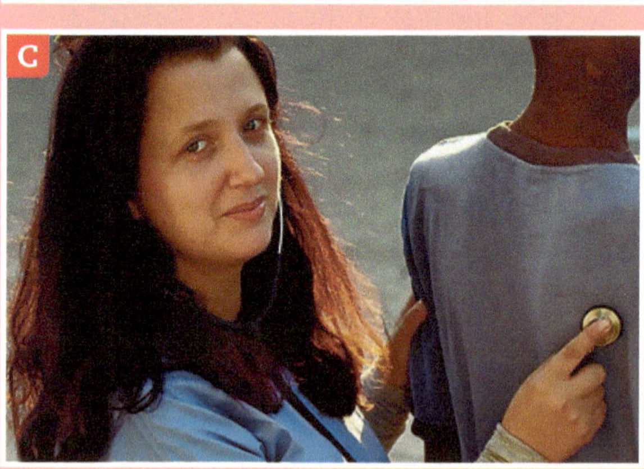

## READING

1 **Look at the photos. What are the people doing? Why might they be considered heroes?**

2 SPEAKING **Work in pairs. Make a list of five people who you think are heroes from people you know locally or at school, people from history, the news, music or sport.**

3 SPEAKING **Work with another pair and compare lists. Categorise your heroes according to their achievements, for example *courage, inspiration, fighting disease, building communities, helping the environment, saving lives*. Some may go in more than one category.**

4 12.01 **Read and listen to the online posts. Which of your categories would each of the three people fall into?**

5 **Match the title to each post (A–C).**

1 Doing good while working out
2 Saving lives in difficult circumstances
3 Playing for a better future

6 **Who or what does *they* refer to in each sentence (1–6)?**

1 Until recently, *they* got this horrible disease. [*Text A*]
2 Through this sport, *they* found hope for a new start. [*Text A*]
3 *They* get fit by helping people in the community. [*Text B*]
4 When you have a conversation with them, *they* teach you a lot. [*Text B*].
5 *They* think she's crazy to give up her research position to go to Haiti. [*Text C*].
6 *They* survived tuberculosis and are now helping others. [*Text C*].

7 SPEAKING **Work in pairs. Discuss the questions. Which of the three heroes in the online posts do you admire most? Why? If you could do something heroic to make a difference to other people's lives, what would it be?**

# WANTED: real-life heroes

**We're looking for ordinary people who have made a difference – people who aren't in the public eye, but who have changed the world around them for the better. Who do you think deserves to win our real-life hero trophy and £10,000 prize? Read about the first three nominees, and then let us know your views.**

### A rowan0719

Polio is an awful disease that, until recently, millions of people suffered from. Today, not many people get it, and there is hope that in the next ten years, this disease will have disappeared completely.

My hero is a polio survivor named Lawan Didi, from Nigeria. I'd like to put him forward for the award. He got polio at the age of three and it left him paralysed and unable to walk. Even travelling to school was difficult and he needed help from his brothers. As a teenager, he loved sport – football in particular – and in 1988, he invented the game of para-soccer with the support of six friends. It is a football-style game for people with disabilities. When they first started playing, the players crawled on the ground, but now they sit on specially adapted roller skates so the players can move faster and play better.

In addition to this, Lawan campaigns for the use of the polio vaccine. Just a few drops of vaccine can prevent a child from getting the disease. Lawan's wish is that one day we can end polio in Nigeria and across the world – he made his dream of playing soccer come true, and he believes we can make this one come true, too. Even if he doesn't win, I hope they will shortlist him for the award – he definitely deserves it.

### B helpinghand_23

I'd like to nominate Ivo Gormley for a local hero award. He set up GoodGym, which is a group of runners that gets fit by helping people in the community. It's now operating in 28 areas across the UK.

I've joined a group in my area. On some days, we clear parks of leaves or paint community centres. Next week we will be planting trees in our local park. We run there, do the job and then we run back home again. The whole session takes about 90 minutes, so it's the equivalent of a session in a gym. As well as getting fit and helping out, it's a really good way of getting to meet other people in your area. By the time I get home in the evening, I will have run several kilometres and I will have helped my local community, too.

We also help the elderly in the community. I do the weekly shopping for an elderly lady called Edith. I do her shopping and then run to her house. I stay and chat for half an hour and then I run home again. We chat about all kinds of things and we have some very interesting conversations. Now it's turned into a friendship and I can talk to her about anything. There is so much you can learn from people from a different generation.

Ivo Gormley should be in the running for the award, and I hope that by the time you read this article, he will have won.

### C w_raven_peak

My candidate for the competition is Dr Megan Coffee. I don't know if you remember, but there was a terrible earthquake in the Caribbean country of Haiti in 2010. Many people needed urgent medical care and there was a risk of a tuberculosis epidemic spreading across the country. Dr Megan Coffee, an infectious disease specialist, got on a plane to Haiti to help. She gave up a research position at Berkeley in the US and went to work in Haiti for no pay. Her family and friends still think she's a little mad for choosing Haiti over Berkeley. I think it was very brave of her to go there in spite of the danger, and she has inspired me to think about volunteering. In September, after I graduate, I will be going to Ghana to work in a hospital there.

A group of local volunteers, many of whom survived tuberculosis because of Dr Megan, is now helping to take care of other infected men, women and children. She has inspired so many people and that's why I'm voting for her.

## Train to THINK

### Appropriate sampling

*In order to reach a relevant and informed conclusion, it's important to conduct research. However, this research should always be done responsibly. One danger is that the research sample is not entirely representative. For example, research might claim that 90 percent of people believe that the government should give a lifetime achievement award to the manager of their country's national football team. If the survey was based on the views of the readers of a footballing magazine, we cannot claim that this result represents all people.*

**8 Would these people agree or disagree with this statement?**

'We need to protect the habitats of our wildlife.'

building developer | farmer
member of the national bird society

**9** WRITING **Work in pairs. You have been asked to find a *Hero of Our Times*. To do your research responsibly, who would you ask to choose the hero? Choose five people who are representative of the population and write a list of questions to ask them.**

**10** SPEAKING **Work in pairs. How would the answers differ across the different people in your list? Discuss with your partner.**

**PRONUNCIATION**
Shifting word stress Go to page 121.

# GRAMMAR
## Future perfect; future continuous (review)

1 **Read the sentences from the online posts on page 111. Which are examples of the future continuous, and which are examples of the future perfect? Then complete the rule with *present participle* and *past participle*.**

1 In the next ten years, this disease **will have disappeared** completely.
2 By the time I get home in the evening, I **will have run** several kilometres.
3 In September, after I graduate, I **will be going** to Ghana to work in a hospital there.

> **RULE:** We use *will be* + [1]_____________ to talk about actions that will be in progress at or around a time in the future.
> We use *will have* + [2]_____________ to talk about actions that will be finished by a certain time in the future.

2 **Complete the sentences using the future continuous or future perfect of the verbs in brackets.**

1 The project will help students who want to study abroad. By the time those students return to their home countries, they _____________ important insights into other cultures. (gain)
2 By the end of next year, 2,000 young people from all over the world _____________ the chance to live abroad and they _____________ new friends. (have, make)
3 A week from today, we _____________ our exams and we _____________ for the results. (do, wait)
4 A Do you think he _____________ his new car by the time he comes to see you?
B No, I think he _____________ still _____________ his old car. (buy, drive)

→ workbook page 108

# VOCABULARY
## Awards

3 **Choose the correct options to complete the definitions.**

1 **nominate someone:** *show a preference for / officially suggest* someone for an honour, a position, a job or an election
2 **put oneself/someone forward for something:** *suggest / search for* oneself/someone for other people to consider
3 **vote for someone:** make your *choice / recommendation*, typically by marking a paper or by raising your hand in a meeting
4 **elect someone:** *choose / reject* someone for an official position
5 **campaign for something/someone:** organise a series of activities to try to *help / convince* people to do something or support someone
6 **be in the running for something:** *have a chance of winning / be likely to lose* a competition
7 **shortlist people:** select a(n) *increased / reduced* number of candidates for final consideration for something

4 **Complete the sentences with the correct form of the words and phrases from Exercise 3.**

1 Jack's decided to *shortlist me / put me forward* for the position.
2 Anna *is in the running / voted* for the award. I think she's got a good chance of winning.
3 My class is *nominating / campaigning* for our Maths teacher to win the Teacher of the Year prize by putting up posters around the school.
4 Gemma's cat cartoon has been *nominated / campaigned* for best animated film. I hope she wins!
5 Mehmet's among the five people that have been *in the running / shortlisted* for the book award. He now stands a good chance of winning the prize.
6 Who is Tim *voting for / electing* in the elections?
7 Amy's class *elected / shortlisted* her as their class prefect and she's done a brilliant job so far.

→ workbook page 110

# SPEAKING

5 **Imagine your class is planning to give awards to the teachers at your school. What three awards do you think should be given? Make notes.**

*most inspiring teacher*
*best public speaker*
*funniest teacher, etc.*

6 **Work in pairs. Compare ideas and agree on just one award category together.**

7 **Share your idea for an award with the class. Hold a class vote and choose a winner for each award category.**

## LISTENING

8 12.03 **You're going to listen to a presentation about the young man in the photos. He did a skydive, but not just for fun. For what other reason do you think he did it? Discuss. Then listen and check.**

9 12.03 **Listen again. Complete each sentence with one or two words.**

1 Stephen did very well at school and had wanted to study ______________ at university.
2 Stephen's mother feared that his father had passed the ______________ on to their son.
3 Stephen was shocked and saddened by his diagnosis, but decided not to ______________ for himself.
4 Stephen came up with a ______________ of 46 things to do while he still could.
5 Stephen wanted to write a book, have a go at ______________ in front of lots of people, break a world record and see a football match live at Wembley.
6 Lots of people from all over the world supported Stephen's cause, including well-known actors, sports people and ______________ .
7 Stephen's mother keeps his ______________ updated.
8 A local band recorded a song, for which the inspiration was Stephen's ______________ life.

## VOCABULARY
### Success and failure

10 **Match the sentence halves. Then write the expressions in italics in the table. Use the infinitive form of the verbs.**

1 When it was announced that John would play the lead role in *Hamlet*, ☐
2 Readers often feel inspired by people ☐
3 Dede *is recognised as* one of the ☐
4 They had great hopes for the project, but *their plans* ☐
5 When he learned about his illness, he wasn't ☐
6 If you really want *to pursue your dreams*, you ☐
7 It's ironic that he believed he was the best and ☐
8 My team wasn't playing well, but they still ☐

a his lifelong *ambition* of performing on stage *had been fulfilled*.
b then *failed so spectacularly*.
c mustn't waste any time and you have to study hard.
d *fell through* at the last minute.
e managed to *pull off a* last-minute *victory*.
f most talented singers in our country.
g prepared to *give up on his dreams*.
h who manage to *overcome adversity*.

| Succeed | Fail | Neither |
|---|---|---|
| *fulfil an ambition* | | |

11 SPEAKING **Work in groups. Think about these questions and note down your answers. Then compare your ideas with your classmates.**

1 Would you rather pursue big dreams and risk failing spectacularly, or not dare to 'think big' at all?
2 Think of someone who has managed to overcome adversity. What adversity did they overcome? What did they achieve? What personal qualities helped them to succeed?
3 If you could pursue only one dream for your future, what would it be?

12 WRITING **You've decided to pursue one of your dreams. Write a diary entry detailing your plans and how you feel. Include at least three expressions from Exercise 10.**

→ workbook page 110

# I just wrote to say ... THANK YOU!

**In our special Saturday column, we give our readers an opportunity to thank someone who's done something special for them. Someone who they never managed to say thank you to at the time. Send us your stories. If we choose yours, we'll send you a £30 book voucher.**

## READING

1 **Read the article quickly. Who was helped by lots of people and who helped lots of people? Was it Matt, Martin or Mandy?**

2 12.04 **Read the article again and listen. Answer the questions.**

1 Why was Matt trying to raise some money?
2 Why did Matt decide to give all his money away?
3 How did Martin become homeless?
4 What did Tara do to help Martin?
5 Why did Mandy start collecting supermarket coupons?
6 Why did Sally call her a 'generous young woman'?

3 ROLE PLAY **Work in pairs. Choose one of the stories. Role play a conversation between the person who wrote in and the person they want to thank.**

## A ticket to walk

When Matt was 12 years old, he was very badly injured in a cycling accident. Two years after the accident, he began raising money for an operation which could help him to walk again. Some time later, he read a story in a newspaper. It was about a five-year-old boy called Jamie, who had only ever walked with the aid of a frame. Jamie's parents were raising money for an operation to help their son walk without the frame.

Matt knew how it felt not to be able to walk and he felt sorry for the little boy. He contacted the newspaper and he arranged for all the money he had raised to be given to Jamie's parents. He did this anonymously. Jamie's parents were able to take Jamie to America where he had the operation. Today he walks to school and he plays with friends – thanks to the remarkable generosity of this now 29-year-old stranger.

'I felt that Jamie had a better chance of walking than I did, and I wanted to help him,' said Matt. 'Hearing that Jamie could walk was amazing. It made giving the money away worth it.'

*A big thank you to Matt from Jamie and his parents. They are eternally grateful to you. It was going to take them years to raise the money. Then you gave it to them. Thank you, Matt.*

## The streets are paved with notes

New York accountant, Martin Goldberg, had some bad luck which resulted in him losing his job and then his home. He didn't want to be a burden on his relatives, so he moved to another town where he spent seven years living on the street and in shelters. He thought he was going to spend the rest of his life homeless. Then, one day, he found a backpack containing money totalling more than $50,000.

Martin decided not to keep this windfall. Instead, he handed it all to the police. They returned it to the grateful owner and the story of the 'good Samaritan' was reported in a local newspaper.

A stranger, Tara White, read the story and she set up a GoFundMe page to raise a reward for Martin. Donations flooded in from around the world, and the page raised $120,000 in no time. This was enough for Martin to rent a house and sort his life out.

*Martin is very grateful to Tara and he has asked us to say that he would love to be able to thank you in person one day.*

## The coupon kid

Mandy Eastwood from Streatham in South London is not your usual 16-year-old. Last year, her single mother Hannah, 43, was struggling to make ends meet on her nurse's salary, so Mandy started finding and collecting supermarket coupons. She saved her mother £2,000 at the supermarket that year. That Christmas, she decided that she would like to help other families, too.

'I didn't have any particular people in mind. I just wanted to help as many people as I could,' she said. 'And I wanted to show them that it's possible to shop very cheaply if you know how.'

She carefully collected 465 coupons for her local supermarket. Then she filled three shopping trolleys with discount food, including meat, vegetables, fruit, cheese and desserts.

'I didn't know exactly what the total would be,' she said. 'It's hard to work it out in your head. I was very surprised when it came to just 10p. That's a saving of £565.10!'

Mandy donated the contents of all three trolleys to a charity which provides food to disadvantaged families.

*'She's a very generous young woman,' said Sally, who works for the charity. 'Her act of kindness has helped a lot of families and they would all like to thank her.'*

## GRAMMAR

Grammar video ▶31

### Future in the past

4 **Read the sentences from the article and then complete the rule.**

1 It **was going to** take them years to raise the money.
2 He thought he **was going to** spend the rest of his life homeless.
3 I didn't know exactly what the total **would** be.

**RULE:** When we want to talk about the future as seen from the past, we use *was/were* [1]_______________ or [2]_______________ .
When we talk about actions that were planned for the future but then our plans changed, we often use [3]_______________ / *were* or [4]_______________ / *weren't going to* … . For example: *I was going to go out last night but I was too tired in the end.* We use *was/were(n't) going to* when a plan was definite.
We use [5]_______________ or *wouldn't* when a plan was less likely to happen or when it was just a possibility or idea.

5 **Complete the sentences with the correct form of the verb in brackets. Use *was/were going to* or *would* to talk about the future in the past. Sometimes there's more than one correct answer.**

1 Last Friday, our teacher announced that the grammar test _______________ probably _______________ on Tuesday, but that she hadn't decided yet. (be)
2 There _______________ a match on Saturday. Then it rained and the match was cancelled. (be)
3 Lily just texted to say she thought she _______________ to come to your party, unfortunately. (not be able)
4 You _______________ Sarah. Why didn't you? (meet)
5 I knew it was going to be cold, but I didn't think it _______________ . (snow)
6 I didn't expect any problems with the test, but I didn't realise it _______________ so easy. (be)

6 **Rewrite the sentences using *was/were going to* or *would*.**

0 Kirsty planned to get home early, but then she had to stay late at work.
*Kirsty was going to get home early, but then she had to stay late at work.*
1 She didn't intend to leave the country, but then it became too dangerous to stay.
2 He had an idea to teach the children to read and write, but he hadn't really thought it through.
3 Their plan was to use football to give the boys more confidence, but then they decided to set up basketball teams instead.
4 She intended to set up a charity to promote the values of tolerance and unity, but so far she hasn't been able to do so.
5 They talked about offering free healthcare to children, but then it became clear that the government had other priorities.

→ workbook page 109

## SPEAKING

7 **Work in pairs. Think about the last two weeks. What things were you going to do that you didn't do? Ask and answer questions and say why you didn't do them.**

*I was going to study for the Maths test.*
*Why didn't you?*
*I had too much work to do for English so I didn't have time. What about you?*
*I was going to have my hair cut.*
*Why didn't you?*
*I missed my appointment.*

## WordWise
### Expressions with *in*

8 **Complete these sentences from the unit so far with phrases from the list.**

in mind | in no time | in particular
in spite of | in the public eye

1 We're looking for ordinary people who aren't _______________ .
2 As a teenager, he loved sport – football _______________ .
3 I think it was very brave of her to go there _______________ the danger.
4 Donations flooded in from around the world, and the page raised $120,000 _______________ .
5 I didn't have any particular people _______________ .

9 **Choose the correct options.**

1 Not all famous people like being in *mind / the public eye*.
2 We got there on time in *spite of / no time* the terrible traffic.
3 I want to go somewhere tonight, but I haven't got anywhere special in *particular / mind*.
4 I really love soft drinks, lemonade in *mind / particular*.
5 I'll have this work finished in *no time / spite of*, and then we can go out.

→ workbook page 110

# DEVELOPING SPEAKING

**1** 🔊 12.05 **Look at the photos. Where do you think the two people are going and what problem do they have? Read, listen and check your ideas.**

**Jake:** This is brilliant. I haven't been on a day trip for ages. And Brighton! I'm really looking forward to seeing the sea again. We can't get there soon enough!

**Meg:** And I'm glad we took the bus, not the train: cheaper, more comfortable, you can see the countryside – what's not to like? Oh, I'm so excited!

**Jake:** Me too. Remind me what time we get there?

**Meg:** 10.30. Gives us a couple of hours to look around before we eat. What do you fancy having for lunch?

**Jake:** Well, at the English seaside, it has to be fish and chips, doesn't it?

**Meg:** Ha, that's right! I'm dying to have some ice cream, too. Well, perhaps I should avoid that temptation! Wait a minute – the bus is pulling over. But it's non-stop. Why have we stopped, Jake?

**Jake:** How should I know? Hang on, the driver's going to say something.

**Driver:** I'm afraid there's a problem with the bus and I can't fix it. They'll send another one to take you all to Brighton, but it won't be here for a couple of hours. Sorry!

**Meg:** Oh no! How unlucky is that? Now we won't get there until after lunch!

**Jake:** The question is, how do we not let this ruin our day out?

**Meg:** I know. My mum gave me some spending money for today, and I think I know a good way to use it. Just let me open this app. There we go. I can get a car here in five minutes, and it'll get us to Brighton in another twenty. Costs a bit, but that's what money's for, right?

**Jake:** Meg, you're my hero! Thanks for doing that. And the fish and chips are on me, OK? And the ice cream, too!

**2** 🔊 12.05 **Read and listen to the dialogue again. Answer the questions.**

1 Why did they choose to travel by bus?
2 What plans do they have for Brighton?
3 How does Meg solve their problem?

## Phrases for fluency

**3** **Find these expressions in the dialogue. Who says them? How do you say them in your language?**

1 … for ages.
2 What's not to like?
3 … do you fancy …?
4 How should I know?
5 How [unlucky] is that?
6 The question is, …?

**4** **Use the expressions in Exercise 3 to complete the dialogues.**

1 A Do you know where Jenny is?
B Sorry, I haven't seen her ______________ .

2 A Let's go out somewhere.
B OK. Where ______________ going?

3 A I love those trousers.
B Me too. They're comfortable and such a great colour! ______________ ?

4 A *Bring Me The Horizon* is on TV tonight.
B I know! ______________ fantastic ______________ ?

5 A We've missed the last train.
B That's right. So, ______________ , how are we going to get home?

6 A Why hasn't she got here yet?
B ______________ ? Call and ask her.

## FUNCTIONS
### Expressing anticipation

**5** **Which of these are said by a) Jake, b) Meg, c) neither of them?**

1 This time tomorrow, I'll be …
2 It's going to be amazing.
3 I'm so excited!
4 I'm really looking forward to …
5 I'm dying to …
6 We can't get there soon enough!

**6** SPEAKING **Work in pairs. Talk about some of the things you've got planned for the future that you're eager to do. Use the phrases above.**

## WRITING

**7** **Write your own entry (150–200 words) for the article on page 114. It can be a true story or one you've made up. For example, you could imagine that you were homeless like Martin and somebody like Tara gave you the money to sort your life out. Think about and make notes on:**

- who you want to thank
- what they did for you.

# LIFE COMPETENCIES

**Temptation is when you really want to do something but you know you shouldn't do it. Temptation is hard to resist, but if we give in to it, we have to live with the consequences.**

1 ▶ 32 **Watch the vlog. What is Will being tempted by? How well does he resist temptation?**

2 ▶ 32 **Watch the vlog again and make notes on the following:**

1 three things he wishes he could do
2 the examples he gives of big and small temptations
3 the consequences that would have happened if he had given in

3 SPEAKING **Work in pairs. Decide what temptations might fit these pie charts.**

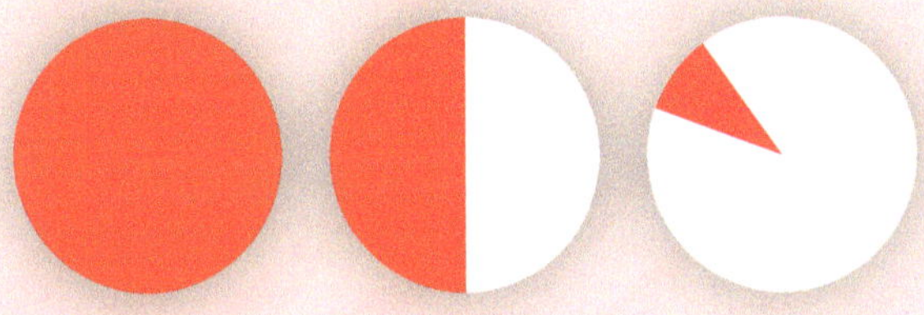

## TIPS ON AVOIDING TEMPTATION

- **Temptation is a part of everyday life, but it can range in seriousness. Borrowing your brother's T-shirt without asking is not the same as stealing one from a shop.**
- **Think about the consequences of giving in to a temptation. Would it really make you feel any better?**
- **Occasionally, it is only natural to give in to a small temptation. But when you do, just try to enjoy it!**

4 **Read the quiz and choose your answers.**

1 **You are struggling in your end-of-year Maths test. You are sitting next to the cleverest kid in the class. Her answers are clearly visible on the page. What do you do?**
a Copy down all her answers.
b Glance occasionally at her answers just to check your answers.
c Don't look at her answers, even though it means you'll probably fail the test.

2 **When buying a magazine for £2, you're given change for £10 instead of the £5 you gave the assistant. What do you do?**
a Put the money in your pocket and walk away.
b Spend time thinking about what you should do, then decide it's too late to go back in now.
c Go back to the assistant, show her the mistake and return the money.

3 **You have decided to get yourself healthier. This means running every day and avoiding all fattening food. When visiting your grandmother, she gives you chocolate. What do you do?**
a Eat it! You don't want to upset her and you can resume your diet tomorrow.
b Take it and decide that you will reward yourself with a piece from it every time you go for a run.
c Thank your grandmother, but explain your situation and ask her to take it back.

5 SPEAKING **Work in pairs. Compare your answers.**

1 Identify the temptation in each situation 1–3.
2 Discuss how you might feel if you chose a different option a–c in each situation.
3 Which of situations 1–3 is the least serious? Why.
4 Which is the most serious? Why?

## Me and my world

6 WRITING **Write a new question for the quiz.**

1 Think of a situation where you were tempted to do something wrong. Write this situation as a question.
2 Write down three possible options – a, b and c.

7 SPEAKING **Work in groups of five or six.**

1 Take turns to pick a new quiz question at random and read it out to the group.
2 Discuss the options for each question.
3 Finally, try to guess who wrote the question and ask them to talk more about the situation and what they did.

# C1 Advanced

## READING AND USE OF ENGLISH

### Part 8: Multiple matching

→ workbook page 115

1 **You are going to read five people's opinions on modern art. For statements 1–10, choose from the people (A–E). Each person may be chosen more than once.**

**Which person expresses each of the following opinions?**

|  |  |  |
|---|---|---|
| I have personal experience of how artists have developed their abilities. | 1 | |
| There are things that people can do far better than machines can. | 2 | |
| The value of a work of art is not only a question of the work itself, but also of one's personal taste. | 3 | |
| True art does not need to be explained. | 4 | |
| Art will always reflect how people, in any period in history, live their lives. | 5 | |
| The ordinary things that we see every day do not deserve to be called art. | 6 | |
| There is no requirement for people to hold the same views about a work of art. | 7 | |
| Art now is not as good as it was in the past. | 8 | |
| The move towards less representational art is not difficult to explain. | 9 | |
| If you look at a work of art and have neither positive nor negative feelings, then it is not art. | 10 | |

**Person A**

People have different ideas when it comes to defining 'art'. My personal opinion is that if something evokes a reaction in the person who sees or hears it, then it can be called 'art'. That said, there's the question of whether the viewer or listener likes it or not, and that's essentially subjective. Beauty is in the eye of the beholder, after all, and that's why I don't have the right to say that what they choose to like isn't 'art'. If you like it and I don't (or vice versa), then we simply disagree.

**Person B**

Most contemporary art is abstract, and I believe there's a simple reason for that. Since the invention of the camera, people are less and less inclined to devote hours of their time and talent to producing a realistic image, which can be done in a second at the push of a button. So art has evolved, necessarily, into something different from what it once was. To me, this is a positive thing – technology, after all, isn't so good at producing abstract images, whereas humans excel at it. Art today is a matter of interpretation, whether you like it or not.

**Person C**

Most of what is on display in galleries these days is simply not art. Art should reflect beauty and as such, represent the very best of human endeavour. Thus, it should strive to improve our lives and also to improve itself – to develop and become better. These days, what we are seeing is a progressive reduction in the quality of life and also of art. Art is something that should always provoke positive reactions in the human soul, and nowadays, the stresses and strains of life require more than ever that art should provide an enrichment of our experience, and be something remarkable and admirable. A pile of bricks does not do this.

**Person D**

Art changes with the times and that is necessarily a good thing. The things that people experience in their lives in the 21st century are distinctly different from what our ancestors experienced. Artists are people too and so the changing human experience will inevitably be reflected in art. Many critics of modern art state that it does not require technique to produce but I would dispute that. As an artist myself, I know that all my contemporaries have studied drawing, colour and so on. Now, whether or not they choose to apply those techniques in what they produce is a matter entirely for them.

**Person E**

I firmly believe that art has to represent something of value to human beings. Something cannot be called art unless it fulfils a number of criteria, and it is not art if it does not require talent and technique on the part of the artist, if it is merely intended to shock an audience, or if it needs some art critic or other to engage in lengthy justifications of its existence. When I look at the products of self-proclaimed artists such as Hirst or Emin, and hold those criteria in mind, then I, for one, am unable to term them art.

# TEST YOURSELF UNITS 11 & 12

## VOCABULARY

**1 Complete the sentences with the words in the list. There are four extra words.**

ageist | failed | head | nominate | optimism | out | pessimist
put | shortlist | steam | temper | through | tongue | vote

1 Don't take him too seriously. He's just letting off a bit of ________________ .
2 I'd like to ________________ my dad for the 'local hero' award.
3 I don't think that joke about old people using technology is very funny. It's just ________________ .
4 He likes to take the opposite view, but I just bite my ________________ and ignore him.
5 His attempts to learn the guitar ________________ spectacularly and he gave up after two lessons.
6 Be careful what you say. She loses her ________________ very quickly.
7 Teresa is such a ________________ . She always thinks the worst is about to happen.
8 I'd like to ________________ myself forward for class president.
9 Do you think people over 16 should be able to ________________ in the elections?
10 We wanted to go camping for the weekend, but our plans fell ________________ at the last minute.

/10

## GRAMMAR

**2 Complete the sentences with the words/phrases in the list. There are two extra words/phrases.**

can | had | has | have | must | were going to | will | would

1 We've ________________ our house broken into three times now.
2 She normally ________________ her hair cut by her mum. Her mum's a great hairdresser.
3 Most phones ________________ be used as cameras, too.
4 I think your cake ________________ have been eaten by the dog. He isn't looking too well now.
5 I've got the worst memory. By the next time we meet, I ________________ have forgotten your name.
6 The ship set sail from England six weeks before it ________________ finally arrive in Australia.

**3 Find and correct the mistake in each sentence.**

1 My dad dyes his hair at the barber's.
2 Police say the fire may caused deliberately.
3 The song got written by all of the members of the band.
4 They will be together 20 years in August.
5 They've just won the cup. Fans would be singing and dancing in the streets all night.
6 For a few scary moments, I thought I am going to die.

/12

## FUNCTIONAL LANGUAGE

**4 Choose the correct options.**

1 A This *moment* / *time* tomorrow, we'll be on our way to France.
B I *can't* / *must* wait.
2 A Take it *easy* / *simple*. It isn't the end of the world.
B Don't tell me to *cool* / *calm* down. I'm really angry about this.
3 A I'm *dying* / *living* to meet Anne's new boyfriend.
B Me too. I'm really looking *ahead* / *forward* to it.
4 A Don't let him get under your *skin* / *head*. He's just not worth it.
B I know – you're right. I don't know why I let him *bother* / *get* to me.

/8

**MY SCORE** /30

22–30 | 10–21 | 0–9

# PRONUNCIATION

## UNIT 1
### Intonation: showing emotions

**1** 1.03 **Listen to the speakers and decide if they are feeling angry (A), cheerful (C), disappointed (D), enthusiastic (E), puzzled (P) or sympathetic (S).**

0 She can be mean to me, but she's still my sister. C
1 But you haven't got a ticket – how did you get in? ☐
2 The homework was difficult, so I'll give you an extra week. ☐
3 My cousin was going to phone but I still haven't heard from her. ☐
4 I need to move out, Mum. I want to be independent! ☐
5 I'm your best friend, Clara. Why didn't you tell me? ☐

**2** 1.03 **Listen, repeat and practise.**

## UNIT 2
### Different ways of pronouncing *c* and *g*

**1 Look at the sentences, paying attention to the pronunciation of the letters c and g in blue. Write the correct phoneme** /k/, /s/, /ʃ/, /g/ **or** /dʒ/ **after each word.**

0 There is concern (/k/, /s/) that teenagers (/dʒ/) are not getting (/g/) sufficient (/ʃ/) sleep.
1 Girls (/___/) are especially (/___/) in danger (/___/) of not getting (/___/) the necessary (/___/) hours of sleep.
2 Experts agree (/___/) that sleep and exercise (/___/) are beneficial (/___/) for your health.
3 The causes /___/ of their anti-social /___/ sleeping habits are biological /___/, /___/.

**2** 2.02 **Listen, check and repeat.**

## UNIT 3
### Unstressed words in connected speech

**1** 3.02 **Read and listen to the dialogue. What do you notice about the pronunciation of the words in blue?**

**Jane** How did you meet your wife, Rob?
**Rob** It's a funny story. My sister crashed into her car. She wanted to apologise and she asked me to go with her.
**Jane** And when you met Petra it was love at first sight!
**Rob** That's right. If it hadn't been for the accident, we wouldn't be married now!

**2 What types of word are unstressed?**

**3** 3.02 **Listen, repeat and practise.**

## UNIT 4
### Telling jokes: pacing, pausing and punchlines

**1** 4.04 **Read and listen to the ending of joke 3 from the listening on page 41. What does P indicate?**

'What on earth are you doing?' he says. 'Running shoes? You can't run faster than this bear!' P And the other man replies: P 'I don't have to run faster than the bear. P I just have to run faster than you.'

**2** 4.04 **Listen, repeat and practise.**

## UNIT 5
### Connected speech feature: elision

**1** 5.02 **Read and listen to the sentences. Then practise saying the linked words in blue.**

1 **Commuters in New York City stopped their mad dash to work to look up in the sky.**
2 Since the authorities thought anyone attempting such a death-defying feat must be crazy.
3 First they shot an arrow across to a contact on the roof of the other tower.

## UNIT 6
### Modal stress and meaning

**1** 6.02 **Read and listen to the sentences. One of the modal verbs in each pair of sentences is stressed and the other is not. Write S (stressed) and U (unstressed) in the boxes.**

1 A I may watch the film tonight – I'll see how I feel. S
B They may be rich and famous, but are they happy? ☐
2 A I might go to the beach – but it looks like it could rain. ☐
B Kate might want to get a lift with us – it's a long walk to the beach. ☐
3 A We could have a problem. We need to look into it. ☐
B My dad could solve most problems. ☐

**2 Circle the correct option to complete the rule.**

We stress the modal verb (rather than the main verb which follows it) when we want to emphasise *certainty / uncertainty*.

**3** 6.02 **Listen, repeat and practise.**

## UNIT 7
### Connected speech feature: assimilation

1 7.05 **Read and listen to the sentences closely. In the pairs of words highlighted in blue, the final sound of the first word changes. How does this sound change in each sentence?**

1 'London Bridge' is a really good book – everyone's reading it.
2 The meditation class was full, so I'm doing yoga instead.
3 Listen to this all-woman band – they're brilliant!
4 We had sunshine on the day of our garden party.
5 After the robbery, she saw a green car speeding away from the bank.

2 **Practise saying the linked words in blue.**

## UNIT 8
### Stress in multi-syllable words

1 8.02 **Read and listen to the sentences. Underline all of the words with three or more syllables and draw a circle above the stressed syllable in each word.**

0 While digging in the sands, Bouchard came across an unusual slab of black rock.
1 Knowing about his emperor's interest in such things, he took it back to show him.
2 The top layer contained ancient Egyptian hieroglyphics.
3 For many years, scholars had been baffled by the inscriptions.
4 The first breakthrough came when scholars realised that all three passages said the same thing.

2 8.02 **Listen, repeat and practise.**

## UNIT 9
### Unstressed syllables and words: the /ɪ/ phoneme

1 9.02 **Read and listen to the sentences, paying attention to the words in blue. Can you hear the /ɪ/ phoneme? This is often used in unstressed syllables and words.**

1 Of the three cases I think the worst miscarriage of justice is the first one.
2 Imagine – she was convicted because of a bullet the police found in her pocket!
3 Since they had no motive, they must have been sent to prison because of prejudice.

2 9.02 **Underline the unstressed /ɪ/ phonemes in the words in blue. Then listen and check.**

## UNIT 10
### Lexical and non-lexical fillers

1 10.04 **Read and listen to these extracts, paying attention to the fillers, shown in blue. How can fillers help you when speaking?**

Well, I didn't really want to go, like, straight from school to university and I'd always wanted to see Australia and New Zealand, so I decided to take a year off, but split it, you know, so the first six months I worked and saved some money.

The headteacher said, 'Look, why not take a gap year and then decide.' Erm … And I thought, well, that's, like, good advice!

Um, at first, I was thinking about going to university to do an Economics course, you know, but then I kind of stopped to think. I mean, university fees are so expensive and you come out in debt.

2 10.04 **Listen, repeat and practise.**

## UNIT 11
### Intonation: mean what you say

1 11.04 **Read and listen to the same sentence said in two different ways. Tick (✓) the sentence where the tone of voice is appropriate and cross (✗) the sentence where it is inappropriate.**

1 A It isn't a problem – don't worry about it, OK?
B It isn't a problem – don't worry about it, OK?
2 A Don't let him get under your skin – he didn't mean it.
B Don't let him get under your skin – he didn't mean it.
3 A Calm down. Shouting won't do any good.
B Calm down. Shouting won't do any good.

2 11.04 **Listen, repeat and practise.**

## UNIT 12
### Shifting word stress

1 12.02 **Read and listen to the sentences, underlining the stressed syllable in each of the words in blue.**

1 A When giving a presentation, you must project your voice so everyone can hear you.
B Jo's really excited about her science project.
2 A The author was happy to sign the new contract.
B Children in poorer countries contract illnesses which could be prevented.
3 A We had to record our voices to practise our English pronunciation.
B She broke a world record at the last Olympics.

2 **Which syllable is stressed in each word?**

3 12.02 **Listen, repeat and practise.**

# GET IT RIGHT!

## UNIT 1
### Habits in the present

**Learners often incorrectly use *use(d) to* when talking about present habits.**

✓ *At school, classmates **tend to** discuss the TV programmes which they watched the night before.*
✓ *At school, classmates **will** discuss the TV programmes which they watched the night before.*
✗ *At school, classmates ~~use to~~ discuss the TV programmes which they watched the night before.*
✓ *Kate **is always taking** my pen and not giving it me back!*
✗ *Kate ~~use to~~ take my pen and not giving it me back!*

**In all of the sentences, *use(d) to* is incorrectly used in order to talk about present habits. Rewrite the sentences using an appropriate form for talking about the present. Try to use a variety of different forms in your answers.**

0 Teenagers use to behave quite rebelliously.
*Teenagers tend to behave quite rebelliously.*

1 People use to form close relationships with friends they have most in common with.

2 My older brother always used to tease me. It's so annoying!

3 My sister often gets on my nerves as she uses to borrow my clothes without asking.

4 Jenny says that her biology teacher always uses to pick on her. It makes her quite upset.

5 Annoyingly, my best friend uses to act rather self-centredly so we sometimes fall out.

6 Elderly people often use to have traditional values.

## UNIT 2
### *would rather*

**Learners often make mistakes with *rather*, failing to use *would/'d* when talking about preferences, and using it unnecessarily in other structures.**

✓ *They **would rather** watch videos than play football.*
✗ *They ~~rather~~ watch videos than play football.*
✓ *Many boys dream of becoming politicians, whereas girls **would rather** become journalists.*
✗ *Many boys dream of becoming politicians, whereas girls **would rather** ~~prefer to~~ become journalists.*
✓ *Do you know where I can have a coffee, or perhaps a beer?*
✗ *Do you know where I can have a coffee, or perhaps ~~rather~~ a beer?*

**All of the sentences contain errors with *rather*. Rewrite the sentences correctly.**

0 Can we meet a bit later? I rather have a lie-in tomorrow morning if you don't mind.
*Can we meet a bit later? I'd rather have a lie-in tomorrow morning if you don't mind.*

1 Would you have a siesta now or go to bed early tonight?

2 Teenagers need more sleep rather than adults.

3 I rather I wasn't such a light sleeper. I tend to wake up several times during the night.

4 Tom's girlfriend has been complaining that Tom's tiredness has made him grumpy and forgetful. Tom would rather prefer not annoy his girlfriend so he's decided to get more sleep.

5 Some dreams have more meaning rather than others.

6 Kate would rather prefer to take a nap now than later.

# UNIT 3
## Conditionals

**Learners often use *would* in the *if*-clause when it's more accurate to use the past simple or past perfect.**

✓ *If **I'd known**, I wouldn't have said anything.*
✗ *If I ~~would've known~~, I wouldn't have said anything.*

**Tick the sentences which are correct and rewrite the incorrect ones.**

1 If Jo hadn't been too ill to play, I might not have had the chance to get on the team. ☐

______________________________

2 The car wouldn't have broken down if you would have had it serviced. ☐

______________________________

3 We would be rich now if we would have won the lottery. ☐

______________________________

4 If they didn't think I was capable of taking on the role, they wouldn't have asked me to step in. ☐

______________________________

5 John really would have been pushing his luck if he would have asked Sam to help him. ☐

______________________________

6 If the photographer wouldn't have photographed the heron he would have missed the woodpecker flying past. ☐

______________________________

# UNIT 4
## Cleft sentences

**Learners at this level often avoid using emphatic structures such as cleft sentences.**

✓ *It's often the unexpected that makes us laugh. (The unexpected often makes us laugh.)*
✓ *What makes us laugh is often the unexpected.*

**Rewrite the sentences using *What* ..., *It's* ... *that* ... or *All* ... to add emphasis.**

0 A sense of humour is simply the ability to see the funny side of things.
All *a sense of humour is, is the ability to see the funny side of things.*

1 The misfortune of others often makes us laugh.
What ______________________________

2 The actions of just two members of the team have made us all a laughing stock.
It's ______________________________

3 Ollie laughed his head off when he saw his teacher playing air guitar to a rock song.
What ______________________________

4 They don't understand that we will have the last laugh.
What ______________________________

5 Simon only said that the show was hilarious.
All ______________________________

6 Many people enjoy watching funny videos on YouTube and it isn't a secret.
It's ______________________________

# UNIT 5
## Gerunds and participles

**Learners often use a gerund when a past participle should be used and vice versa.**

✓ ***Cooked** properly, Brussels sprouts can taste really nice.*
✗ *~~Cooking~~ properly, Brussels sprouts can taste really nice.*
✓ ***Based** on their recent exam results, all the students will probably do well.*
✗ *~~Basing~~ on their recent exam results, all the students will probably do well.*
✓ ***Talking** loudly, the students walked down the corridor.*
✗ *~~Talked~~ loudly, the students walked down the corridor.*

**Choose the correct option.**

1 *Jumping / Jumped* out of her chair, she said, 'Let's go!'
2 *Discovering / Discovered* in time, a lot of serious illnesses can be cured.
3 *Catching / Caught* outside in the thunderstorm, we ran for shelter under some trees.
4 *Seeing / Seen* from far away, the mountain path didn't look that long.
5 All this noise is making me *confusing / confused*.
6 The new stuntman is a real daredevil *comparing / compared* with the last one.

# UNIT 6
## Modals

**Learners often confuse the different modals – *may, might, can, could, will, won't*.**

✓ *I hope you **will** like it.*

✗ *I hope you ~~would~~ like it.*

✓ *You **won't** believe it when you see it.*

✗ *You ~~can't~~ believe it when you see it.*

**Correct the error and rewrite the sentences.**

0 I will be grateful if you could help me tomorrow.
*I would be grateful if you could help me tomorrow.*

1 If Jenny wears that outfit tonight she would be the centre of attention!

______

2 Although I am interested in reading about celebrities, I will not describe myself as obsessed.

______

3 When people suffer from Celebrity Worship Syndrome, they won't function properly in their normal lives.

______

4 You wouldn't find much difference between those two celebrities. They're both famous for doing very little!

______

5 I asked if she can help me stay out of the limelight at the party.

______

6 You will be an up-and-coming child actor, but you still have to do your homework!

______

# UNIT 7
## Substitution

**Learners at this level often avoid using substitution with words such as *so, neither, either, that, those, ones*. This can make sentences sound repetitive.**

✓ *People's idea of beauty is very different to **that of** 100 years ago.*

✗ *People's idea of beauty is very different to their idea of beauty 100 years ago.*

**Rewrite the sentences using substitution.**

0 Fiona is going to buy some new trainers this weekend. She's going to buy the trainers she saw on sale. (ones)
*Fiona is going to buy some new trainers this weekend. She's going to buy the ones she saw on sale.*

1 Some people find these kinds of activities fun, but I'm not someone who finds these activities fun. (those)

______

2 The survey revealed that none of the students exercised more than twice a week and the teachers didn't exercise more than twice a week. (neither)

______

3 It brings a smile to my face when I see the delight on a baby's face or on a child's face when they eat chocolate for the first time. (that)

______

4 I get shivers down my spine when I watch a horror film and Becca gets shivers down her spine too. (so)

______

5 Tom doesn't agree with people having plastic surgery for cosmetic reasons and also Sally doesn't agree with people having plastic surgery. (either)

______

6 A Do you think I'll lose weight if I take up running?
B Yes I think you'll lose weight if you taking up running. (so)

______

# UNIT 8
## Relative pronouns with determiners

**Learners often confuse the different relative pronouns; *who, whom* and *which*.**

✓ *I'm the one **who** would be the best person to do that.*

✗ *I'm the one ~~whom~~ would be the best person to do that.*

**Rewrite the sentences correctly using *who, whom* or *which*.**

0 There were about 100 people at the conference, many of who came from Russia.
*There were about 100 people at the conference, many of whom came from Russia.*

1 He spoke in broken English, most of who I was unable to understand.

______

2 As well as speech, people communicate with gestures and facial expressions, both of what can greatly aid understanding.

______

3 My grandad spoke a northern dialect compared to whom standard English might seem like a different language!

______

4 I met several people at the party, one of which was the most conceited person I've ever met!

______

5 Mandy might have brought her hairdryer with her, in what case I'll borrow it from her.

______________________________

6 Oliver has had many jobs, but interpreting for the United Nations was the job to whom he dedicated himself the most.

______________________________

# UNIT 9
## Negative inversion

**Learners at this level often avoid using negative inversion or use it incorrectly. Typical learner mistakes relate to word order or the omission of the auxiliary after a negative or restricting adverb.**

✓ ***Never have I*** *heard such rubbish!*

✗ *~~Never I have~~ heard such rubbish!*

✓ ***Little does she*** *know he's not who he says he is.*

✗ *~~Little she knows~~ he's not who he says he is.*

**Rewrite the sentences beginning with the negative or restricting adverb given, paying attention to word order and including any necessary auxiliaries.**

0 The members of the jury had never heard such a story before.
Never *before had the jury heard such a story.*

1 The defence lawyer didn't realise that her client would be found guilty.
Little ______________________________

2 The witness gave false evidence, but also committed the crime himself!
Not only ______________________________

3 People don't often think it's fair to be able to pay to jump a queue.
Rarely ______________________________

4 The children are absolutely forbidden to go in there – it's where I'm keeping all their Christmas presents.
Under ______________________________

5 The thief made a full confession and then immediately retracted it.
No ______________________________

6 The witnesses did not withhold evidence – that did not happen!
On ______________________________

# UNIT 10
## Reporting verbs

**Learners often use the wrong preposition, omit the preposition, or make mistakes with verb patterns after reporting verbs.**

✓ *He accused me* ***of*** *cheating in the exam.*

✗ *He accused me ~~for~~ cheating in the exam.*

✓ *They decided* ***to go*** *to the beach.*

✗ *They decided ~~going~~ to the beach.*

**Rewrite these incorrect sentences correctly.**

0 I need to congratulate Emma for the great presentation she did in class today.
*I need to congratulate Emma on the great presentation she did in class today.*

1 The politician denied to have promised a reduction in student fees.

______________________________

2 In the end, the government agreed for a change in the school curriculum.

______________________________

3 Chloe invited Georgina for the wedding.

______________________________

4 The researcher confessed altering the test results in order to show a better outcome.

______________________________

5 Helen suggested me that we go ice skating.

______________________________

6 My dad insisted to pick me up after the party.

______________________________

## UNIT 11
### Passive with *get*

**Learners often use *get* in passives, using it with stative verbs or adjectives where *be* should actually be used.**

✓ *The baby **was** very loved by its parents.*

✗ *The baby ~~got~~ very loved by its parents.*

**Tick the correct sentences and rewrite the incorrect ones.**

0 Tom gets thought to have a bit of a temper, but he's actually quite calm. ☐
*Tom is thought to have a bit of a temper, but he's actually quite calm.*

1 Jim got knocked over by a cyclist the other day. ☐

2 The fence got broken by a motorist who crashed his car. ☐

3 Which road user gets more liked – the cyclist or the motorist? ☐

4 After a week at the sports camp, I'm sure we'll get exhausted by all this exercise. ☐

5 Mrs Summers got disappointed with her son. He had promised to give her a lift to the station, but he didn't turn up. ☐

6 The film got enjoyed by all who watched it. ☐

## UNIT 12
### Future in the past

**Learners often make errors when referring to the future from a past perspective, using *will* instead of *would* or *is/are going to* instead of *was/were*.**

✓ *I thought I **would** be sick.*

✗ *I thought I ~~will~~ be sick.*

✓ *Everyone believed he **was** going to leave school, but he didn't.*

✗ *Everyone believed he ~~is~~ going to leave school, but he didn't.*

**Tick the correct sentences and rewrite the incorrect ones.**

1 Jack and Chloe are going to eat at the Italian restaurant, but they changed their minds and went to the Chinese instead. ☐

2 You said there would be plenty of legroom, but there wasn't. ☐

3 He is going to leave school, but not until he's taken his exams. ☐

4 Sally and Jim are going to go on a round-the-world trip, but their plans fell through when Sally's father fell ill. ☐

5 If I'd known I am going to fail so spectacularly, I wouldn't have bothered trying! ☐

6 Did Mike really think that I will invite him to my party? ☐

# STUDENTS A & C

## UNIT 5, PAGE 51

**Student A**
**Think of reasons to agree with the following statements.**
**Make notes and then discuss in pairs. Finally, talk about your real opinions.**

- A doctor who treats a patient suffering from a life-threatening virus is taking a greater risk than the world's most audacious stuntman.
- Before someone engages in any kind of death-defying action, they should have to prove to a panel of experts that they've assessed the risk.

## UNIT 5, PAGE 53

**Student A**
**You believe the following ...**

Base jumpers are irresponsible and their 'sport' should be banned.

Extreme scuba diving looks like the most amazing sport. You'd love to try it.

Tightrope walking isn't fun; it's ridiculously dangerous.

**Try to convince your partner.**

## UNIT 10, PAGE 94

**Student A**
*Which should your government invest in – more teachers, more sports facilities, better-equipped science labs or after-school clubs?*

You think that the government should invest in more teachers. Students B, C and D disagree with you. You must try to convince them.

**Student C**
*Which should your government invest in – more teachers, more sports facilities, better-equipped science labs or after-school clubs?*

You think the government should invest in better-equipped science labs. Students A, B and D disagree with you. You must try to convince them.

## UNIT 10, PAGE 97

**Student A**
**Tell your partner about the following news, item by item. Also react to their news.**

School Summer Holidays to be Scrapped

Compulsory One Term Work Experience to be Introduced for all Sixteen-Year-Olds

New Minister for Education Says 'No More Homework'

A *The government is going to increase spending on education.*

B *I'm glad to hear it. That's the best news I've heard in ages. Schools really don't have enough money.*

## UNIT 11, PAGE 104

**Choose a situation. Imagine you feel extremely angry about it. Think about how you would explain the situation and how you feel to your partner. Make notes.**

1 You lent something to a friend three weeks ago and they still haven't given it back.

2 Someone said something unkind about the clothes you're wearing.

**Work in pairs. Take turns to tell your partner about your situation. Your partner should try to keep you calm.**

# STUDENTS B & D

## UNIT 5, PAGE 51

**Student B**

**Think of reasons to disagree with the statements. Make notes and then discuss in pairs. Finally, talk about your real opinions.**

- A doctor who treats a patient suffering from a life-threatening virus is taking a greater risk than the world's most audacious stuntman.
- Before someone engages in any kind of death-defying action, they should have to prove to a panel of experts that they've assessed the risk.

## UNIT 5, PAGE 53

**Student B**

**You believe the following …**

Base jumping looks amazing and you'd love to try it. Base jumpers take risks but they know what they're doing.

Extreme scuba diving looks terrifying. The risk of being trapped underwater or running out of oxygen is very real.

Tightrope walking looks like so much fun; it must be exhilarating to do it.

**Try to convince your partner.**

## UNIT 10, PAGE 94

**Student B**

*Which should your government invest in – more teachers, more sports facilities, better-equipped science labs or after-school clubs?*

You think the government should invest in more sports facilities. Students A, C and D disagree with you. You must try to convince them.

**Student D**

*Which should your government invest in – more teachers, more sports facilities, better-equipped science labs or after-school clubs?*

You think the government should invest in after-school clubs. Students A, B and C disagree with you. You must try to convince them.

## UNIT 10, PAGE 97

**Student B**

**Tell your partner about the following news, item by item. Also react to their news.**

School Day to be Extended by Half an Hour

Government to Increase Spending on Education

Government Bans Mobile Phones from School Grounds

**A** *I agree. And I've also heard that they plan to extend the school day by an extra hour.*

**B** *They've got to be joking! We're already spending too much time at school.*

## UNIT 11, PAGE 104

**Choose a situation. Imagine you feel extremely angry about it. Think about how you would explain the situation and how you feel to your partner. Make notes.**

1 You got a poor mark for some homework and you think it deserved a better grade.

2 Your favourite team lost a very important match because they played really badly.

**Work in pairs. Take turns to tell your partner about your situation. Your partner should try to keep you calm.**